Passion for Christ,
Passion for Humanity

Passion *for* CHRIST,
Passion *for* HUMANITY

**International Congress
on Consecrated Life**

BOOKS & MEDIA
Boston

Library of Congress Cataloging-in-Publication Data is on file at the Library of Congress [http://www.loc.gov/Z3950/gateway.html].

Cover art: (Left icon) "St. Photini (the Samaritan Woman) at Jacob's Well," Holy Transfiguration Monastery, 278 Warren Street, Brookline, MA 02445. Used with permission. (Right icon) "The Good Samaritan," Fifth Archdiocesan District of the Greek Orthodox Archdiocese of Australia [http://members.optusnet.com.au/~goawa/]. Used with permission.

ISBN 0-8198-5954-0

Published by Pauline Books & Media, 50 Saint Paul's Avenue, Boston, MA 02130-3491.

Printed in U.S.A.

www.pauline.org

Pauline Books & Media is the publishing house of the Daughters of St. Paul, an international congregation of women religious serving the Church with the communications media.

1 2 3 4 5 6 7 8 9   11 10 09 08 07 06 05

CONTENTS

ABBREVIATIONS

CfL   *Christifideles Laici*

EN   *Evangelii Nuntiandi*

GS   *Gaudium et Spes*

IL   *Instrumentum Laboris*

NMI   *Novo Millennio Ineunte*

PC   *Perfectae Caritatis*

RHP   *Religious and Human Promotion*

SaC   *Starting Afresh from Christ*

VC   *Vita Consecrata*

PRESENTATION

José María Arnaiz, SM
General Secretary, USG

This book compiles the work of the First International Congress of Consecrated Life organized by the UISG [International Union of Women Superior Generals] and the USG [Union of Superior Generals]. Their work merited a structure to situate, explain, and thus better understand the rich and vital theological reflection that emerged during the proceedings. From the outset, the Congress issued a clear message without neglecting procedures that were participative. This was a moment of grace. However, this paper speaks not only about the proceedings of the Congress, but also about its presenters. The presenters reflected and listened to the Spirit, who assisted all of us through our work and will continue to assist us in the challenges that lie ahead. For clarity's sake, we will recount the history and the theology important for these proceedings.

Before the Congress

1. We Felt the Need for a Congress

In late May 2001, the Union of Superior Generals and the International Union of Women Superior Generals felt the need to organize a

Congress. It would be the first held in common and the first to be international in scope, involving the presidents of the national and international conferences. Nearly ten years have already passed since the publication of the Apostolic Exhortation *Vita Consecrata,* and it was clear that a different kind of Congress was needed.[1] The Congress needed to engage members in a manner that was participative and reciprocal, involving men and women of different cultures and age groups. The participants needed to be aware of and listen to the diversity within the group. The participants were required to look for the major signs of vitality given to us by a Spirit at work in contemporary expressions of consecrated life in order to identify and discern future directions. We desired to incorporate intercultural and interreligious perspectives in this Congress. We needed to include the experience of those who govern (Superior Generals) as well as the intuition and creativity found in the area of theology (theologians, presidents of schools of theology, magazine editors). Equally important was incorporating the energy of young people. Taken as a whole, the Congress could be the authoritative and relevant voice of men and women religious as well as a voice for the young.

2. The Objectives of the Congress Were Born

A group of six people from both unions formed a visioning team in September 2001. Their role included the following:

- To assess the actual situation of the lives of religious men and women.
- To formulate fundamental priorities with special attention to the innovative and the original.
- To analyze the significance, effectiveness, and relevancy of consecrated life.
- To raise awareness of the shared responsibility required of the participating unions and conferences in consecrated life.
- To discover, welcome, and reinforce innovation. To recognize emerging forms in consecrated life—signs of vitality, prophesy, and hope.

- To create a spirit, a spirituality, and a praxis of communion in the Church and in the world.
- To acknowledge the many opportunities for communion among the charisms and the need for communication between various structures.
- To place consecrated life at the heart of the Church.

3. Our Objectives Required a Process and a Spirit

To realize these objectives, it was necessary to construct a process. The process had three steps, beginning with the preparation and development of the Congress. The first step involved the identification of that which is new in order to discern the direction to which the Spirit is prompting us to go. These new promptings would then propose the manner in which we might respond. The Spirit, which animated the entire work of the Congress, was present from the very first stages of preparation, most recognizably in the "action words" of the *Instrumentum Laboris*[2]:

- *To receive:* This means that we listen to, see, and describe those things that the Spirit offers us. For example, we examine our motivations for engaging in the work of evangelization.
- *To allow ourselves to be transformed:* Transformation is possible when we are open to learn and discern the many directions in which the Spirit is moving us.
- *To initiate a new praxis:* New praxis means that we are willing to offer proposals that enable transformation, restructuring, and innovation, which in turn helps us change our concrete praxis. The demands of these proposals are twofold: personal and communal conversion as well as the transformation of the institutional structures and environment.
- *To celebrate:* An authentically celebratory attitude must be present at the Congress. This requires the capacity to praise, symbolize, contemplate, enjoy, ask for pardon, intercede, and express gratitude.

4. We Found a Title and a Theme

In October 2001, we first contacted the General Superiors, the presidents of national conferences, as well as a number of theologians to gather their first impressions and reactions regarding the proposal to convene a new Congress. We asked them to submit suggestions about the theme and the mode of preparation.

The visioning team compiled the feedback and presented it to the executive commission of the union. After lengthy discussions, they settled upon the theme: "Passion for Christ and Passion for Humanity." The commission wished for the Congress to reflect upon the passion *of Christ,* a passion *with Christ,* and a passion *for Christ.* The whole notion centers upon Christ's passion for humanity and for the men and women who embrace consecrated life. In many ways, this passion was regarded rather as "compassion." Consecrated life, now more than ever, requires wisdom and profound commitment to focus upon this theme and to live out its implications. Supporting topics were the re-launching of consecrated life with special attention to the spiritual, communal, joyful, and hopeful dimensions of the mission and the search for innovative approaches at the beginning of the new millennium.

5. We Searched for an Icon

In 2002 through the beginning of 2003, the visioning team made its initial preparations. During this time, a central commission was created along with a variety of other commissions. In addition, a general secretariat and an executive secretariat were appointed. In order for the Congress to reach its objectives, it needed organization, structure, process, participants, and content. During this preparatory stage, there was room for thorough and much needed reflection upon the state of consecrated life based on the document, *Vita Consecrata.* This renewed call to action prompted many pages of theological reflection about consecrated life during this particular stage. Much of the reflection emerged from a contemplation of two images: the Samaritan Woman at the Well and the Good

Samaritan.[3] We believe that this choice was correct. We looked for an inclusive "icon" that led the one contemplating these images to a passion *for Christ* and *for humanity.* The contemplation of these images offers a choice that brings consecrated life back to its principal reference point, rooted essentially upon the Gospel as a "foundational standard." The Gospel standard allows us to examine our misdeeds and our weaknesses (our "husbands"), which also carry with it the seeds of radical choice and prophecy.[4]

Ultimately, the results attained by the visioning team came through hard work.

6. *We Elaborated Upon the* Instrumentum Laboris

At the beginning of 2003, we began a working document. In addition to this, we constituted an international commission comprised of 14 people. Our criterion for the commission remained unchanged. We wished to allow men and women religious of different cultures and nationalities to participate in a Congress that allowed for creative theological reflection upon consecrated life. A first draft was composed after a meeting in October 2003. On this occasion, we composed a second text written for a more select group of respondents to obtain their initial reactions. In February 2004, we viewed the definitive text, which became the *Instrumentum Laboris.* Although it was lengthier than expected, it was well received and the commission received a substantial number of comments. The publication of this working document began a more intensive period of preparation and collaboration among the members of the commission. This document was not merely a recitation of a theology already well known to religious. The document presupposed that participants were familiar with previous documents. The first section of the *Instrumentum Laboris* contained reflections on sociology and Scripture. The second section dealt with discernment and the refoundation of consecrated life. The document seeks a revitalization of consecrated life as well as a structure to achieve this end. The third section moved us to action. It is important to listen to the Spirit and to discover where the Spirit is creating newness in consecrated life—especially those opportunities for creative fidelity.

7. We Gathered Reactions to the Working Document

Beginning in March 2004, the secretary of the Congress began to receive feedback on the *Instrumentum Laboris*. In many ways, the Congress had already begun. From the outset, it was clear that the *Instrumentum Laboris* would die with the beginning of the Congress. We did not wish to create another draft with the same material. We thought it necessary to reflect seriously on the new material that arrived in order to articulate it well and offer it to the participants. An appointed theological commission saw the work to its completion in a spirit of collaboration. The commission was comprised of participants living in Rome, but hailing from all parts of the world. By the beginning of October, they published the document, "From the Well to the Inn," that sought to synthesize and interpret the contributions of the many respondents. The document places us between the well of the Samaritan woman and the inn of the Good Samaritan. It invites us to go and "do likewise," to resist passing "by on the other side."[5] The participants received the document at the opening of the Congress along with an accompanying introduction from Bruno Secondin, O.Carm., and Diane Papa, OSC, who asked the participants to reflect on a "present that has a future."

8. We Identified Guidelines for Reflection in the Congress: Discernment in Order to Refound

As the time of the Congress drew near, the organizers felt it necessary to elaborate further on the guidelines for reflection. They set down nine points that identified the main initiatives and ideas in preparation for the opening of the Congress. The same Roman theological commission completed their work, assisted by the secretary of the Congress and a number of other facilitators. It is practically unnecessary to say that those in consecrated life already have many theological affirmations regarding their state and their work; what they lack is a new way of proceeding. Men and women who have embraced consecrated life are encouraged to open their eyes to discover that which is new. Many men and women in consecrated life have already been moved by the Spirit and have begun to live this new way of being. Our strengths and resources cannot be reduced to a mere exercise in survival. The organizers of the Congress asked the participants to develop the willingness and determination to act as refounders of their respective congregations. They are already capable of tapping into the mystical dimension of their own vocations to sustain the life and mission of consecrated life.

During the Congress

9. *Some 850 Samaritan Women and Good Samaritans Speaking, Listening, Sharing, and Celebrating*

On November 23, the Congress officially began. Therezinha Joana Rasera, SDS, president of the Congress, reminded us that the challenges that lie ahead for religious require that we be united. The participants and the presenters of the Congress numbered about 850 religious—all wishing to learn to be Good Samaritans. The participants wanted to follow in the footsteps of the significant persons of the Gospel and enter the school of the Samaritan woman in order to live a significant and fruitful consecrated life at the beginning of the new millennium. To do this, they must both listen and speak. The function of the conferences was to continue a conversation begun almost four years ago. In her presentation, Dolores Aleixandre, RSCJ, saw the participants as seekers of wells and pathways. João Batista Libânio, SJ, described today's religious men and women as Good Samaritans, and he spoke of the realities and challenges facing us. Timothy Radcliffe, OP, identified us with Samaritans who read the signs of the times, especially in a post-September 11 world. Sandra Schneiders, IHM, offered her comments on the future of consecrated life in the Church. Six people who had previously read the presentations were asked to highlight important insights and add what

they considered suitable according to the lived experience of consecrated life within their own cultural contexts. This group included Marie Thérèse Gacambi, ASN; Bernando Olivera, OCSO; Judette
Gallares, RC; Jean Ilboudo, SJ; Mani Mekkunel, SG; and Barbara
Bucker, MC.

The Congress gave special attention to the message of the Holy
Father on the final day as well as to a presentation by Monsignor
Franc Rodé, CM, the Prefect of the Congregation of Institutes of
Consecrated Life and Societies of Apostolic Life.

10. Dreaming of the Future to Determine Common Themes: Convictions and Actions

After having listened to a variety of experiences during the first days,
the participants felt the need to move on to the concrete—to speak
of how each one arrived at an answer to the call of the Spirit. The
Congress thus chose fifteen common themes. Working groups dis-
cussed the themes and proposed convictions and actions. After much
work, the list of themes was presented to the secretary and
to the facilitators of the Congress. More than themes in consecrated life, we were interested in exploring the roadblocks and signs
of vitality. We needed new convictions and lines of action to take the
significant steps forward in the future. The fifteen themes were as
follows:

1. Justice and peace and the suffering of humanity;
2. Inculturation and incarnation of consecrated life in a culturally pluralistic world;
3. Interreligious dialogue;
4. The art and artistic dimensions of consecrated life;
5. Social communication and the transmission of values;
6. Liberating the prophet and solidarity with the marginalized;
7. The prophetic dimension of our lives: consecrated celibacy;
8. Plowing the lands of the Sacred Scriptures;
9. Thirst for God and the search for identity;

10. Enduring formation: personal conversion and collective transformation;
11. Congregational culture;
12. Community as missionary;
13. Sharing with the laity;
14. Leadership and authority;
15. The ecclesial dimension of consecrated life.

The final document included the principal convictions that emerged from the discussions. It was difficult to gather concrete lines of action. Not all the lines of action held the same interest or weight of importance among the different groups, forms of consecrated life, and those of different continents and age groups. The religious institutes were left with the task of sifting through the information and making choices. Religious institutes must find where to dig the wells and the paths that lead there, to choose the inns that will revitalize consecrated life and the companions for the journey. As stated in the last open forum of the Congress, religious institutes must identify those who thirst, who are capable of bearing water, and who are experienced at watering. These small places where paradise flourishes will benefit us all a great deal.

11. Producing a Synthesis of What We Lived and Heard

The position of the central commission of the Congress was clear from the beginning. They did not wish to produce a large document in the style of the *Instrumentum Laboris*. Nor did they desire to leave without showing some fruits from their days together as well as their delicate efforts at reflection. After extensive discussion, they finally decided to produce a brief, final document of six pages in all. It was a combination of information and declaration, of reflection and proposal—all oriented toward action. The document highlighted the crucial and delicate moment in which we lived. The Congress seemed to validate an important beginning that emphasized rich intuitions, reference to the Scriptures, prophetic

sensibilities, images, and poetic overtones. In a word, we gathered
the principal elements of our journey during the Congress to serve
as a guiding compass. The work was arduous. The task was entrusted to a group of nine people from diverse cultures, whom we
called "listeners." These men and women listened attentively from
the first moment of the Congress. However, their work consisted not
only in listening, but also in speaking and writing. The group would
have to formulate and express the fruits of the Congress at its conclusion. They made several successive drafts on what they heard and
lived. Finally, they produced a generally well-regarded document
that could serve to continue the spirit of the Congress and move its
varied participants and diverse groups to action.

After the Congress

The expectations for the Congress were high. At times, the organizers were anxious and preoccupied. The General Superiors had
the foresight to suggest that November 27 did not mark the end of the
Congress but its beginning. There were many well-qualified assistants
who suggested multifaceted ways of continuing this lived spirit, this
proposed method, this specified journey, this launched project, this
renewed form of life in the Church, this deeply held sentiment, this
prophetic call to action, this overpowering passion for Christ and for
humanity. An immense task lies ahead. A blueprint for the international revitalization of consecrated life was issued. The final text is
to actually write these hopes into our daily lives.

12. The Task Ahead

The Memory of What We Lived

This week has been one, large, grand, festive liturgy celebrating
consecrated life. Religious men and women have sung and danced,
proclaimed and acclaimed, asked for pardon and expressed gratitude
to God. They have implored and praised, lifted their voices, sought
conversion to the Good News not only for those present but also for

all those who could not be present at the Congress, including the laity and the rest of the Church. The mass media lent a helping hand. The 850 religious men and women became a great community of intercession that prayed in silence and acknowledged that consecrated life was a sacrament that both signified and created the life of grace.

The Task of Articulating the Experience Lies Ahead

There were a diversity of opinions expressed, some contradictory, some completely new. There is a call for an effort grounded in reflection to articulate what has been expressed. The participants said more than once that the anthropology of consecrated life must be deepened and that it is necessary to rethink, in the light of postmodernism, the vision of the human person underlying the understanding and practice of consecrated life. An in-depth dialogue must be initiated involving the theology of consecrated life in Europe and the developing models in Asia, Africa, and Latin America. The task proper to theologians is to read these "texts," which they situate in their proper contexts and encounter their "pretexts" in order to deepen, develop, and expand the horizons of consecrated life. There are already open forums on the national, continental, and international levels, but other forums may be opened.

The Task of Naming This New Articulation Lies Ahead

If consecrated life is always more inclusive, more collaborative (between men and women, as in this Congress), more north and south, integrating more the life of the laity and consecrated life, more intercongregational and intergenerational, closer to the poor, more mystical and prophetic, then consecrated life in the future will be different than we know it now. We will move away from a model of consecrated life marked by Europe and North America toward a more universal form. The voices from Africa, Asia, and Latin America were heard clearly in the Congress. Certainly, this symphony would not be complete without hearing the voices of European religious men and women.

It is necessary to move away from a model of consecrated life ordered around religious institutes toward one ordered around religious families. There must be a movement away from a consecrated life marked by congregational identity and works toward one that embraces the notion of an intercongregational consecrated life; a movement away from a consecrated life without imagination to one that has discarded its fears and offers new generations the rich legacy it has received, lived, and preserved. All these geographical and cultural movements can bring about a transformation of consecrated life—a truly creative fidelity and a radically new evangelical outlook.

The Desire to Live What Was Proposed

The historical impact of the accomplishments of the Congress for Consecrated Life will be gauged by how it affects daily life. We cannot forget that the works of the Spirit are like a fine mist that falls slowly and continuously, but bears great fruit; so it is with the Congress. This is necessary if there are to be new forms of consecrated life.

Passion for Christ and Passion for Humanity

To lose these two passions means that we lose our souls. In fact, we must cultivate and intensify these passions. They are like a fire that communicates warmth and yet does not die out. These passions and signs of the Spirit are the point of departure for a new beginning.

A Desire to Use a New Language
When Speaking of Consecrated Life

The Congress confirmed that we listen more closely when we are convinced of and filled with enthusiasm for this form of Christian life. We must use a new language to speak of consecrated life. The language carries with it communion and the call to be passionate; it is creative and filled with images. The language is poetic, evangelical, and binding. It is not helpful to be simply rational and discriminating. The very language that separates can now lead to unity. It should allow us to communicate the significance of consecrated life to modern men and women.

The Intention to Organize Another Congress

Some suggested that the next Congress should not take place in Europe. In the intervening time, there should be opportunities for meetings. It is important in this historic moment that men and women religious be allowed the opportunity for dialogue, encounter, interaction, and communion.

The Task of Communicating to Many What Was Lived by a Few

It is our hope to communicate effectively what has been thus far an intuition, a powerful message of life, a unique experience of confidence in the Lord, of the absence of fear and the power of living hope. One can only give hope if one possesses it. The Holy Father invites us in his message "to offer a lost humanity, deprived of memory, a credible testimony of Christian hope." Let us begin to nourish this hope and share it with the members of our communities. It is then that consecrated life evidences solidarity and radiates appeal.

At the end of the Congress Álvaro Rodríguez, FSC, reminded us that this is the path to success. He urged us "to invent, innovate, and move ahead stripped of everything alien to the Kingdom." The fire for the passion of Christ and for humanity belongs to us. The pages of this book are meant to pass on this spiritual fire to the reader. It is the symphonic voice of experience on the theology and praxis of contemporary consecrated life.

Notes

1. John Paul II, Post Synodal Exhortation *Vita Consecrata* (Boston: Pauline Books & Media, 1996).

2. The working document composed in preparation for the Congress.

3. Cf. Lk 10:25–37; Jn 4:1–42.

4. Cf. Jn 4:18.

5. Cf. Lk 10:31, 32, 37.

WITH A PASSION FOR CHRIST AND A PASSION FOR HUMANITY

Instrumentum Laboris

Introduction

I. At the Beginning of the Twenty-First Century

1. Jesus Christ, our Risen Lord, the Mediator of the New Covenant and of the Kingdom is our contemporary. He does not belong to the past, nor is consecrated life, our form of Christian living, a thing of the past. Currently, in some countries the phenomenon of aging has had a dramatic impact on consecrated life, while in others the average age of religious is much younger. In recent years, new forms of monastic and consecrated life have been added to the centuries-old forms we have known. Some of the charisms that arose centuries ago have taken on new aspects, which have given them new vitality. Following the Second Vatican Council, consecrated life received a great impetus and underwent important changes. Present sociocultural and religious contexts demand transformations that are even more decisive. In the midst of many contemporary changes, we perceive the validity and relevance of the important values that constitute our form of life, and we feel the urgency of living these values

in an intense and significant way for ourselves and for others. We are living in a time of grace and challenge.

2. The passion that Christ felt for humanity, shown throughout his lifetime, and in a singular way on the cross, is also not something of the past. It continues through all of history, in which we find clear signs of its fruitfulness. At the beginning of the twenty-first century, Christ shares the crosses of millions of persons in various parts of the world. Today, his call for consecrated men and women is demanding and life-giving. It is a call to follow him passionately and, motivated by his compassion, to share his passion for each human being.

II. The Congress

3. We want to be attentive to the voice of God, to the teachings of Jesus, and to the urgings of the Spirit that constantly open new horizons and prompt us to a new evangelization. We want to be attentive to the challenges that the Church places before us, attentive to the needs of present-day society and to the needs of consecrated life. For this reason, representatives of consecrated life from all over the world will gather in this Congress. We want to listen to these voices from an intercultural perspective, careful to include the perspectives of men and women. We want to bring to this task all of our experiences as superior generals, presidents of national and continental conferences, women and men theologians, directors of centers for theological reflection on consecrated life, and editors of reviews on consecrated life. The young religious who are present will contribute their enthusiastic faith, attuned to present-day cultural values. We want to continue the reflection and discernment begun with the Synod on Consecrated Life, and to discover the new things that the Spirit is bringing to life in us (Is 43:18–19) at the beginning of the third millennium (VC, no. 13). From these foundations, we wish to offer some proposals and practical steps to rekindle our hope and sustain us along the path on which the Spirit is leading us.

a) Objectives of the Congress

4. The overall objective of the Congress is to discern together, with a global awareness, what the Spirit of God is bringing about among us, where the Spirit is leading us, and how we can respond to the challenges of our times, thus building up the Reign of God "for the common good" (1 Cor 12:7).

5. This objective is composed of the following *particular points:*

- to discover and discern the validity of "the new" that is emerging among us;
- to accept and promote this newness as a gift from God and an expression of commitment;
- to strengthen the spirituality and mission we share with the People of God and to foster communion and solidarity among consecrated men and women;
- to commit ourselves to sharing our passion for Christ and for humanity in new contexts: consecrated life is urged to make cultivating a "passion" for God and for human beings a priority (VC, no. 84);
- to be the voice of consecrated life for consecrated life.

b) The Method and the Spirit of the Congress

6. This *Instrumentum Laboris,* which is an expression of a serious and ongoing group effort, makes the objectives of the Congress concrete. Prior to the development of this document, the Congress on Consecrated Life was announced along with four questions to help us discover signs of vitality, challenges, obstacles, and dreams. A "Visioning Group" analyzed the responses received from the questionnaires and worked to focus the theme, inspiration, objectives, and process of the Congress.

Faithful to the replies received, the "Theological Commission" now offers this *Instrumentum Laboris,* which aims to offer a creative synthesis that reflects certain intuitions for future directions. We are sending this *Instrumentum Laboris* to all the participants of the Congress for their reactions and contributions for its enrichment.

During the Congress, the participants will delve more deeply into the themes, which will be developed through the various conferences, exchanges, and proposals.

7. The *Instrumentum Laboris* we are presenting seeks only to guide the preparation of proposals that will likely arise from our global and shared discernment during the Congress. In this *Instrumentum Laboris,* we present the different elements, areas, and aspects that may help to focus or direct our work.

8. We deeply desire to express the "spirit" of the Congress in the following verbs or dynamic attitudes that inspire the *Instrumentum Laboris's* particular "components" and us in the writing of this document: welcome, transform, begin anew, and celebrate.

> *Welcome:* implies seeing, discovering, listening to what the Spirit offers, and perceiving how the Gospel moves us to respond.
> *Transform:* implies openness to learning and discerning the spirits that move us.
> *Begin anew:* suggests a willingness to be decisive and to make proposals that help transform, restructure, innovate, and rethink our concrete actions. Such proposals demand both personal and communal conversion and transformation of environment and structures.
> *Celebrate:* evokes an authentically celebrative attitude, needed throughout the Congress. This demands an ability to create symbols, to contemplate, to be joyful, to ask pardon, to intercede, to give thanks, and to praise.

c) The Icons: the Samaritan Woman and the Good Samaritan

9. The theme of the Congress, "With a Passion for Christ and a Passion for Humanity," finds its inspiration for discernment and proposals in the Gospel icons of the Samaritan woman and the Good Samaritan. Both symbols, not traditionally applied to consecrated life, offer inspiration in this moment of need.

10. The Samaritan woman met Jesus at the well. She felt attracted in her heart to his person, his mystery, and his message. For him she abandoned her water jug—that is, her former life—and became a witness to and sower of Good News (Jn 4:5–42). One day a Samaritan man met another half-dead human being, a victim of robbery and violence. He felt his heart moved to compassion. Therefore, he altered his journey because of this person. He became his "neighbor" and took care of him with great generosity (Lk 10:29–37). The Samaritan woman and the Samaritan man are symbols of the pathway along which the Spirit is leading consecrated life today and of the love and compassion that the Spirit is arousing in our hearts. This double icon has been a powerful force of inspiration throughout the history of spirituality. It also pours out its transforming energies on consecrated life today. The Samaritan woman and the Samaritan man are sinners, yet they do not lack grace and openness to goodness. We consecrated women and men are very much like them, and we feel challenged by the Samaritan woman's thirst and desire for living water and the Samaritan man's compassion for the wounded on life's byways.

11. We are experiencing a crucial period in our history. As a world, a Church, and consecrated life, we experience the exuberance of life, as well as terrible signs of death. The Spirit leads us toward sources of life and, simultaneously, toward those brothers and sisters who lie prostrate and dying on life's paths.

d) Perspective: Discernment for Refounding

12. We understand consecrated life to be a gift of the Spirit given to the Church for the world. The Church is mother and teacher. It is a field of action and mission for consecrated persons (EN, nos. 8, 24). In the People of God, consecrated life is at the service of the Reign of God, which is breaking forth in our world. We must be attentive so that the world and the new culture coming to birth will have a human face and that the Church will be a "sacrament of humanization." For this to become a reality, consecrated life needs a

radical revitalization that will give it a new face. Everything in this document is directed toward beginning a discernment of this new process, which has already been initiated by some religious men and women, some communities, and some congregations. This discernment will continue during the days of preparation for the Congress, will be deepened during the Congress, and ultimately it will be shared with the whole of consecrated life. While we intend to include the contributions of the theology of consecrated life, ecclesiology, and anthropology, we will not develop these lines of thought.

e) The Logo

13. The message of this document is captured with strength and beauty by the *logo*. The logo is made up of many dots—representative of the many that make up the world, humanity, and God's Reign. The women and men in consecrated life constitute millions of these dots. In the drawing's composite, there is a movement in which one symbol flows into the other in a continuous rhythm. They come to the center, to the essential, to the love that envelops all. They also go outward, to the world that represents the Body of Christ, the People of God. This dual movement flows from the cross, the sign of life and hope. In its entirety, the logo evokes the heart of every religious in which passion for Christ and for humanity merge together into one dynamic. The colors—red and blue—remind us of the force of Christ's grace that penetrates humanity with all its tenderness and vigor. Consecrated life desires to participate in this movement. The call to zeal, to intensity, to mission, and to conversion is very much present in this significant symbol. The glorious cross of Christ draws us to itself; it transforms us and sends us on mission.

PART ONE

The Reality That Challenges Us

"Jacob's well is there and Jesus, tired by the journey, sat straight down by the well." (Jn 4:6)

"And when he saw him, he passed by on the other side. But a Samaritan...was moved with compassion when he saw him...." (Lk 10:31–33)

14. As Jesus taught us, in the signs of the times we discover the will of God, the innovative action of the Spirit, the direction in which we should move, the presence of God, and God's designs for us. The comments from those who answered the questionnaire for the Congress have helped us to glean insights and to suggest a profile of consecrated life in these times.

15. When we look at our reality at this moment of history, in this world, in this Church—at everything that forms our experience—we ask ourselves various questions:

- What is the Holy Spirit raising up in consecrated life today?
- How do we identify it, describe it, and present it?
- How are we initiated into it and how do we form ourselves for it?
- How do we describe the leadership that it needs?
- How do we discover the obstacles to its existence?
- To what new "wells" and paths is this emerging consecrated life drawing us?
- What can we call this process of newness in which we are involved?

16. The following is a presentation of the challenges and opportunities for grace that we have recognized, as well as the obstacles that make our dreams impossible or difficult, and, more concretely, our passion for Christ and for humanity. The four *great fidelities* mentioned in the document, *Religious and Human Promotion,* are important criteria for us: "Fidelity to [humanity] and our times, fidelity to Christ and the Gospel, fidelity to the Church and her mission in the world, fidelity to consecrated life and the particular charism of each Institute" (RHP, 1980, nos. 13–31). We are also faithful to our current reality and to the great spiritual and ecclesial realities. These two perspectives are intertwined and mutually nourishing. We will consider each reality or situation in relation to consecrated life in order to see the influences and challenges present. Our objective is to be "ready to respond with the wisdom of the Gospel to the questions posed today by the anxieties and the urgent needs of the human heart" (VC, no. 81).

Challenges and Opportunities

17. Consecrated life, now more global than ever, feels challenged by various new phenomena. Included among these challenges are: 1) globalization with its ambiguities and mythology; 2) human mobility with its migratory phenomena and accelerated processes; 3) the unjust and destabilizing neoliberal economic system; 4) the culture of death and the struggle to promote life in the face of such challenges as biotechnology and eugenics; 5) pluralism and growing differentiation; 6) postmodern attitudes and mentality; 7) the thirst for love and the distortions of love; and 8) the hunger for the sacred and secularistic materialism.

18. Such challenges place us in a field of tensions and opposing forces that we can neither forget nor minimize, making it all the more necessary to discover where the Spirit is leading us in this *"novo millennio ineunte."* What opportunities is the Spirit offering us for growth, innovation, and refoundation? What practical decisions inspire us to grow and renew? Toward what formation processes are we heading? What are the difficulties or stumbling blocks awaiting us?

I. Globalization with Its Ambiguities

19. We are dwellers of a global and planetary world. Thanks to new technologies, information easily circles the entire planet and creates economic, political, and strategic dynamics—even unthought-of and unsuspected ones. We feel closer to one another and are better able to understand our differences. Nevertheless, since these dynamics are at the service of unofficial powers with immense influence, particular interests, and neoliberal ideologies, they have very negative and discriminatory consequences. They generate poverty, humiliate the dignity of peoples with few resources, impose only one neoliberal economic model, and marginalize cultures, peoples, and groups that do not serve their interests.

20. Consecrated life is also involved in the process of globalization. Our charisms are rooted in new religious and cultural places and contexts. These differences convert our institutes into transnational communities that enjoy the same global identity. Nevertheless, there is a danger that the predominant culture in the institute will impose itself on others and thus impede the process of inculturation and the expression of the charism in new contexts (VC, nos. 73 and 79). This universalizing model can have similar negative consequences to those of the neoliberal project, going against the poor and the excluded.

21. The challenge of globalization can become an opportunity to recognize the unity in the diversity of this world so loved by God. A prophetic commitment to justice, peace, and care for creation is a dimension of the Christian mission in which the Church and consecrated life oppose the neoliberal model of globalization and defend a model of global consciousness without excluding or impoverishing anyone ["global consciousness" translates the Spanish *mundialización* (— Trans.)]. This form of global sensitivity opens us to real possibilities for an inculturation and contextualization of our charisms as well as a closer collaboration with other congregations and with other forms of Christian and human living.

II. Human Mobility and Its Migratory Phenomena

22. Diverse political and social conflicts such as poverty, wars, political instability, and religious intolerance are among the causes of the various waves of migration changing the complexion of some nations. Large sectors of humanity feel displaced, uprooted, and dispersed throughout the world. The constant struggle for survival in such circumstances hinders the transmission of traditions, balanced education, and healthy, dignified development. The migration of peoples challenges us in that in welcoming others, we put our own Christian and religious identity at stake. From this arise admirable attitudes of hospitality and receptiveness, but also xenophobic, ethnocentric, and racist attitudes that we cannot tolerate.

23. In consecrated life, we also experience the mobility characteristic of the times. We are called to be Exodus communities and persons who wish to have an attitude of dialogue with life and culture, an openness of mind, and a capacity for transformation. In an unjust and divided world, we need to be signs and witnesses of dialogue and trust, of communion and communal love (VC, no. 51).

24. Today, consecrated life has an opportunity to meet people in their mobility. It has an opportunity to share with many men and women the sense of uprootedness from one's own cultural identity as well as the process of adapting and of creating new syntheses. Consecrated persons have to be "Samaritans" in knowing how to welcome, accompany, and care for these wounded and marginalized persons. Their mission takes on essential overtones of hospitality, compassion, and interreligious and intercultural dialogue (VC, no. 79). All of this presupposes that consecrated life undergo a profound restructuring of lifestyle, mentality, and programs.

III. Unjust Economic Systems and New Forms of Solidarity

25. Another great challenge is the exclusion to which great sections of humanity are subjected in the name of the current process of globalization. An economy of exploitation generates wants and new types

of poverty (cf. NMI, no. 50) that ultimately lead to an ongoing depreciation of life. The liberalization of the world economy has not managed to avoid evil effects, which crush the weak and less developed peoples and countries.

26. As consecrated men and women, we can picture ourselves involved in this economy, which excludes many. This challenge really tests the truth of our solidarity with the poor, the excluded, and those whose right to life is threatened. It also tests our commitment to their liberation. We recognize that this solidarity is an essential part of our faith in Jesus, of the prophetic dimension of our consecrated life, and of our following of Jesus. The evangelical counsel of poverty should become more and more a personal and communal practice of solidarity with the poor, of detachment, of giving freely, of trust in Providence, and of simple witness (VC, no. 82).

27. Consciousness of unjust economic systems also offers us the opportunity of confronting our lifestyle with the Gospel and with the urgent needs of the poor. It challenges us to establish an economy of solidarity that is critical of present economic systems. It calls us to put our resources and institutions at the service of the poor and of creation by actively participating in the defense and promotion of life, justice, and peace through collaboration with other religious and civil organizations.

IV. Life Threatened and Defended

28. Life is abundant and fruitful in nature and in humanity. An appreciation, defense, and passion for life are shown in many ways today. There are persons and organizations working on behalf of the poor, human rights, and peace. At the same time, the great steps forward in the sciences, biotechnology, and modern medicine constitute a sign of hope and fear for humanity. This is particularly true for consecrated men and women, who are committed to *promoting and protecting human life.*

29. There are numerous *signs of violence and death* in our world. Life on our planet is threatened (e.g., contamination and lack of water, deforestation, pollution, toxic wastes). Human life is devalued from conception to death (e.g., abortion, violence against women and children, sexual violence, totalitarianism, terrorism, wars, the death penalty, euthanasia). The sources of life and fertility are being manipulated often without scruple and without ethical criteria. At times, one has the impression of scientific showmanship. Religious fundamentalism of many kinds provokes a violence that could be called "sacred" and from which we ourselves are not exempt.

30. The challenges are numerous, above all for consecrated men and women who serve in the field of health care:

- ethical challenges: abortion, euthanasia for the terminally ill, the use of therapeutic cloning and embryos for the healing of some degenerative diseases;
- the challenge of great endemic and epidemic diseases, such as HIV, malaria, Ebola, SARS;
- challenges in the field of justice: e.g., the moral acceptability of the pharmaceutical industry warehousing medicines while the poor die for lack of medication. Consecrated men and women could be these poor, sick people as well as the defenders of their human rights.

31. This dramatic situation opens new opportunities for us. We can no longer live without being deeply affected by these situations that impact Mother Earth and our human community. We should be attentive so as not to become co-responsible for a "culture of death." Our apostolic plans make no sense if they do not incite us to serve with greater devotion those whose lives are diminished or lead us to establish a true "culture of life."

V. Pluralism and Increasing Differentiation

32. We live in a pluralistic world, and we are more sensitive than ever to differences of ethnicity, culture, religion, gender, and generations.

The acceptance of pluralism renders our way of thinking and acting difficult and complex. Some cultures are excluded. Respect for differences and pluralism often conflicts with networks of particular interests. The majority often prevails over the minority, force over reason, economy over solidarity, law over freedom, gender exclusion over gender inclusion, dictatorship over democracy. The tendency to a single way of thinking and the leveling of every playing field cause great tension and distress.

33. Consecrated life embraces pluralism and diversity now more than at any other time. Consecrated life itself is called to be diverse in its members and in the charisms that the Spirit gives it. For this reason men and women in consecrated life feel uncomfortable in uniform ecclesiastical or social systems and in monocultures that are closed or non-participative. The challenge of dialogue, on all levels, attempts to shape a new style of consecrated life. At the same time, we need to acknowledge that many times consecrated life has also imposed cultural forms, ways of acting, ethnic fanaticism, and caste differences. Mature religious obedience, an exercise in attentive listening to God's desires and those of others, in free submission and in an integrated personal and community commitment, helps us to respond adequately to this challenge.

34. This task becomes an opportunity when we are capable of entering into communion with those who are different from ourselves. Individual charisms are recognized, freed, and put at the service of others. Consecrated life that respects and promotes differences in gender, age, culture, rites, and sensitivities acquires a notable quality of being a sign in our world. In this way, consecrated life gains a better understanding of pluralism in our society and is better equipped to defend it and to illuminate it with the wisdom of the Gospel.

VI. Postmodern Mentality and Attitudes

35. The so-called "postmodern mentality" is a globalized phenomenon that affects younger generations above all. They are more sensitive to the reality that surrounds us and more receptive to pluralism and complexity, and, as such, they are more vulnerable. This, in turn, fosters feelings of uncertainty, insecurity, and instability, and leads to a narcissistic tendency to look for pleasure in the present without any responsibility for or hope in the future. It should not be surprising, then, that there arise fundamentalist, reactionary movements seeking to establish security by restoring the past.

36. In consecrated life, we also see that the complexity of our world and a *postmodern* mentality produce, especially in younger generations, a more complex and less defined type of personality. This has particular effects on the life and mission of consecrated persons. It shows up in attitudes more tolerant of diversity and more centered on the subjective, and less interested in accepting long-term and definitive life commitments. Everything becomes relative in relation to subjective feelings and needs for temporary commitment. We see from this the necessity for finding ways to live the Gospel authentically and creatively in this new postmodern culture.

37. This postmodern attitude gives us an opportunity to recognize our own limitations and to avoid the triumphalism of the past. It should also make us more vulnerable and compassionate, both toward our own communities and toward all people. We see an opportunity in this to regain our compassion for the suffering of our world. The sense of temporariness and the cultural difficulties with permanence/stability could lead us to study possibilities for proposing forms of consecrated life *"ad tempus"* (VC, no. 56; and *Propositio,* no. 33), which would avoid giving the sense that someone who has joined consecrated life for a time has deserted or abandoned it.

VII. The Thirst for Love and the Distortion of Love

38. We perceive in our world a deep thirst for love and intimacy expressed in so many different forms that sometimes we feel disturbed.

There is a desire for the kind of marriage and family that becomes a home and communion, security in the midst of a hostile, strange, rapidly changing, and violent world. We are very aware of how difficult it can be to work at a love relationship, how it can be continuously interrupted and may even fail and end in self-centeredness. There are various reasons for difficulties in this area: a cultural dominance of one gender over the other (machismo or sexism), patterns of employment imposed by outside forces unfavorable to the stability required by the family and couple, a desire for autonomy and self-realization, etc. The number of divorces is high, and, at the same time, life expectancy is longer. Greater possibilities for relations between persons of the same or of the opposite sex have appeared. It is obvious that the institutions of marriage and the family, such as we have inherited them, are in crisis. All of this generates a "distortion of love" difficult to manage.

39. The Church laments the fact that her message and doctrine—laid out in more integrated and educational schemas—are not sufficiently embraced and carried out not only by society, but also by her own faithful. This situation has also affected consecrated life both in the living out of celibacy or consecrated chastity and in community and interpersonal relationships. The constant flow of those who leave this form of life, the sexual scandals, and the affective immaturity of members indicate that this situation is unsatisfactory to more than a few, who also do not find ways of getting beyond the obstacles and blocks. The celibacy we profess in consecrated life demands a mature, generous, fruitful, and healthy way of living affectivity and sexuality. This witness becomes a prophetic gesture in a society like ours, so greatly marked by eroticism (VC, no. 88).

40. A theological and anthropological reflection of this sort cannot be limited to this topic and to problems related to celibacy or community life. It is true, however, that in speaking of celibacy and community life we need to keep in mind the contributions of the new anthropology. Only in this way can we respond to new situations and have a better orientation for formation in love and celibacy, empha-

sizing the relational and integrating the dimension of spirit and body. This anthropology should influence the other areas of consecrated life as well. We have not always been on target in formulating the implications for formation and vocation ministry, for multiple interpersonal relationships, for forms of government and organization, and for language. If we do not pay attention to the human substratum that sustains consecrated life, we could easily be building on sand.

VIII. *Thirst for the Sacred and Secularistic Materialism*

41. This theme is not placed at the end because it is less important, but because it is the key that gives meaning to everything already said. An authentic renewal of consecrated life and a revitalization of its mission arise out of a healthy and lively spirituality. We see in our world a thirst for the sacred and a longing for spirituality, for meaning, and for transcendence. On the other hand, overconfidence in ourselves, in power, in technology, and in wealth moves us far away from the ultimate Reality. In our world, new idols are being adored that prevent the adoration of the one and true God. A secularized vision of reality is globalized, especially in wealthy countries, and we find ourselves immersed in a world devoid of transcendence, a world that is syncretistic, agnostic, and functional; in other words, a world without a soul.

42. Both in the Church and in consecrated life, the secular environment also favors a tendency toward idolatry expressed in a cult of the media, of the powerful, of institutions, customs, ritualism, and laws. This makes conversion to the only Absolute and Necessary One difficult. It also makes a passion for God and for the Reign of God difficult. Today, the challenge of a deep experience of God and of a passion that is mission-oriented, innovative, and prophetic is seen as conversion to the living God. Hunger for God nourishes our Exodus, and mission gives meaning to our Christian and consecrated vocation. Moreover, we should see that the new experiences and forms of spirituality are not only fruits of human searching, but also true calls and challenges of the Spirit for a society and humanity that have

not found the paths of transcendence, but still eagerly search for the mysterious face of God (VC, no. 84).

43. The thirst for God and a healthy spirituality for our times, together with an idolatrous and secular tendency, offer us the opportunity to purify our vision of what is religious and to find new modes of expression, thus living out our passion for the God of the Covenant. Consecrated life will recover its identity if it appears and acts as a witness to God, as an announcer of God's reign, and if it makes use of serious spiritual means to listen intelligently and empathetically to the sentiments of the human heart. It will thus offer services of spiritual paternity and maternity to our contemporaries in need of them. Witness to the true God also demands that consecrated persons be prepared to risk, in the extreme case, their own lives, even unto martyrdom (VC, no. 86). This situation offers us new opportunities for evangelical creativity in announcing the Risen Jesus.

44. A spirituality that is able to face as an equal the challenges and expectations of the men and women of our times must be nourished with daily, prayerful listening to the Word. We need to strengthen ourselves to meet the demands of the paschal mystery that we celebrate daily, to insert ourselves in the not always easy or defined pathway of God's people in this world, and to enter into a welcoming dialogue capable of discerning the utopias and wounds of present-day humanity. Only through this experience of life in the Spirit as a point of departure can we encourage and animate a new epoch in the history of the coming of the Reign of God and in the history of consecrated life. According to different cultural and religious contexts, this spirituality must give more emphasis on the elements of interiority or historic commitment, but it can never falter in its continuous search for a dynamic balance between these two perspectives. By encountering God, we encounter a great love for the human being, especially the "little ones" and the frailest. By encountering the poor and the wounded, we are moved in our deepest being and we see in them, however disfigured and scorned, an image of God.

Obstacles

45. It is sometimes difficult or impossible to walk the paths along which the Spirit directs us. Consecrated life appears to be held back with locked brakes and blocked by various obstacles. For some of these we are the cause; the Church and the world in which we live are the cause of others.

I. Obstacles Caused by Ourselves

a) Personal and community limitations

46. Our institutes seem blocked, in the first place, by the limitations of their members. These limitations include the continuing aging of members and of the institutes themselves in some countries; the development of new vocations, who are sometimes affected by family or social traumas or are inadequately chosen or poorly accompanied in the formation process; the excess of work that burdens some members; and the superficiality of discernment or the lack of serious initial and ongoing formation. These limitations also restrict the capacity of institutes to respond to the challenges of our times and places. In turn, this reduces and, in some cases, swallows up our passion for Christ and for humanity. Therefore, the programmatic vision expressed in our documents very often exceeds our actual possibilities and we are stuck in the first stages of developing an unrealistic utopia. This generates anxiety and frustration. Solemn theoretical proclamations and language remote from everyday life speak more of human cunning than of evangelical wisdom.

b) Infidelity and a lack of vocational response

47. Another obstacle comes from our infidelity or lack of response to our vocational gift. A middle-class mentality or strong sense of being well established, engendered by an excessive interest in comfort and goods, and a lack of evangelical simplicity born of excessive attachment to material goods, suffocates openness and a spirit of mission.

It blurs a contemplative vision and numbs us in the presence of the poor and marginalized, thus hindering an authentic life of communion.

48. Direct or indirect involvement in sexual and economic scandals and in the abuse of power destroys our credibility, our moral and evangelical authority, and paralyzes the implementation of our projects. To be in touch with reality, we cannot ignore these serious facts. It is difficult to weigh the consequences, but there is no doubt that all of this puts into question the evangelical radicality of this kind of life, which should shine with brilliance.

c) Fears and shutting out

49. The action of the Spirit is blocked within us when we allow ourselves to be motivated by a fear of taking any risks and refrain from making suitable decisions that might displease a dominant group or authority. Fear paralyzes. It reduces our capacity to risk and moves us to seek secure positions. We become traditionalists, conservatives, persons closed to renewal and innovation.

50. When superiors allow themselves to be influenced by fear, a weak leadership develops that attempts to please everyone and everything. As a result, authority becomes very indecisive or too subservient to higher authorities. In a word, such superiors are more willing to please than to act. It is difficult to exercise authority and obedience in an evangelical way in this situation. Today we lack men and women with sufficient moral authority to lead communities in creative fidelity to their charisms.

51. Groups that try to hinder Conciliar renewal and impose their laws on certain aspects of life and in certain circumstances change the collective charism into something routine and decadent. In these cases, creative persons are looked upon with jealousy and are controlled. The most they are permitted to do is to make some superficial changes that do not threaten the status quo. Thus "new wine" is poured into "old wineskins" (Mt 9:17).

52. Fear leads us to search for securities, which in turn lead us to close ourselves up within our own little world, be it religious, ecclesiastical, provincial, or national. We become inordinately attached

to our own language and culture and to isolation in our charism or religious tradition. We become blind to the signs of the Spirit and we kill all initiative and creativity for responding to the great urgencies of our times. There is a pressing need for a new inspiration from the Second Vatican Council that will make us daring and striking in our faithful living of the Gospel.

II. By the Church and Society

53. The Church is the Body of Christ in continual growth (MR, no. 11). Consecrated life finds living space, expansion, and growth within the Church. However, it feels blocked wherever a closed ecclesiastical system dominates, be it on the universal level or in particular local churches, where the system is distrustful and suspicious of the evangelical freedom that so often moves consecrated life. In such circumstances, consecrated life seems relegated to an inferior position and unappreciated in relation to other more docile groups. In some places, the initiatives and labors of consecrated life are dulled and suffer discrimination. If it then opts for conformity with the situation, it loses touch with its most prophetic source. If it opts for the exercise of its prophetic vocation, it is excluded. The prophetic dimension, so essential to consecrated life, must be nurtured and promoted (VC, nos. 84–85).

54. The societies in which we live influence us powerfully, in such a way that their obstacles are our obstacles and their virtues are our virtues. We have only to mention the obstacles proceeding from dictatorial regimes, societies that are extremely "closed in on themselves"—without any openness to global realities—and societies immersed in materialism and secularism. There are many groups, currents, and cultural tendencies that block us: the lack of credibility on the part of principal organizations (political parties, labor unions, social projects, religious organizations), the collapse of the "great utopias" which make the struggle for a better future that much more difficult, and the presence of terror and violence. All of these make us more insecure and fearful every day and everywhere.

III. *The Hope Obstacles Cannot Crush*

55. The realities that challenge us do not crush our hope. Our times are the time of our God of the Covenant, of our God "always greater," of our God whose gifts surpass our desires.

56. As consecrated persons, we are living through crucial moments for humanity and for the Church. We have to make decisions of great importance for the immediate future. We are being presented with decisive options: we can gladden life or make it difficult; grow in communion or create greater distances between us; be conquered by difficulties or face them. We do not have time to spare. New realities demand new responses. God is speaking to us through these new situations and challenges. Our responses must be rooted in reality, but they must also come to birth and be nourished with the wisdom of God and the Word, through whom God comes to us and enlightens us, provokes us and draws us out, purifies us and guides us, and inspires us anew. This is the hour to listen to God's voice. The present period in the history of consecrated life is not its finest hour, but neither is it its worst. It is *our* hour, the one that we have been given to form and make prosper with a faith that acts through charity and makes hope possible.

57. We cannot live an ideal kind of consecrated life far removed from reality. Neither can we talk about a future outside the real world or shape a future out of a dying paradigm. It would be good to regain the ability for a true revitalization using the models proposed, while accepting the necessity of testing fragile solutions without deciding everything beforehand.

PART TWO

Enlightenment: The Symbol

"And when he comes, he will tell us everything."
(Jn 4:25)

"What is written?... What do you read there?"
(Lk 10:26)

58. Facing the realities that challenge us and the obstacles that paralyze us, we turn to the Word of God for light and strength just as our Founders and Foundresses did. "From familiarity with God's Word they draw the light needed for that individual and communal discernment, which helps them to see the ways of the Lord in the signs of the times" (VC, no. 94). The Word of God invites us to discern God's will, what pleases God, what is the more perfect (Rom 12:2), to discern God's ways through the signs of the times and to act with fidelity and wisdom.

59. We want to be enlightened in our discernment, as we have said, by two biblical symbols: the narrative about the meeting of the Samaritan woman with Jesus at Jacob's well (Jn 4:1–42) and the parable of the Good Samaritan (Lk 10:29–37). In their contribution to the Synod of 1994, consecrated women have already used the first symbol. Here we use it to affirm the passionate, spiritual search for living water, for the "contemplative passion" that all of us—consecrated men and women—carry in our hearts and which only Jesus can satisfy. We propose the second symbol as an example of active and diligent compassion toward every person, wounded in body and spirit. Both symbols can inspire our discernment and offer us new perspectives and wise direction as we begin this new century. New and fresh horizons are opened to us that can orient us in the actual context in which we live.

Samaritan Woman, Samaritan Man

60. Against all the common expectations of those times that a Samaritan would behave in a way conforming to the will of God, the two protagonists are involved in a process of transformation expressed in gestures and particular reactions that can inspire our lives. Consecrated life, both feminine and masculine, sees reflected in both symbols its spiritual adventure of passion for Christ and passion for human beings.

I. The Symbol of the Samaritan Woman: Thirst and Liberating Dialogue

61. The story of the dialogue with the Samaritan woman in John's Gospel appears in the context of people's first reaction to Jesus: Nicodemus, the Jew, who wanted to know clearly but resisted in part because of his skepticism (Jn 3:1–21); the Samaritan woman, who is fascinated and thus led to the new (Jn 4:1–42); and the pagan official, who is converted with his whole family (Jn 4:46–52). Traditionally, the entire fourth chapter of John is considered as a baptismal catechesis. In her life journey, the Samaritan woman meets Jesus (Jn 4:1–42). Jesus, tired from his journey, is sitting by Jacob's well. Moved by God the Father's suppliant love, and challenging the prejudices and taboos of his time (Jn 4:27), he begins a dialogue with the woman by asking her for a drink. Her initial resistance does not disturb Jesus. Their dialogue develops through the woman's answers and Jesus' seven statements. The conversation touches both of their hearts. Jesus breathes deeply, asking to be believed. He speaks of true worship in spirit and in truth (Jn 4:23–24); he entrusts her with his deepest secret, telling her that he is the "Messiah who is to come" (Jn 4:26). The woman feels the strength of his words and the deep attraction of his person. Slowly she discovers the mystery of this man who offers her living water and the possibility of a new relationship with God beyond the institutionalized worship practiced on the mountain or in the Temple.

62. This woman bears in her heart a history of wounded relationships. Perhaps she goes to the well at an unusual hour so as not to be seen. She no doubt knows some elements of religious practice, but needs something new and more profound. When she finds it, she becomes a new person. The water jug symbolizes well the emptiness of her life. Jesus perceives the interior malaise that has been the cause of her past adventures. He reveals, with a certain rhythm, the worries he discovers in the woman. She is transformed, passing from irony to a seduction that disarms her, from emptiness to a plenitude that enthuses her. She begins to reflect and to trust. The mysterious Master does not condemn her, but he speaks new words to her that touch her heart, which is thirsting for depth in relationships. The meeting with Jesus transforms her into a messenger: she runs to the city and challenges her neighbors with the announcement of a "Messiah" who knows without condemning and directs the thirsty to the waters springing forth to life eternal (Jn 4:39). Her water jug, a symbol of human thirst and affections that have never been satisfied, now becomes useless. She lets it go (Jn 4:28). Meanwhile, Jesus announces to his disciples that the harvest is ripe and it is time to reap (Jn 4:35–38). The woman sows faith in Jesus among those townsfolk and then brings them to him (Jn 4:39).

63. We can find in this biblical account an icon of our vocation as an experience of encounter with Jesus and commitment to the proclamation of the Gospel. In this meeting place—totally void of all sacred signs—the dialogue opens the heart to the truth; it reveals and heals. God shows himself fragile and thirsty in Jesus. God's thirst meets the woman's thirst, our thirst. He who asks for a drink is willing to offer a new drink: eternal water that transforms life. The relationship becomes a game and a glance, confidence and new birth. Jesus does not fear restless humanity. His serenity and interior freedom allow humanity, represented in the woman, to be the protagonist, to dance at the rhythm of its restlessness until it finds the living water that springs forth to life eternal. Jesus' thirst and the thirst of the woman are the guiding thread of a liberating dialogue that heals

interior wounds, which have been incurable to this point and made more intolerable through racial and religious prejudice. The "indigent" love of God in Jesus invites us—a restless humanity—to drink and freely offers us the Water of Life.

64. We see reflected in the woman that many times we have been wounded in our mutual relationships, and that we thirst for truth and authenticity. We also discover that we are incapable of understanding our affections, behind which our wounded hearts hide. Meditating on this text gives the light of the Word to our life. Simple and ordinary circumstances of life are pleasing to Jesus; they are transformed into special moments of grace and revelation. This woman's capacity, despite her shady past, to gather people is surprising; yet at the same time it teaches us to have confidence in little things and in limited resources. The prejudices with which the disciples observe this scene (Jn 4:26–27) reveal a chauvinist mentality that still exists in our times. But it is Jesus' serenity, born of a clear consciousness of his mission, that allows him to patiently wait for the right question and the moment of total confidence. The disciples go into the town to buy something to eat; the woman goes back to town alone, but she is responsible for many other Samaritans following the path of faith in "the Savior of the world" (Jn 4:30–42).

II. The Icon of the Good Samaritan

65. On the road of life—as the parable tells us—a Samaritan met another person, whom robbers had left half-dead. Deeply moved by this sight, he took care of him (Lk 10:25–37). Maliciously interrogated by a teacher of the Law concerning what one should do to enter eternal life and who is one's neighbor, Jesus first of all refers him to the Law—the principle commandment—and then, to clarify the concept of neighbor, Jesus gives an example in the form of a story through which he changes the question. The important question is not knowing who is my neighbor in order to love him, but rather, having the disposition of heart to be moved to compassion and to approach those in need as *neighbor.* Here is the passage of

an understanding of neighbor as the object of attention, which includes some and excludes others, to that of the subject who lives loving closeness to all, because only active compassion makes us neighbors.

66. We can distinguish between the Samaritan of the tragic hour—the one who helps the victim of the thieves, where he is found immediately and effectively to prevent his death—and the Samaritan of the following day, who organizes the convalescence of the injured man according to the demands of the times and the economy, asking others to collaborate.

67. In this text, pastoral and theological tradition has found a reflection of wounded humanity abandoning itself, and the compassion of God that, through his Son, descends to heal it. This interpretation is based on the verb "to feel compassion"—*kai esplanchnisthè*—used here as well as in the narrative of the widow of Naim (Lk 7:13); it is what motivates the father to run toward the Prodigal Son (Lk 15:20). This beautiful and suggestive interpretation is still valid and teaches us to have the same sentiments of Christ and to kneel, as he did, before a wounded and violated humanity and to help with all means the wounded and abandoned, who lay half-dead on the peripheries of our society.

68. In this parable, we see how Jesus puts aside, in his evaluation, those who are signs of religious power when they are unmoved by compassion, while he gives center stage to a man moved to make poor and humble gestures of healing with oil, wine, bandages, his beast of burden, and the inn. The Samaritan offers immediate help as "first aid," but he also asks the innkeeper to "take care of him" and, for this reason, he cares for, helps, and respects him for an extended time. For the Samaritan, the needy victim was constantly on his mind, and his preoccupation was such that he returned to check on his treatment and to pay the costs. He does not shift his worries onto another's shoulders, but rather they become a stimulus for active solidarity. The final invitation of Jesus "to do the same"

(Lk 10:37) is directed toward practical consistency and not theoretical principles.

69. Today, the Samaritan's road is an immense space where crowds of men and women, children and the elderly who are "half-dead" bear the wounds of every type of violence inflicted on their bodies and their souls. Innumerable are the faces disfigured by violence and injustice: the faces of emigrants and refugees in search of a new homeland, of exploited women and children, the elderly and the sick abandoned to their own fate, of those humiliated by racial and religious prejudices, of children traumatized in body and spirit, of those disfigured by hunger and torture. These are the scourged of the earth, on the margins of society throughout history, who beg for a creative compassion that transforms traditional charitable institutions in response to the new urgencies and who give new testimony to their neighbor. To be a neighbor means, in fact, to view situations from the perspective of the poor who are at the end *(éschaton)* of society and, basing the deciding criterion on the Last Judgment (Mt 25:31–45), starting from their requirements and from the process of healing and liberation. The main challenge today consists in changing priorities in order to promote dynamics of neighborly compassion.

70. The most important challenge is to enter into action, giving priority to those in need, to persons and not to business, to the healing processes and not to the sacred norms that strip us of compassion—as in the case of the priest and the Levite. The people of the "institutions" did not know how to free the imagination of charity. They continued on the road in order to keep themselves pure in the legal and cultural sense. However, the man who exercised his religiosity and worship in an unacceptable form, even to the point of being scorned by the official religious leaders, showed himself the only one capable of practicing charity. Free of external religious projects, he had a merciful heart and soul.

When we are profoundly moved, even poor resources such as oil, wine, and bandages are transformed into signs of great and deep values. It is necessary, however, for us to get off the beast of burden that makes of us privileged persons and that separates us from so many travelers who have no dignity, home, or means. It is necessary to pour over their wounds the oil of our contemplation, because it is not an egotistical and solitary self-seeking, and the wine of our tenderness and gratitude return hope and the desire to live.

71. The Samaritan community forms itself around Jesus. It is the community of those who are with Jesus, who share his compassion for humanity, and who are sent, as was he, to preach. They also receive the power to expel demons (Mk 3:15) and to cure the sick, anointing them with oil (Mk 6:13). This is how the true community of Jesus is formed in a world of violence and injustice.

Consecrated Life As "Samaritan"

I. Keys to Reading

72. Contemplated together, these icons show us how the consecrated life is born from a vocational experience that takes place in an encounter and dialogue of life with Jesus, who calls us, and with those who are in most need. The Samaritan woman and the Samaritan man urge us to bring to light our wounded relationships of consecrated life so as to embrace them compassionately, heal them gratuitously and diligently, pouring over them the oil of contemplation and the wine of tenderness and gratitude. Both images allow us to sit at so many "wells," where disturbed and needy hearts that lack new liberating hope go to slake their thirst or to walk the roads where we find the poor who need our help; to dialogue calmly and without prejudice, not calculating time or prestige; to share our passion for the water that truly satisfies, revitalizes, and transforms; to get off our "high horses"—privileges, rigid structures, sacred prejudices— to bind ourselves to the fate of the crucified of the earth and to struggle against all violence and injustice, in this way beginning a new phase of healing and solidarity.

II. The "New Model"

73. Under the impulse of the Spirit, who is guiding us along the path to complete truth (Jn 16:13), there is a consecrated life emerging with new characteristics. We feel ever more strongly the necessity for an intense contemplative experience lived amidst the anguish and hopes of people, especially the most fragile and insignificant. A new model of consecrated life—born of compassion for the wounded and downtrodden of the earth—is being defined around new priorities, new models of organization, and open and flexible collaboration with all men and women of good will. The elements that have characterized this Christian vocation in history, and express its great and rich tradition, are gathered in a new synthesis. This permits consecrated life to recapture the Gospel as its first norm, the great commandment of the Covenant as its central element, and fraternity as a proposal and prophecy in a divided and unjust society, living the passion for humanity with a great drive of imagination and creativity. The experience of being in the midst of the poorest and the excluded has given new configuration to consecrated life as Samaritan life that announces the Gospel with new expressions. "How many consecrated men and women have bent down, and continue to bend down, as Good Samaritans, over the countless wounds of the brothers and sisters whom they meet on their way!" (VC, no. 108)

74. Thus, a new image of the paschal Church, the servant, enriched by the testimony of martyrs, is emerging in the midst of much fragility. There are widespread examples and experiences of solid and fraternal communities, prayerful and daring, constant in doing good and vigilant in compassion, courageous in initiatives and joyful in hope. "Does not this world of ours also need men and women who, by their lives and their work, are able to sow seeds of peace and fraternity?" (VC, no. 108)

PART THREE

Toward Action

"Give me a drink!" (Jn 4:7)

"Do this and life is yours! ... Go and do the same yourself!" (Lk 10:28, 37)

75. Jesus' insistent words to the teacher of the Law are today directed to us: "Do this and life is yours!" For consecrated life, the two icons are a stimulus and a program for living and commitment. Ours is the hermeneutic task of interpreting in every place and time the way to transform these into reality. In consecrated life, we have given certainty to many things, and, at times, simply by the fact of our knowing and speaking about them. However, we should only do this for what we live.

76. Above all, we recognize that we are not lacking in voluntary effort. God is already acting in us and with us. There are indications of newness, precursors of the gift that we are being offered and we should already know. However, there are also areas or fields in which we must demonstrate our willingness to collaborate with grace and to show the creative and imaginative power of our freedom and the "creativity of charity" (NMI, no. 50).

Indications of Newness: Where Is the Spirit Leading Us?

77. The Holy Spirit continues to act in the world, in the Church, and in us. Signs of life and hope appear everywhere. Those who are sensitive to the Spirit and truth "know the gift of God" (Jn 4:10), and they know what must be done to live and give life. There are signs of all of this in consecrated life, which we need to know how to read and interpret. Above all, we need to

know how to enter into the processes that permit us to bring to fruition what we are beginning.

I. The Power of the Fountain, Source of the Living Water

78. From the Second Vatican Council to today, consecrated life has made a great effort to return to its sources, to encounter God's gift. It has sought to re-encounter the Word through its founding inspiration and identity.

79. The *Word of God* has been placed at the center of consecrated life and it animates all its aspects. We listen to it with the whole People of God in the context of our times. Consecrated life "has re-encountered the Word" (VC, nos. 81, 94). In the Word, we find the strength to live, the direction to walk, and the stimulus for our projects. The Word is the basis of our incarnated and inculturated spirituality. The Word nourishes all of the aspects of our life: prayer, community, and mission. In a particular way, this has been attained through the discovery and diffusion of the ancient tradition of the *"lectio divina."* Thus, the Word is made wisdom that "questions, directs, and shapes our lives" (NMI, no. 39). Nourished by the Word, we are transformed into "'servants of the Word' in the work of evangelization" (NMI, no. 40).

80. In some religious institutes, there has been a return to the *original inspiration of their Founders and Foundresses,* according to the spirit of the Second Vatican Council (PC 2). Where this has happened, the institute has been able:

a)   to perceive the permanent freshness of its charism and its gathering, transforming, and prophetic strength (VC, nos. 84–85); to return to the origins of an institute has made us "feel ourselves family";

b)   to understand that the inherited charism is a gift for the whole Church and, as such, should be shared with others (VC, nos. 54–56);

c)   to discover a new reality expressed in new language: "shared charism," "shared spirituality," "shared mission," "shared community" (SaC, nos. 30–31);

d) to modify our understanding of the institute to the end of feeling ourselves as "family," to put life back into our sense of Church and shared consecrated life;

e) to see our enthusiasm reborn and to recover the creative dream of the origins in new contexts, responding to new needs (VC, no. 37);

f) to redefine our identity not only starting from "essential elements," but also in correlation to all the forms of Christian living, from the humble service of all and an attitude of sharing (CfL, no. 55); and

g) to respond to the request of the laity and ordained ministers to share our spiritual inspiration.

II. The Meetings That Transform: We Have Gone to Drink from the Same Well

81. The Spirit of God continues to create the "new," continues to speak to us through the prophets, and calls us to loving fidelity and apostolic audacity (VC, no. 82). In consecrated life today, there are traces of the Spirit's renewing presence. There are new *"encounters"* that transform and give new life, but also new questions and challenges (VC, no. 73). Creation is an encounter, as are incarnation and redemption. Because these encounters are fruitful, they must take place in the *"meeting tent,"* as was the case with Moses (Ex 33:7). In the process of refoundation, already initiated, consecrated life has slowly passed from isolation and distance to dialogue, sharing, communication, presence, and interaction. New ways of relating have multiplied.

82. Among the most significant and important encounters, and those with greater consequences for consecrated life, we need to note the following: encounters between men and women and between religious and "laity." Through these encounters, we are slowly learning how to drink from the same well and to walk with both feet through the life of the Church and of society, listening with our two ears and seeing with our two eyes. Encounters between different cultures and

generations are increasing. We are learning how to live with cultural diversity and with people of different ages and to see these differences as a great richness. Encounters between religious and the poor: the experience of insertion, solidarity, and shared life with the poor has been very fruitful when this has occurred (VC, no. 82). Encounters between believers and non-believers have taken place, as well as encounters among members of different religions, which also bring together different churches. We are trying to break many kinds of barriers and divisions, to build bridges and create communion. We are also discovering the richness of the different forms of consecrated life within different traditions through dialogue and exchange. A great richness for religious is the encounter with Mother Earth. The ecological dimension can bring about important consequences for our mission and spirituality (VC, no. 103; NMI, no. 56). The encounter among different congregations, from simple collaboration to confederation, federation, or fusion (VC, nos. 52, 53), allows us to put in relief what is essential and common to consecrated life without losing the aspects specific to each group. This will contribute to finding the new paradigm that all of us seek in one way or another.

83. These encounters, seen as events, processes, and grace, delineate the indispensable dimensions of the new modes of consecrated life. They are already becoming a reality, but they need the creativity and insight of many in order to take shape in the present journey of the Church and society. All of these encounters are demanding and we often initiate them, but later we do not follow through on them. Nevertheless, in and through these encounters new forms of evangelical life are emerging, which are simple, radical, ecumenical, inserted among the people, flexible in structure, welcoming, and attentive to symbolic language, to the present rhythms of life, and to the demands of deep communion with God and with persons (VC, nos. 12, 62).

III. *The Language of Water That Gushes and Flows*

84. The signs of vitality that the Spirit is raising up in consecrated life have stirred in us the need to express the new in a new way, with a new language, and with the creation of original, symbolic schemata. This is why we speak of "new paradigms," "new models," "new forms," "refounding," and of "creative faithfulness." The form of life modifies and shapes the language, and the language modifies and shapes the form of life. It is not strange that the new forms of living consecrated life are changing our forms of expression and organization, and that these new words change our ways of living as well. Consecrated life has always been a laboratory of new cultural and organizational models, thus expressing authentic evangelical values in different contexts and in different cultural and religious conditions. In consecrated life, there has existed a strong tendency toward inculturation that is still present in our times and that we should re-actualize (VC, nos. 6, 98).

85. In the first place, we have discovered the necessity for new expressions and methods to announce Jesus Christ and the Reign of God for our times. Consecrated life that knows it is called to share in the great project of the "new evangelization" is conscious of the demand for a "new fervor" or a new spiritual language that unites mission and spirituality, community and individuality, body and spirit. Lastly, it knows that the option for the poor and excluded is an unavoidable expression of this new evangelization (NMI, no. 49).

86. Some symbols and symbolic language of the past lose their force and are replaced by other forms of communication, which are better adapted to contemporary culture. Contact with sociocultural and ecclesial realities humanizes, renews, and adapts us. A different sensitivity is being born among us, and the Holy Spirit is carrying us toward new forms of mission and life. All of this requires of us a serious commitment to cultivate the gift that God is giving us.

IV. New Relations in a Church of Communion: Plentiful Fruit from a Well-Irrigated Land

87. The ongoing development of an ecclesiology of communion, which comes from the Second Vatican Council, has continuously invited all the members of the People of God to walk together on the paths of sanctity, evangelization, and solidarity. The confession of the Triune Mystery and the acknowledgment of the active role of the Holy Spirit in the Church as an expression of fecundity, communion, and missionary dynamism, have revealed the richness of different vocations and forms of life within the Church, emphasizing the relationship and the reciprocity between them (cf. VC, no. 55). All of this is extending, and at the same time, qualifying these relationships so that it is possible to live deeply our being daughters and sons of God, the fraternity, and the mission inherent in all Christian vocations. Fostering the spirituality of communion proposed by John Paul II (VC, no. 46; NMI, no. 43; PC, no. 22), the Church is made more visible as a community of believers and apostles. The Church's missionary horizons are widened, dialogue is made more fruitful in all directions and with various spokespersons, the paths of solidarity are expanded, or, in other words, the spirit of "the Samaritan" is lived (*Ecclesia in Asia,* nos. 31, 34, 44).

88. In these last years, the relationships of consecrated persons have been extended, multiplied, and improved. There are relationships not only with the Bishops, but also with the laity, and in a particular way with those who share the same charism and mission. There are relationships with diocesan priests, who provide connections to many other relationships with leaders within Christian communities, as well as with all those who, with good will, work toward the world's transformation. We consecrated persons seek to enter the network of solidarity as an alternative to impersonal globalization. We are conscious that this involves and implies conflicts. We think that it is our duty to prevent the dangerous effects of globalization and to sustain the initiatives of those organizations working to cre-

ate this awareness and encourage a profound thirst for communion. At times, however, we do not know how to live this commitment and, at other times, it is not well received.

Response to the Gift: Imaginative and Creative Strength

89. Our Lord invites us: "Do this and you will have life!" We have to put this into action. The Congress invites consecrated life to initiate and continue a new praxis, to take decisive and serious steps forward. In doing so, we give ourselves a two-fold goal that corresponds to a two-fold urgency in consecrated life. It will require of us intensity and zeal, in other words, a passion for Christ and for humanity. It demands focus and clear goals and objectives. In this section, we want to envision and make our own the future God desires for us, describing in the best possible way the responses we must make to God's proposals.

90. It is not easy to indicate what needs to be done in order for consecrated life to be significant in society and in the Church. From the pedagogical perspective it is very important to indicate, as did the Church before the Second Vatican Council, what is not going well, what is ending, what has neither present nor future. This helps us to concentrate our energy on what is most necessary.

91. We propose to follow some reflections and questions to orient our discernment in the Congress. The questions emerged from the consultation carried out.

I. Witnesses of Transcendence

92. In a time when the experience of the mystery of God is fading and in some cases entirely extinguished, or in other cases interfered with by an extremely diverse religious pluralism, we feel the call to emphasize and reveal the inherent religious value of all aspects of life.

93. The religious experience given to us, and which we cultivate, is an experience of God the Creator, who has acted as redeemer of history and made himself *Emmanuel,* becoming incarnate in Jesus of Nazareth. Thanks to the Spirit, who has been given to us, we who possess a vocation to consecrated life try to become a memory of the lifestyle of Jesus of Nazareth. We wish to be his witnesses to the ends of the earth and a manifestation of his passion for God and his compassion for people, promoting in all its forms the religious dimension of life, the basic richness to which all contribute and in which all participate.

94. For us, to announce Jesus with our lives, our gestures, and our actions is the quintessence of our evangelical vocation. For this reason, we ask ourselves: *What are the changes that are becoming necessary in our religious, institutional, and communitarian systems to make our lives more evangelical?*

II. Inculturation

95. Consecrated life will not survive or fulfill its mission if it is not inculturated in the diverse places and contexts where it is found. To follow the process of inculturation, "which entails discernment, courage, dialogue, and the challenge of the Gospel" (VC, no. 80), is a vital question for consecrated life and a proof of its authenticity looking toward the future.

96. The Spirit is moving consecrated life to diversify, to incarnate, to revitalize itself. These processes of inculturation are demanding, but, when carried out well, they emphasize the original elements of the foundational charism. *What proposals can we make so that this becomes a reality? What are the obstacles that we perceive in the traditional organizational, formational, spiritual, or anthropological models?*

97. The face of consecrated life is changing. A multi-centric and intercultural communion is always more necessary. We have to learn the new art of the ecclesiology of communion. *What con-*

sequences does this new perspective have on our structures of government, formation, pastoral experience, and cultural and spiritual language?

III. Community Life, Affectivity, and Sexuality

98. Community life is a reality deeply rooted in consecrated life (VC, nos. 42, 45, 51). It takes effort to live it well. The "new consecrated life" looks for "new communities." *What lines should we follow in order to refound, psychologically and evangelically, our communities in these new times?*

99. Within the "disorder of love" so evident in our times, our community life could become a means of affective stability and living together inspired by faith and open to complete fulfillment. Relationships are less rigid and impersonal than in the past. They allow for adequate manifestations of affection and tenderness, and give greater attention and care to physical and emotional well-being. However, an excessively erotic mentality and context would be a danger for us. Let us acknowledge that, with the help of divine grace, we can speak of our life as a reclaiming of the primordial project of God for humanity: "in the beginning, it was not so" (Mt 19:8). From this perspective is born a new way to understand celibacy as an evident consequence of the relationship between genders and a more integrated vision of sexuality. *What should we say and do in regard to this?*

IV. Spirituality

100. We form part of a humanity thirsting for spirituality. The cries for a life in the Spirit are expressed in so many ways that it is necessary to characterize them. Of us, consecrated men and women, our brothers and sisters expect a particular spiritual contribution that affects our language and our experience of life and mission (VC, no. 102). The Spirit is calling us to exercise the ministry of spiritual paternity/maternity in a new way, open to the future, entering in interspiritual dialogue not only to give and teach, but al-

so to listen, accept, and receive (NMI, no. 56; GS, no. 92). This is our challenge.

101. The new realities being born are affirmed where healthy spirituality is cultivated. Its basic point is to care for the faith and the prayerful experience of our life. *How do we do this? What do we do to make consecrated life—by vocation and charism—a laboratory of spirituality, a space for the cultivation of the Spirit and the spiritual that dwells in everyone?* (VC, no. 6)

V. Sharing with the People of God and Our Pastors

102. A consciousness of the reciprocity proper to an ecclesiology of communion will lead us to feel interdependent in all forms of Christian life. In a special way, the laity, whom the Spirit is raising up, are becoming for consecrated life inspiration, support, and accompaniment to help it go forward in a renewed and fruitful manner (VC, nos. 54–56; SaC, nos. 30–31).

103. Consecrated life shares its charisms with other forms of Christian living, especially with the laity, and participates with its charisms in the services and ministries of others. Situated within the living network of the Body of Christ, the Church, consecrated life— especially women and the laity—can contribute to generating new models of ecclesial identity that demand recognition, encouragement, and integration. From the experience we have accumulated, we ask ourselves: *What orientations should we follow along these lines of relationship and mutual identification in the form of life and mission?*

104. The mutual communion between pastors, laity, and religious is felt, with always more power, as an intrinsic demand of docility to the Spirit, who guarantees the relationships between ecclesial members. Institutional interests and pragmatic pretensions are put aside or postponed. The dynamics of information, dialogue, and participation are spreading throughout the Church, in which ministers and charisms have their precise places and functions. There is an always greater sharing of spirituality and

concern for the proclamation of the Reign of God—two matters definitely at play. *How do we think, feel, and act together according to the Gospel?*

VI. The Symbolic Capacity Beginning from the Authenticity of Our Life

105. We have lost our sense of the symbolic with the passing of time. The world of symbols in which we live requires serious adaptation in the realm of meaning. Lack of imagination or fear has transformed us into mere custodians of symbols that are either insignificant or have value merely as a museum piece or legend. We lack adequate expressions for the authentic values incarnated and lived in consecrated life. As the *Instrumentum Laboris* of the Synod on Consecrated Life reminded us: "Our life has in society a critical, symbolic, and transforming function" (IL, no. 9). This function demands many changes if it is to be eloquent and effective. On the point of our significance, we ask ourselves: *What language are we using? How are we presenting it? What are we transmitting? How should we live so as to be significant?*

VII. Poverty and Human Suffering

106. A consecrated life that desires a guarantee of fruitfulness must read itself in the vein of service, accompaniment, and solidarity with those who are in pain or misery. It will have to find the way to be like the Samaritan woman who seeks, along with all the thirsty, the living water in the fountains and the wells of memory and happiness. It must tend wounded faces without forgetting to continue the fight against violent and unjust systems that cause suffering. *How can we do this? What do we have to say about this challenge?*

107. A return to a life of poverty, solidarity, and compassion has always been the key element in the process of refoundation in the history of consecrated life (VC, nos. 75, 82). In our society at present, many people live with superfluous things in such a way as

to irresponsibly damage Mother Earth. Through our vow of poverty, God calls us to live only with what is necessary and, if possible, with what is indispensable. This option allows us to be generous in sharing and giving and free in receiving and requiring. *How can consecrated life promote a change from a life based on the superfluous to a life based on the necessary?*

VIII. The Area of Ecumenical and Interreligious Dialogue

108. We can understand mission as a movement of the people—inspired by the Spirit—toward the Reign of God, to which consecrated life contributes something particular. It bears witness before humanity to the saving plan of the God of the Covenant and becomes for all a symbol of a faithful response to that pact. The principle commandment of love, of solidarity, gives rise to the Covenant relationship among all people, and is expressed through a real commitment to justice, peace, and care for creation. In this particular historical moment, the communitarian, intercultural, religious, and ecumenical dialogue of life is the name of the mission; it is a question of life or death for all the evangelizing and missionary activity of the Church. In our institutes, we have sensed this for some time now, and we are looking for new models of missionary insertion and Gospel proposals.

109. The presence and action of religious in the area of dialogue help consecrated life to widen *"the space of its tent"* (Is 54:2), to be revitalized and establish life-giving connections. By re-enforcing this presence, we reaffirm the kind of consecrated life that the Spirit stirs in our times. *What initiatives should we begin to take to shape our mission in character with authentic dialogue?*

A Process to Follow

110. The Congress is a milestone in the history of consecrated life. Will it be a significant moment within this history? We want to affirm this and to thank our God for what the Holy Spirit is bringing

to birth in consecrated life at the beginning of this new millennium. There is no doubt that a process has begun that will be united to the many experiences of the past sixteen centuries.

111. The fidelity the Spirit is raising up among us brings us to give consistency, continuity, and security to the initiative begun. For this reason, we want to discern, discover, and propose how formation should be shaped to ensure continuity in this new consecrated life and how government should be structured in order to animate this new phase in the development of consecrated life.

I. A Government for Structural Transformation

112. Consecrated life has structures, organization, and functions of government that correspond to its glorious history. But we should be building the future. This requires a profound change in institutional mentality that makes possible the emergence of new institutions and forms of government in which this new life would not be suffocated. In all its forms, consecrated life appears in the Church as a series of energies not always taken advantage of and sometimes wasted, and at other times used in a repetitive way. Internal reorganization—not only of each institute, but also of all institutes—intercongregational dialogue, and bridges of collaboration and integration are clear initiatives to which the Spirit is leading us. However, it is clear that structures have to be "light" and animated through dialogue, co-responsibility, and the Gospel. *What would we propose along the lines of institutional refounding? What should those who govern religious institutes do to put the structures of their institutes and projects at the service of the mission?*

113. In great part, consecrated life depends on its economic structures. A large part of its missionary enterprise depends on money, as do its formation processes and its globalization, but it can also be a counter-testimony. Although economy is not the most important aspect of consecrated life, its influence has always been great. All reforms or new forms of consecrated life have given spe-

cial attention to poverty and economy. The complexity of world economics and unbalanced and unjust economic systems has a notable influence on the economics of institutes. *What can we say about this? How do we shape economies of solidarity? How do we organize an economy that serves mission?*

II. A New Formation for a New Form of Consecrated Life

114. We want to shape consecrated life to be authentically "Samaritan," that is, with a thirst for God and constantly moved by compassion. Our responsibility in the face of what the Spirit is bringing to birth among us demands communal discernment (VC, no. 74) and serious commitment to the development and implementation of formative and spiritual guidelines that will make its growth and consolidation viable. In this we must faithfully follow the criteria expressed in the Post-Synodal Exhortation, *Vita Consecrata:* "Formation is a dynamic process by means of which individuals are converted to the Word of God in the very depths of their being and, at the same time, learn how to discover the signs of God in earthly realities" (VC, no. 68).

115. The ecclesiology of communion affects formation processes from different perspectives. A model of joint formation is emerging from the People of God, and we cannot remain indifferent to its presence. In foundational moments, on the other hand, formation tends to "go to the essential," to the heart, the font of life. We are living in a time in which the ecclesiology of communion asks us to learn together—all forms of life—what it means to be *"Christifideles."* It is only by starting from this point that we will be able to understand ourselves in charismatic co-relationship. *What are the implications of these perspectives for shaping formation processes?*

Conclusion

116. We sense that our forms of consecrated life are in a time of transition, but our hearts burn, thirst, and search for the living water, especially when we are able to listen to God, who speaks to us on the way. We experience a passionate love for Jesus and a loving compassion for our brothers and sisters. Therefore, we are able to encounter and publicly recognize him as the *"Savior of the world"* (Jn 4:42). We well know that the fire of love can intensify or fade, widen or shrink, be contagious or isolated. It is also possible for it to go out.

117. We do not want to become stuck in "the glorious history." Rather, we want to "look to the future, where the Spirit is sending [us] in order to do even greater things" (VC, no. 110). For this reason, we are not interested in defending presumed vested rights, but rather to serve better and more, faithful to our vocation. In this way, we purify ourselves and recover a new fruitfulness. Thus, we become credible in a Church that is being reborn in this *"novo millennio ineunte."* This is a serious and urgent demand.

118. We can count on the promise of the Spirit that makes all things new and "intercedes for the saints according to the designs of God" (Rom 8:27). We are assured of the compassionate and life-giving presence of Mary, symbol of fruitfulness, the Mother of all life that is born. Consecrated life, when it has desired to initiate a new phase in its historical journey, has always looked to and invoked Mary. Through her and in her it has lived its days of new Pentecost. Under her protection, all consecrated persons implore of the Spirit "the courage to face the challenges of our times and the grace to bring to all humankind the goodness and the loving kindness of our Savior Jesus Christ" (VC, no. 111).

FROM THE WELL...TO THE INN

Bruno Secondin, O.Carm., and Diana Papa, OSC

Introduction

It is not our intention to summarize the *Instrumentum Laboris,* even less to communicate in great detail the responses and reactions to it. Approximately 100 contributions were sent to the Congress Secretariat, and a number of contributions have appeared in reviews, on websites, etc. All those who responded deserve our thanks. This interpretive synthesis is a response to the collaboration we have received. Suggestions, further development, additions, and critiques are presented here in three large sections: text, context, and pretext. A rereading, both horizontal and dynamic—which we could call meta-textual—will help to open our history to new horizons and new adventures, both evangelical and charismatic.

Responses to and Proposals Concerning the *Instrumentum Laboris*

1. The Text

Many appreciated the positive, multifaceted, and encouraging tone of the text. The presentation of the great sociocultural themes in a realistic style, both sincere and provocative, was also very well received. Many recognized the osmosis between the phenomenological vision and the theological and ecclesial interpretation open to taking up the challenges and finding new paths of creative fidelity. Sometimes the density of the synthesis on certain complex issues produced paragraphs that were too general or too dense, making immediate comprehension of the content difficult. Everyone realized that the text "will die" during the Congress and, therefore, there will not be an "improved second edition." Nevertheless, we also received observations for clarifying the text, making additions to it, improving it, rejecting aspects of it, and completing it.

a) The Biblical Icons

Many expressed pleasant surprise over the two Gospel icons and, above all, for the method used to present and interpret them. In reality, the method is more symbolic and allusive than technical or exegetical. People liked the call to the processes of interior transformation experienced by the Samaritan woman and the Good Samaritan. The possibilities of original applications to consecrated life were noted, with emphasis on the nontraditional aspects or the aspects not usually considered.

The method of *lectio divina* has shown itself to be a rich source of inspiration not only on the spiritual level, but also in practice. There were some notes for enriching the interpretation by underlining the details not commented upon (e.g., how the Good Samaritan spent the night, inverting of typical roles—the Samaritan woman speaks about theology and the Good Samaritan shows tenderness and care—the sacramentality of the body, the scribe who questions, the ecological elements, etc.)

b) Some Critiques

Some rather well developed critiques also arrived. We quote some of them here. Someone thinks that the following of Christ, which constitutes the true basis of consecrated life, was not in evi-

dence; others consider the two figures (feminine/masculine) an artificial couple; someone thinks that we feel ourselves "Samaritans"
much too quickly, while we are among the "wounded" and perhaps
also among those who wound. Someone also noted the lack of a communitarian context in these icons. Others do not like the excessive
human initiative, which does not seem to take into account the theme
of election and the primacy of the experience from above (it is God
who calls).

Stories remain open to uncertain outcomes and this generates
perplexity in those who want things well defined. The word "re-foun-
dation" seems to be easily accepted, but is not justified with solid
reasons. The preference in the type of consecrated life tends toward
the apostolic life, leaving monastic and contemplative life almost
on the margins. On its part, monastic and contemplative life also
desires to live with full rights in the Church under the dynamic action of the Spirit. Among the new experiences, a reference to the
models born within consecrated life or within new ecclesial movements is lacking, etc.

There are a number of references, though, to inappropriate or
equivocal expressions, missing elements, perspectives that are too
Western (European and from the time just after the Council), or too
masculine or surprising, such as the "consecration *ad tempus,*" etc.
In a few cases, the critique is followed by a concrete proposal. Some
well-developed proposals touched on ongoing formation, on some
cultural aspects of modernism, on "new models" of consecrated life,
on the feminine identity of consecrated life, on the reformulation of
the vows in postmodern terms or in terms of interpersonal relationships, etc.

The third part of the *Instrumentum Laboris* posed some questions on various aspects to be developed and clarified, and on perspectives for action in the future. These were not given much
attention; in fact, responses to the specific points are rare. We do
not have, therefore, significant contributions on those points except
where explicitly requested with specific questions.

2. The Context

The most important issue on which the comments reflected was the current situation of consecrated life. Many interpreted the situation in terms of "crisis" and of confusion of orientation and of options. Others preferred to use the expression "chaos" to point to a context with opportunities as well as dangers. Finally, others liked to speak of the complexity and of situations that are "multiversal." They dealt with analyses of practical aspects (e.g., works, structures, organization, fragmentation, aging, cultural traditions), of religious cultural aspects (old models of spirituality, of language, and of life; new pedagogical and psychological needs; new sociocultural situations; paradigm change), and of the ecclesial and current social context, which is in a process of rapid transformation. We will make a general presentation on the major themes.

a) The Ecclesiological Dimension

There are very interesting comments on the theme of ecclesiology. It was reaffirmed that consecrated life develops in the midst of the Church and for the Church, always forming part of its holiness and of its very life and mission. We took up the ecclesiology of communion, strongly promoted by the Second Vatican Council and afterward, up to the most recent documents. Now, however, there is an ongoing regression. We see that the Church is ever further from the realities and problems of our world, looking at them as from on high without profound compassion, almost as one "passing by." Legalism and indifference make the prophetic word sterile in the Christian people. The "spirituality of communion" is much proclaimed in words, but, in reality, it results in a reduction of areas of autonomy and prophecy. Prophecy is forced into hiding and that generates distrust. Consecrated life feels the effects of this problematic ecclesial situation, receiving a significant restraint on the journey toward authentic renewal. The process of refoundation, begun practically forty years ago in the light of the Council guidelines, suffers serious damage from it.

Among the many reactions added as commentary to the *Instrumentum Laboris,* one sentence particularly reflects these times: "Who can affirm that in these times consecrated life does not appear half-dead [like the man who fell in among thieves]?" Consecrated life, at this time, really is experiencing a period characterized by contradictory signs. On the one hand, there is evidence of a profound weariness, of inertia, and of uncertainty concerning identity, evidenced in the fear of the future and in the crisis of a clear public image. One example is the debatable televised appearances of religious men and women presented in many forms. Contemporaneously, there are also many personal and communitarian testimonies that concretize the radical and growing desire for commitment in discerning the signs of the new being raised up by the Holy Spirit and in the effective work of integrating these fruitfully into the proper charism.

Such signs of newness and creative fidelity in so many responses support the conviction that it is still possible for consecrated life today to play its prophetic role. It is still possible for it to live its unique vocation and mission in the Church and for the Church, at the same time creating newness and calling everyone to a fidelity rich in love and apostolic boldness.

b) The Secularized and Postmodern Context

Some wanted to give lengthier clarifications regarding the sociocultural context, for example, on the crisis of modernism and postmodern culture; the false readings concerning the "rebirth of the sacred"; the dialogue among religions and cultures; the communication, both pervasive and symbolic, on the centrality of the body and affectivity in the present culture; the credibility crisis of institutions; globalization as resource and challenge; the search for new and affectively gratifying relationships, etc. Perhaps there is some truth to saying that the *Instrumentum Laboris,* in its description of the variety of sociocultural phenomena, did not include a true and sufficient spiritual discernment. The spiritual reading of the crisis of these times could have pointed to and stimulated a more effective guiding wisdom, which would go beyond a rapid glance at phenomena that are, in reality, very complex.

According to some, it is necessary to be on guard against adaptation to a secularized mentality, consumerism, and various forms of individualistic or bourgeois mentalities. It is necessary to set ourselves up as a counter-cultural project founded on a deep and solid experience of God and a radical following of Christ. Some saw in the document's general plan—and thus, in the plan of the Congress—a concerning deficiency, because the overly horizontal perspective and the usual evaluations of the current evils are repeated without arriving at concrete and livable proposals. These found the development in the *Instrumentum Laboris* "general," vague (light) and imprecise, for example, concerning new religiosity, gender differences, the concept of the Church and its institutional forms, the "blocks" hindering the realization of ideals, the new models of consecrated life and its possibilities for the future, and renewed spirituality itself.

Others, instead, saw in the *Instrumentum Laboris* a serious and precise description of the current context in which we all are living, with its disquieting shadows, but also the opportunities and stirring challenges. They were in agreement, for example, on the wide range of problematic situations set in relief in the first part, but also on the decisive points for consecrated life described in the two sections of the third part. Also the two areas to which the document called attention at the end and for which it requested proposals—formation and government—were seen as strategic and decisive. There is need for further guiding clarification, which is awaited from the Congress in a definite and concrete way. In the pedagogy of formation and the realistic solutions for the complex issues of ongoing formation—areas considered important—it seems that shared models and tested solutions are lacking.

c) To Be Attentive and Incarnated

There are those who recognize that the entire cultural system characterizing consecrated life, and with which it is expressed today, is weak in its ability to communicate, backward with respect to cultural sensitivities, and set in other presently obsolete cultural worlds (PC no. 3 already stated the necessity of updating on this point). Thus arises the suggestion for a definite "updating" of paradigms and the presentation of the major values: the vows, community, witness, anthropology, life-vision, the sense of well being and the religiosity of life, affectivity, corporality, dignity of the person, need for co-responsibility, etc. According to some, consecrated life will never be understood because it belongs to a different world and is founded on an experience of transcendence, which few know how to appreciate and interpret. These people like to insist on the aspect of the "mystery" of this ecclesial vocation.

Therefore, they are convinced that it is not adapting—in practice, assuming current secularized values—that will make consecrated life understood and place it in dialogue in the new areopagi. Consecrated life must preserve its identity and irreducibility, even to the point of paradox. Returning to monastic roots—that is, to the radical and intense passion for the contemplation of God—consecrated life will become truly capable of a prophetic and transparent witness. Not many proposed the return to a monastic paradigm of consecrated life, but perhaps this is also implied in the insistence—from many—on a significant spiritual concentration. This nostalgia also appears among the characteristics of various new experiences of consecrated life, where the management of works moves into second place in order to give a privileged position to the quality of liturgical prayer, community life, hospitality, commitment to a wise discernment of history, spiritual dialogue, manual labor, and openness to culture and other religions.

For many, the most serious challenge and the most urgent turning point could be that of developing and living an intense spirituality, characterized by a radical following of Jesus, a profound experience of God, and a new passion for humanity. In consequence, consecrated life frees itself from the burdensome management of works in order to move on to sharing in the suffering of the poor and of the excluded with more flexible structures and initiatives. Some elements of the two icons were also brought up to reassert this: the thirst for living water, feeling and tenderness, the breaking of taboos, care for the body, new mediation, emotional and compassionate participation, etc. At the same time, the prejudices of the disciples and ethnic hostility, as well as the legalistic rigidity of the priest and the Levite, are recalled as warnings with regard to some of our own hypocrisies.

3. The Pretext

The ample phenomenology and the various proposals for responding to the gift received, described in the *Instrumentum Laboris,* gave many the pretext for courageously enlarging the horizons and topics. We will summarize some more frequently developed issues.

a) Compassion and Formalism

One person had the courage to say that the Church has lost its sense of "compassion," taken up as it is by the safeguarding of its organizational system and by concerns for formal orthodoxy, for the sake of which it sometimes reaches excesses of rigidity and even repression. The Church itself—as an institution and the People of God—ought to take more seriously the aspect of community *simper reformanda,* because, in truth, in many things it bears the signs of cultural and religious frailty. In times of the scarcity of resources and of the social marginalization of the religious element, the danger of making sacred the traditional patrimony could be transformed into fanaticism and fundamentalism. Flexibility and updating without discernment can also cause disasters and confusion in the charismatic identity. With a certain frequency, these two polarities are also seen in the responses.

There are signs that reveal a widespread schizophrenia in the world of consecrated persons, as is the case in the Church as well, where it is believed that theoretical proclamations are enough in themselves, even without translating them into practice—as if spreading a layer of a varnish of good intentions would suffice to give rise to radical transformation (cf. EN, no. 20). This transformation requires slow and laborious processes therefore full of risk, and evangelical boldness marked by a mysticism that nourishes prophecy (cf. VC, no. 80). We must remain vigilant to keep at a distance from the Gnostic illumination of theoreticians and verbal proclamations without praxis.

b) Exploring New Meanings

The breaking of taboos evident in the two icons—passing through the dialogic dance of the Samaritan woman and Jesus and the innovative compassion of the "heretical" Good Samaritan—should be our inspiration to break with many of the current ecclesiastical and cultural taboos, and to narrate histories and not only to expound theories and universal assessments. The Congress itself must become an event capable of showing a more charismatic and free elaboration—participative not on paper only—and an integration between charisms that reduces fears and secular separations.

It is not possible to live a life according to the Spirit simply by "dreaming" of this new life; a process of radical transformation is required, as already glimpsed in the two major players in our icons. It is necessary to begin to search for new wells of living water, to relearn near wells similar to those "left to us as a heritage by our father Jacob" the revealing and healing art of dialogue, in company with all those thirsty for sincere affection and a religiosity that is neither rigid nor too vague. It is necessary to set out along the streets that go down from the "holy" Jerusalem toward the "depression" of Jericho, that is, from the comfortable and privileged life of the "sacred temples" to the hellish depths of oppression and violence. It is necessary to go more deeply into these precarious places in order to gather the "wounded" and entire nations "half-dead," to raise them up, care for them, and carry them to safety, giving one's whole self and not just "two denari."

c) Richness of the Icons

Many particulars of the icons offered the "occasion," a pretext, for developing comments that were often very original. Among these were the thieves who resorted to violence, for husbands and their symbolic significance, for the scribe who asks for a theoretical answer, for the beast of burden and the bandages; but also for the unfortunate "half-dead" man, for the disciples who were prejudiced against the woman, for the abandoned water pitcher, for the time of day, etc. The presence—also noted in the comments of the *Instrumentum Laboris*—of an interior process of transformation of people was equally broadened in many other aspects of the experience of faith and spirituality.

From the viewpoint of the impact of the communication of ideas, the icons and their symbolic and metaphorical meaning were very successful because they launched broader and more original senses that are only vaguely present in the biblical text. They were very much appreciated and stimulated creative reactions.

4. *"It Is I Who Speak to You... Take Care of Him"*

Let us now try to draw some conclusions from the many-sided reactions to the *Instrumentum Laboris* that we have described up to now. We can speak of the icons as two "small doors" that opened vast and fascinating horizons. We could call this reading meta-textual (or even hyper-textual), because it tries to bring together theory and practice, existence and project, realism and utopia. To borrow an image from Asia, it is the exercise of the "third eye," that of intuition and emotion, which penetrates the reality that remains invisible to ordinary vision. Let us now identify some focal points around which it will be possible to summarize what was said implicitly and explicitly.

a) Between Paradox and Mystery

Various responses placed consecrated life in the realm of paradox. What consecrated life proposes to live and communicate is in disconcerting contrast to the currently accepted cultural values, in which a notable reduction in authentic contact with life risks moving along on a virtual wave to the detriment of deep relationships. This spreads a mentality that seems to narcotize in the person

- the need for interior unification because of fragmentation;
- the need to focus on essentials because of the excessive consumption of the superfluous;
- the need to structure times of spontaneity, consciousness, and interiority because of the neurotic acceleration of time.

Therefore, consecrated life places itself as an alternative to the current ways of acting through the radicality with which it desires to take up certain evangelical proposals and the very life of Jesus of Nazareth (cf. VC, no. 22). Because of this, it loves to speak of the following of Christ in almost literal terms, seeking to make contemporary that lifestyle and the options that characterize it. Many people deem it is necessary to return to this form, following in the footsteps of Jesus and transforming this following into a serious norm of life without either taking anything away or becoming hypocritically bourgeois. It is the call to a "transfigured" and "configured life in Christ" (cf. VC, no. 19) that renders the Father visible, leavening history with the creator Spirit and broadening the horizons that limit existence.

To this decisive and publicly evident aspect, it is necessary to add that of gratuitousness, of the squandering—completely irrational in the eyes of most—of resources and projects for passion and compassion, for service and adoration (cf. VC, nos. 104–105). Clearly the frequent stress on a spirituality equal to today's challenges and provocative for the present aphasia is a sign of the need to dismantle the great apparatus of works and structures, even glorious ones,

for a more simplified and sober life giving greater emphasis to a gratuitous, immediate, and impassioned presence. The works are still
numerous and important; they are a source of prestige, but also of
problems. The majority of people almost see in these "the signs" of
the identity and of the mission of consecrated life.

Many asked for the courage to subject to verification this gigantic apparatus, in which lives are often trapped and "half dead."
The current mental and material structures often hinder or halt the
movement of the living water of the Gospel in history, smothering
evangelical freedom through compromises that do not make the presence of the Spirit credible.

We note, therefore, the necessity of recognizing the signs of
"sickness of spirit" because of burdensome works and lifestyles that
warp persons. The poor look to us, they make requests of us, and they
wait for us to structure our time as God's time for our brothers and
sisters in order to make real here and now God's plans in history,
building a world of justice, peace, and joy. There is need for
"Samaritans" who descend from their beasts of burden and who are
not hindered or absorbed by structures, so that they may gather the
"half alive" and carry them to new inns of healing and freedom with
care, gratuitously, tenderly, and in a concrete way.

Finally, there is the prophetic aspect that is associated with two
points already mentioned and that gives to both an illuminative and
explorative tension that is not purely functional or organic. Prophecy
has an aspect of continuity with the past and the present not on a
superficial or phenomenological level, but on a level of depth and future projection. With creative fidelity (VC, nos. 37, 85), the prophet
shows that the present is not enough for anyone and scrutinizes the
present for signs of the flowering of the seed of the future sown by
the past in the ground of history. By means of his or her ministry,
he or she communicates that God always takes care of humanity,
even when the darkness of history can make one think that God does
not exist or that God has forgotten the men and women of our time.
The prophet does not break with the past or cling to the present but

places them both in an explosive and fruitful tension toward the future with creative fidelity. This disconcerts those who enjoy a lazy or scared maintenance or who adore "memory," mythologizing and preserving it as if it were a fetish.

b) Apocalyptic Provocation

Consecrated life has always been considered a "goad" announcing a future: that of the Reign of God. It extends itself toward what we all await, or rather, it gives an anticipated presentation (or *prolepsis*) of the future (VC, no. 26). This comes with the detachment from many forms of "possession" and self-realization, considering these transitory or non-vital for entering into the Reign of God (to possess goods, to marry and to have children, to live independently, to pursue a career and power...). Consecrated persons emphasize the great guiding values of the Gospel message in view of the final encounter: love, prayer, hope, faith, liberty, communion, detachment, vigilance, supplication, contemplation, etc. By narrating the Gospel with one's life, or rather, becoming the "living memory of Jesus' way of living and acting" (VC, no. 22), consecrated persons help the men and women of the present times to recognize the traces of God in the beauty of their existence.

The entire qualitative structure of consecrated life—that is, the vows, community life, gratuitousness, service, prayer, spiritual struggle, etc.—ought to have this eschatological pressure, this sense of the "beyond" and of the pre-eminence of the "Other." The world is waiting for persons who live out their existence with wonder, with gratuitousness, and with gratitude, persons who pray and who structure time and space under the banner of love. The same solitude that many people endure as an evil can be reinterpreted by consecrated women and men as a constitutive element of human existence, the place where God is present, who, loving the person, reveals to them their uniqueness. Consecrated life is authentic when it is lived not as a flight from the world and history, but as a ferment and stirring within history. A new heavens and a new earth are emerging, and

God, who is the absolute New (cf. Rev 21:1–7), lives within our limitations, causing them to explode, and bringing about the new heavens and the new earth.

Today, there is an appeal for knowledge of how to bring together professional knowledge and ongoing formation, cultivating a deep culture that enables us to look at history with an open mind and heart, ready to show the paths of hope to our contemporaries. Humanity needs to meet men and women who are moved with passion in the mystical dimension of life, who know how to hear the voice of silence, who are in contact with the flow of existence common to all, and whose words resonate with their life in God. The world needs to see living persons who assume the sentiments of Jesus Christ in daily life (Phil 2:5), and who are witnesses through justice, peace, pardon, mercy, tenderness, freedom, beauty, gratitude, solidarity, meekness, love... (cf. VC, no. 27).

From this point of view, it seems that references to the apocalyptic aspect found in the *Instrumentum Laboris* were not redeveloped and reinforced in the responses and reactions. A strong and decisive "apocalyptic goad" is lacking in consecrated life today. Rather, it seems to be committed to a "reform" of watered-down updating, to a weak "refoundation" in which everything is relativized and profaned in the name of an awaited fullness deprived of shocking apocalyptic provocation of meaning and purpose. We might hypothesize that this weakness of apocalyptic thought and the low profile of responses to its challenges is one of the causes of the fragility of the message consecrated life gives today. In this culture truly shaken by an apocalyptic fear that paralyzes everyone, a different apocalyptic projection is necessary, and consecrated life must work at finding alternative responses.

c) Empathetic and Healing Function

Clearly, these icons move toward an ambient of healing. The wounded and confused Samaritan woman and the attentiveness and tenderness of the Good Samaritan toward that "half-dead" traveler are placed in relief. We can translate these aspects with certain immediacy in the many types of charitable services carried out by consecrated life. All of this goes on very well, but does not finish here. Many requested a serious effort to explore ways of building a new society, beginning with the depths of mercy, making the body dance and giving flesh its meaning as sacrament of grace and of hope. Above all, a request was made for knowing how to recognize new ministries of mercy and solidarity.

Also, without particularly insisting but with a frequency that, taken altogether, appears interesting, there were many who gave great importance to consecrated life as a "therapeutic experience." This concerns first of all the members of consecrated life and their own existence: thirst for life and social wounds, lost relationships and wounded feelings, marginalization and a need for tenderness can become a cry and entreaty and must be brought back to a liberating path always open to new ministries. Therefore, it is necessary to be insistent so that the entire system of life and organization of consecrated men and women becomes capable of offering healing and support, care and not violence, a "dancing" liberation and not neurotic repression and suspicion of everything.

One reads in *Vita Consecrata,* number 87: "Thus, while those who follow the evangelical counsels seek holiness for themselves, they propose, so to speak, a spiritual 'therapy' for humanity, because they reject the idolatry of anything created and, in a certain way, they make visible the living God. The consecrated life, especially in difficult times, is a blessing for human life and for the life of the Church." Developing this intuition of a therapeutic function of consecrated life for humanity and joining it with empathetic participation opens new perspectives. Is it worth asking, beyond personal perfectionism and a view of repressive ascetical renunciation, how consecrated life can carry comfort and hope to a collective way of thinking and seeing that has been traumatized by many tragedies and social and political absurdities? This could involve the vows being lived and interpreted as new ways of interpersonal relationships and of cultural ferment, that community life be a realistic reference point as a cultural model for many situations of injustice and conflict (cf. VC, no. 51). The witness of reconciled communities that relate as equals, respecting the diversity of roles as well as in reference to the service of authority, is precious. The same use of goods and material resources and the way of deciding and of developing a mature psycho-affective identity ought to be evangelically authentic. At the same time, it should be communicative and liberating, as well as a force that destroys deceitful and oppressive structures. Therefore, human formation in all its requirements is urgent. It becomes an important support for freeing and purifying the roots of existence, often made arid by the encrustation of infantilism and false needs accumulated over time. In order to do this, refoundation at different levels is necessary.

d) Starting from Incarnation

From the analysis of the two icons emerges the urgency of having a different kind of relationship with the body and corporality. For a long time a strong emphasis on spiritualism, to the detriment of the integral development of the person, has caused consecrated life to be disincarnated, confirming entire generations in the conviction that enjoyment is an evil and that the body is a kind of "sickness of the spirit" and the place where sin is found. The book of Genesis (1:31) says that the newly created man was very beautiful and his body was made in the image and likeness of God. Now, because of the mystery of the incarnation—in which the Son of God takes a body completely like our own, except sin—consecration cannot leave out the positive aspects of the body and of corporality. In a time when corporality is desecrated in many forms, consecrated men and women can make visible the beauty of God's masterpiece by fully taking up their proper corporality, experienced as the "temple of God" (1 Cor 3:16).

Integrating harmoniously the biological, psychic, social, and existential levels, consecrated men and women tell, through their internal integration and communitarian unity, how to experience the body fully. In a time when materialism or spiritualism alone are exalted, men and women who are deeply human, evangelical, sexually integrated, and continuously giving of themselves can attest to the joy of living appropriate corporality and wonder face to face with the other. Redefining life from a theological and anthropological perspective of the incarnation of Jesus Christ, the human face of God, means to give God the possibility of making himself visible and salvific in history through the corporality of each consecrated man or woman.

e) Sowing New Hope

Consecrated life embraces the cross with Christ, as a symbol of every obstacle and resistance to the "good news." It takes up the same cause in the face of every unjust and manipulative system of religion. With this witness to men and women of today, the infinite love of the Father for humanity and God's fidelity draws everything toward the new life given through the Resurrection of Jesus Christ. There are many in the world who are beaten and robbed, left half dead on the edges of civilization, and for them God has a depth of compassion and tears of pity. They are God's children. Their dignity trampled upon, they are waiting for a deeply human presence through which they might experience the closeness of God. A love without end (cf. Jn 13:1) does not grow numb trying to protect its own legal purity, nor is it consumed in a closed and sterile spiritualism. Love constantly asks consecrated women and men to establish deep, intimate, and meaningful relationships in a society with its fragmented ethos.

In these times, the number of persons who live ever more purely virtual relationships is growing, and they appear as shipwrecked survivors of the spirit adrift on their on-line life raft. In a certain sense, they give themselves a new identity, one that is fluid, interchangeable, almost a puzzle. It is as if they were in a labyrinth without goals or a way out, where losing one's self and finding one's self are the same thing. At the same time that the meta-network connects everything and everyone, life has no more secrets; it is the death of intimacy and tenderness, of privacy and freedom. In this context, men and women of God are called to spread identity and hope, goals and reasons for living, remaining in authentic relationships even when the other is disconnected. It is the new way of being "fishers of souls," through very different net(-work)s than those of the Sea of Galilee.

If the interruption of the way into the future due to the frailty of projects and expectations recalls the fear and death by bulimia of the present, consecrated women and men can save the world from desperation and from "not thinking" by constructing and reconstructing bridges of relationships at whatever level, making visible the invisible with passion for humanity (cf. VC, no. 27). This seems to be the true new frontier of mission for all members of consecrated life and for all charisms.

To Continue the Journey...

From the responses to the *Instrumentum Laboris* it is possible to be disillusioned with a consecrated life that seems to hobble along and to be short of breath, above all in the northern hemisphere where consecrated life is going through a phase of weakness in grand ideals and gospel projects. Or it is possible to have a positive confidence in the southern hemisphere where there is lively and even tumultuous growth, but consecrated life has not yet succeeded in giving a stable form to new inculturated models that are satisfying for cultures very different from those of the West.

Therefore, the conviction emerges, with strong and rather widespread evidence, that this ecclesial and cultural change of vast and new dimensions is an appeal from God and a novel chance in our history. The only choice is one of courageous discernment in faith, with a prophetic imagination. This time of weakness and the decomposition of our patrimony and projects in the northern hemisphere, and of growth and prophecy in the southern hemisphere, can become a time of grace (a true *kairós*) in the most intense and fruitful sense. The geographical and cultural shifts can become a new stage of refoundation and of evangelical radicality revisited with new eyes.

It is a matter of living in history and dirtying one's hands, without pretending not to see or "passing on the other side," fearful and confused, worried only about our "legal purity." It is a question of always returning to seek new, living water at the "pure and perennial fountains of the spiritual life" (cf. DV, no. 21). We must know how to entreat the Lord humbly so that he might give us the eyes to see the needs and the sufferings of our brothers and sisters. It is a question of being attentive, listening to the Word with the ear of the heart in order to recognize the hour in which "the Father seeks worshipers in spirit and truth" (Jn 4:23), in order to be, beyond our frailty, servants of the Word in the new historical areopagi. In the daily human fabric, as in the great horizons of globalization today, we are asked to be prophetic witnesses to truth and freedom, to justice and peace, to tenderness and solidarity.

Consecrated persons, fragile and enamored women and men, compassionate and realistic, must nurture—narrating and living—the parable of wounded existence that grace heals, testimonies of painful disquietude that dialogue returns to authenticity, provocative reactions that recall theoretical curiosity to a transformation into compassionate practice, weaving gestures of occasional meetings that compassion wraps with new hope.

THE GUIDING THREAD
OF THE CONGRESS

1. At the beginning of the Congress, special attention was given to the reality of the consecrated life *(Vita Consecrata)* in a period of transition toward different ways of being and living. This transformation has resulted in a deep *purification* with its beginnings at the Second Vatican Council and then moved ahead in the following decades. At the present time, we, consecrated men and women, live in a moment of grace, and these are truly challenging times.

2. To move ahead in this moment of evolution for humankind and for the Church requires passing through a *crisis* that involves everyone. For some this crisis is due to a combination of circumstances; for others, it is structural. These issues are not marginal to consecrated life, but they challenge the theological understanding of what this life is all about. The consecrated lifestyle in the present moment is in crisis. The sociocultural, political, economic, and religious aspects of the modern world are extremely challenging. In some continents, there is complete "chaos," insofar as the identity of consecrated life is completely blurred. It has grown faint. Much creativity is necessary, which is not easily found in many men and women religious. Nevertheless, creativity is crucial to the proper incarnation into the local "milieu" that religious are called to express.

3. It is difficult to address properly the serious challenges that we face. As part of Christian life, consecrated life, as it presents itself to today's world, has lost its appeal. To render it fruitful becomes an uphill task, as is experienced by religious men and women, as well as by other members of the Church and of society. It is our duty to offer a different alternative. To do this, the light of discernment is necessary; thus, we will know where the Spirit wants to lead us. Well-made discernment opens the door to authentic revitalization. It will be a discernment of reconversion, in the dimension of being and doing, of feeling and thinking, and of interacting and communicating. In this discernment, we must not forget that the image of the identity of consecrated life is blurred. New forms of consecrated life have come into being, and different ways of living consecrated life have developed for the laity.

4. In trying to answer the questions coming from within and without consecrated life, *errors* have been and continue to be committed today. These errors have made evident certain weaknesses, roadblocks, inertia, and sins and, at the foundation, the radical poverty that characterizes consecrated life today. All this translates into fatigue, a lack of revitalizing experiences and of vision to discern the direction to take and the road to follow. Therefore, the reading of the past and the present should not be triumphalistic but humble, "Samaritan." At the beginning of the new millennium, religious men and women have many "question marks" concerning consecrated life's true identity and the way to live it. From the Congress we see evidence of the urgent thirst for authentic relationships and abundant healing.

5. Motivated by this, the Congress wants to emphasize above all the radical essence of consecrated life. From a global point of view, we can call this the desire for a quest. Mary Magdalene sought her Master (Lk 20:14). Consecrated life looks for a meeting with Jesus. This quest includes the intensification of the theological dimension of our lives and the charismatic dimension of consecrated life and of every Institute. It requires a new lucid and compassionate meeting with human reality the cultural, social, and religious aspects of

the present moment. Consecrated life needs mystical experiences, passionate souls, and prophetic vision.

6. In this way, a *different* consecrated life will be made clear. For some the present model of consecrated life is exhausted because it no longer renders alive, in present contexts, the great intuitions of our Founders and the accumulated experiences of contemplative, fraternal, and missionary life of the past centuries. Only in deep communion among ourselves, with the Church, and with the men and women of our times will we discover the necessary alternative and the way to revitalize consecrated life—an alternative that presumes a rebirth in today's sociocultural and religious situations. The roots are the same: the Gospel and our Founders. We have to sow and grow in new soil and to begin a new spring. This requires that we dare to put the new wine of consecrated life into new wineskins: that is, in structures that are simple, friendly, helpful, and open. Though this is a difficult task, it is vital. Let us not remain stuck in the present or even less in the past, let us reach out to the poor and the needy; it's the only way to open up to the future. This is the great proposal of Jesus, "the one who calls into being things that are not."

7. This Congress aims at creating an overarching dialogue that will help us to begin a new *process*. There is much to be done. Let us be aware of it. We have to hit the target by offering suitable proposals for the present times. Therefore, we must drop certain things and begin to realize others. If we keep on doing the same things in the same way we have until now, we will have the same results we have now. The Spirit of the Lord is upon us. He bestows on us the power to restructure in order to revitalize and the power to revitalize in order to found anew. He gives us the grace to die and to be born again, to leave behind and to maintain that which in consecrated life responds to the present historical moment. The Congress is intent upon continuing a process, which the Spirit had already begun in us. It calls for a conversion at the personal and communitarian level, the transformation of environment and of structures, and the capacity to put our trust in the Lord.

8. This process must be animated by a spirit. From the start, *hope and passion* are essential to initiating and continuing this process. Spiritual things are like a light rain; they require patience and courage to bring them to life. We need not arrive when it is already too late. Hope is needed to discern the signs of life in consecrated life, to identify, distinguish, articulate, celebrate, and recognize them as a new point of departure for a new period. Under the action of the Spirit something new is coming to life (Is 43:18–19), a new way that for some is a new form of consecrated life. We have to succeed in articulating it with a profoundly theological and spiritual dialogue and place it at the service of the Kingdom of God. Consecrated life feels the urge to foster the "passion" for God and for humanity.

9. This is what the Congress must show. This is what it must leave to the religious men and women of the world who have greater need of *faithfulness, vision, and daring.* With its proposals and answers, consecrated life has repeatedly surprised us throughout the course of history. This Congress is being held to give consecrated life the opportunity of surprising us again. What we will live, do, say, and hear will give us the certainty that the Spirit of the Lord is creating new things in consecrated life, and for this we give praise and thanks to God. We would like our hearts to be set on fire, as were those of the Samaritan woman and the Good Samaritan. Let us put into practice what we will gain from this Congress. To revitalize consecrated life means to nourish hope, to be passionate in living our daily life, being at the service of the Church and of the world. The commitment is not lacking in those present at this Congress and in all those generously dedicated with their dreams and responsibilities, their reflections and actions, to a consecrated life devoted to the salvation of the world.

OPENING TALK

Therezinha Joana Rasera, SDS
President of UISG

With immense joy and a very full heart we welcome you to this Congress for Consecrated Life. And here we are, coming from all corners of our planet, aware of our thirst for depth and renewal, to drink the water from the well of life and hope.

The world, especially the poor of this world, expects us—religious women and men—to be persons of hope, a hope that is able to enlighten their lives and strengthen them while they continue to struggle for the recognition of their human dignity and for a more significant and happy life. We may say that this is Christian hope, with faith and charity as companions. It is a hope born from the resurrection of Jesus that creates—in the face of oppression and death—a new space for life.

We are representatives of consecrated life from the whole world. Of those participating in this Congress there are: 95 from the African continent; 250 from the Americas (South, Central, and North America); 92 from the Asian continent; 16 from Oceania and 394 from the European continent, which totals 850 men and women religious members from the five continents: members of the General Curias,

Presidents of the National and Continental Conferences, theologians, young religious, directors of spirituality centers and of some magazines.

We also have some special guests: Bishops, members of the Congregation for Institutes of Consecrated Life and Societies of Apostolic Life, of the Congregation for the Evangelization of Peoples, and representatives of various ecclesiastical movements.

To each and every one a hearty welcome.

We are aware that the outcome of this Congress will depend on each of us. It will depend on our active and effective participation irrespective of our category. For this reason, we invite you to feel at home, thus contributing to an atmosphere of openness, simplicity, spontaneity, joy, and active participation. For our work together, it is very important to listen actively and attentively to the Spirit, who will reveal to each participant through our dialogue with the different cultures and expressions of consecrated life present. Our attentive listening will lead us to welcome and make the necessary changes required today.

Welcome to share the pain, frustration, insecurities, fears, the searching and success, dreams and hopes, which fill your hearts.

Welcome to be open to new horizons and to give dynamic life to our future, to our history with the conviction and prophetic courage of our Founders and Foundresses.

We do not yet know the fruit of this Congress. However, we know that we want to discover alternative ways to our present reality, to walk courageously so that our presence may nourish hope for a future of greater justice and solidarity, where political, economic, affective, religious, and other relationships will be according to the plan of God's Kingdom.

We are aware that those who follow in the footsteps of Jesus of Nazareth also challenge the empire of death and the power of the oppressors of this world, and will risk and accept the loss of their own lives for others, so that they may have "life, and have it abundantly" (Jn 10:10).

Following the example of Christ, who, "though he was in the form of God, emptied himself, taking the form of a servant" (Phil

2:5–11), consecrated life is invited to rid itself of everything that may impede its prophetic power. Beginning from our ideas about God, which are often far from the concrete reality and the life experience of the people, consecrated life needs to let go of the image it has of itself, an image so often imprisoned behind secure walls that separate and alienate members from the suffering and the cry of the poor.

If we contemplate today's world, many questions arise:

What is the Holy Spirit raising up in consecrated life today?

How do we identify it, describe it, and live it?

How do we discover the obstacles to its existence?

To what new "wells" and paths is this consecrated life leading us? *(Instrumentum Laboris)*

These days we will ask ourselves similar questions. We want to be attentive to the answers that the Spirit will inspire and to open ourselves to the questions not yet asked.

The *Instrumentum Laboris* points out many challenges. "We, as consecrated persons, are living through crucial moments for humanity and for the Church. We have to make decisions of great importance for the immediate future. We are urged to have attitudes of hope, justice, and solidarity for all peoples of our times so that they can live in dignity. We are being presented with decisive options: we can gladden life or make it difficult; grow in communion or create greater distances between us; be conquered by difficulties or face them. We do not have time to spare. New realities demand new responses" (no. 56).

For this reason, we are invited to participate in this great assembly through dialogue and discernment, sharing our gifts and inspirations in order to "manifest the gift of the Spirit for the common good" (1 Cor 12:7).

The theme of this Congress, "Passion for Christ, Passion for Humanity," takes its inspiration for discernment and action from a double icon contained in the Gospel: the Good Samaritan and the Samaritan woman.

Both personalities from Samaria were accepted as inspiring symbols because they can be a significant response for consecrated life in our times.

The story of the Samaritan woman gives us the insight that Jesus, in his reply to his followers, includes all people. Jesus came to eliminate divisions, often created in the name of a religion or of God, which have the disastrous consequences we all know. The Samaritan woman's dialogue with Jesus touches her personal, intimate life and that of her people, causing her to enter into a conversion process.

Everyone here is also moved and invited by the Spirit to draw near to the Gospel again, and, as Jesus' followers, to accept God's loving invitation to change our lives from individualism to solidarity, from rational coolness to sensitivity and humanization of relationships, from prejudice to accepting the dialogue with the differences among us, from war and violence to peace and justice, from the appearance of strength and power to a stronger resemblance to the Servant of Yahweh in order to be worthy of our vocation as missionaries of the Good News!

We are called by the Spirit not to accommodate ourselves to a precise order, or to adjust to a supposed spiritual superiority or to a belief that our consecration includes us in an automatic process of sanctification and of being witnesses of the sacred. Often our consecration turns us into Pharisees and counter-witnesses. Thus we remain on the margin of any change or transformation, "continuing our lives without calling anyone or proclaiming anything, because we believe our works justify our means and fears," as is clearly described by Bishop Pedro Casaldáliga in reaction to the *Instrumentum Laboris*. He continues by saying: "We are accustomed to believing that we need to appear modest and prudent, and that prophecy shapes only a few among us. We are afraid to appear ridiculous before the 'foolishness' of the Gospel. We are afraid to lose our personal or communitarian security. We could annoy certain benefactors, certain authorities, or certain hierarchy. We fear the cross and persecution, which cannot be avoided if we wish to radically live our following of Jesus."

Consecrated life cannot overcome its crisis if it does not enter into a process of self-evangelization, which obliges us to return to the source that generated our history. We have to touch again the strength and the power of the transformation of our charisms. From the very beginning, our Founders and Foundresses made it clear that our charism express a powerful Gospel truth capable of transforming our own lives and the reality around us. None of our institutes was created to be the continuity of a static situation, of non-life; quite to the contrary, they were begun by choosing life and incarnating the option for the poor.

Through her personal encounter with Jesus, the Samaritan woman was able to visualize a new horizon of spirituality and its meaning for her life and, consequently, also for her people. She dared to dialogue with an unknown Jew, exposing herself to something new. Thus, she went beyond the institution in search of meaning for her emptiness. And she found a source of Living Water!

The parable of the Good Samaritan begins after Jesus thanks his Father for "having hidden these things from the wise and learned and revealing them to children" (cf. Lk 10:21). In reality, the first person who tries to confound Jesus is a "wise and learned" expert in the Law. St. Luke emphasizes that the lawyer asks the question: "What should I do to inherit eternal life?" (Lk 10:25), not because he was interested in the truth, but "to confound Jesus." In returning the question, Jesus makes it clear that the lawyer already knows the reply because he cited the commandment: "You shall love the Lord, your God, with all your heart, and with all your soul, and with all your strength, and with all your mind: and your neighbor as yourself." Jesus told him quite simply: "You have answered correctly; do this and you will live" (v. 28).

But the man insists: "And who is my neighbor"? (v. 29) Jesus does not allow himself to be trapped in a theoretical and sterile discussion, but suddenly brings the discussion to the practical level by telling the parable of the Good Samaritan. After having finished, Jesus asks the lawyer: "Who do you think proved to be a neighbor to the man who fell among the robbers?" The lawyer is forced to recognize that the one who became a true neighbor to the suffering person, the one who showed mercy, was a Samaritan. At the end, the lawyer hears from Jesus: "Go and do likewise" (v. 37).

We are invited to form a "Samaritan" consecrated life, with a thirst for God and constantly motivated by the practice of mercy, ready to move from a place or situation for the sake of the mission. Such a call puts us in crisis and, if we want, leads us into a process of discernment. We need the courage to read and to welcome the signs of the times; we have to have the boldness to act prophetically. Thus, consecrated life will have to move from its self-centered concerns to transparency and a passionate following of Jesus Christ. The two persons from Samaria make it clear to us that the true expression of consecrated life lies in our approach to the world of the excluded and of those who are living outside the circle of globalized societies. Only this will give meaning to consecrated life, for which it is searching so insistently!

Dear Sisters and Brothers, I welcome you "to be immersed in the spirit of this Congress, which is one of welcoming the voice of the Spirit of God, of allowing ourselves to be transformed, and of beginning a new practice."

To welcome implies openness, active listening, sharing what the Spirit is offering, and being moved by Gospel issues.

It is possible to be transformed if we remain open to learning and discerning those spirits that move us.

We are sensing new horizons and therefore are dreaming of relaunching consecrated life in all its dimensions of spirituality, solidarity, justice, and hope for the mission.

We are discovering the validity of new expressions that are arising among us, and we wish to accept and promote these new expressions as a gift of God and as a new commitment.

We want to strengthen a kind of spirituality and mission to be shared with the People of God, as well as to strengthen communion and solidarity among religious of both genders.

We want to commit ourselves to experience "passion for Christ and passion for humanity" in new contexts. "Consecrated life is urged to cultivate a passion for God and for human beings" and to be the voice of consecrated life capable of challenging itself where it is present in the world.

I welcome you to make this Congress good news for today's world. We are here to continue being a gift of the Spirit for the Church and the world!

SEEKERS OF WELLS AND ROADS: TWO ICONS FOR A SAMARITAN CONSECRATED LIFE

Dolores Aleixandre, RSCJ

At a small museum in Nazareth there is an interesting capital on a column from a very ancient church. It depicts a woman (Faith?) wearing a queen's crown. Moving forward, she holds in one hand a scepter topped with a cross; in the other she clasps the hand of a man (Peter? an apostle?), who is hesitating, led very reluctantly in a direction he'd rather not go.

The two figures bring to mind very different attitudes. The "guide" seems self-assured. She uses the cross for support and, receiving strength from it, takes the initiative to grasp the man's hand to get him to follow her. He resists, pulling back, afraid. With his right hand held fast in the woman's left hand, he has lost face and goes forward led by Faith. He holds his cloak in his left hand, as if he were afraid to be seen naked by those looking on. He is not embracing Faith; rather, Faith is the one who takes him by the hand, like a prize, and does not let go.[1] An interesting detail of the capital is that while one can clearly make out the facial features of the man being "led," those of the "guide" are undefined. Looking at the capital, we can hazard a guess about what may have happened in the past, but the future is open-ended and we can only imagine how things might turn out.

This image comes to mind as I begin to reflect on the icons of the two Samaritans—the woman (Jn 4:1–42) and the man (Lk 10:25–37). I propose that we allow them to give a specific face to the faceless figure, the one guiding the other by the hand, and that we identify ourselves with the second figure. We can all see ourselves represented in this figure, men and women in the Church who have embraced the particular form of love that the Father has allowed some to grasp, that we call the "consecrated life." We will once again be faced with the surprise that following in the footsteps of the Lord leads to the most diverse outcomes.[a]

Let us allow these two Gospel personalities, unnamed in the texts (perhaps so that we who gaze on them might substitute our own names), to take us by the hand and be our mystical guides as we follow the Risen Lord. The message that reverberates in them has the power to take hold of us and bring us beyond where we are today at the beginning of this millennium. It is not for us to know clearly where we are being led; we are to consent to their promptings and allow ourselves to be brought along without trying to control the journey's outcome. An ancient hymn of the Church prays: *Per tuas semitas duc nos quo tendimus* (Along your paths lead us where we want to go). Right at the start let us avoid the danger of beginning from ourselves and our response. The ever-flowing love of a God who loves us passionately exerts its attraction on us through these two icons. Our part will come later on in the form of "passion for God and passion for humanity" in response to that love.

As in the creation accounts in Genesis, we are going to attend a drama in three acts. Beginning with the initial scene of emptiness, chaos, and need, we will contemplate the Lord's creative action in people and see their transfiguration at the end of the narratives. Although we will center our attention on the two icons of the Samaritan woman and the Samaritan man, we will engage in conversation with a third person: the scribe who dialogues with Jesus in Luke's narrative and comes across as being ambivalent. Will he find out how to gain "eternal life" as did the parable's Good Samaritan? Will he accept Jesus' invitation and allow himself to be formed "in his image and likeness"? Luke doesn't reveal the scribe's reaction, and that undetermined outcome, that leaving things up-in-the-air, allows us to see ourselves reflected in him today, our freedom challenged by the same invitation he heard from the lips of Jesus: "Go and do likewise."

We will also take a look at the other persons with secondary roles in the two scenes: the Pharisees, whom John portrays as prompting Jesus to decide to leave Judea behind and head for Galilee, passing through Samaria; the disciples, who bring food to Jesus and are upset when they see him speaking with a woman;[2] the Samaritans drawn to Jesus by the woman's testimony; the man attacked by robbers and left half dead; the priest and the Levite who passed by the wounded man as if he weren't there; and the innkeeper who agreed to care for him.

We are not going to view these people as if we were sitting in a studio audience. We will view them as our contemporaries, aware that their stories, attitudes, and reactions can be our own. We will welcome the good news that the creative work we witness taking place in them invites us today to allow ourselves to be shaped by the creative hands of the One who accomplished his transfiguring work in them.[3]

1. "In the beginning" there was nothing

As happens in the creation narratives, these two Gospel scenes begin with a situation of "chaos," need, and emptiness.[4] The participants appear to lack crucial knowledge and ability. The woman who encounters Jesus at the well and the man who ministers to the robbery victim are both Samaritans, people who are at odds with the establishment, of dubious reputation and objects of suspicion. The woman represents the idea of "not-having": "she doesn't have" a husband, and the man with whom she lives "isn't her husband." She has the burdensome task of heading to the well every day to draw water; she is a prisoner of ethnic and religious conventionalism, and she speaks about them openly with Jesus. Her later behavior—taking the initiative to "evangelize" the people in her village—is an audacious act for a woman.

Concerning the scribe, he doesn't know how to gain "eternal life" and he is searching for a feeling that he is "justified." Although there seems to be a vast difference between him and the woman, their common situation of being vulnerable and searching for life unites them. The woman is yearning for the "living water" of which Jesus tells her, and the scribe desires to possess "eternal life." In one way or another, this need for life makes them participants in the drama of the wounded, "half-dead" man in the parable.

Jesus is also forsaken and vulnerable: he is a stranger; he is thirsty and has no jar with which to draw any water from the well. In his encounter with the scribe, Jesus also seems to be at a disadvantage: an expert in the law is "staring him in the face" and intends to "put him to the test." Can this Galilean from Nazareth measure up to a learned man's argumentation?

Jesus has chosen an unusual and dangerous itinerary that takes him through the hostile territory of Samaria. His asking a woman to give him some water breaks with the conventional manner of relationships between Jews and Samaritans and between men and women. Measured according to the customs of the time, his conduct is offensive and reprehensible. In the presence of the woman, Jesus seems to be characterized by "not having," which in John's Gospel always describes a deficiency and the risk of remaining outside life's mainstream ("They have no wine..." 2:3; "I have no one to put me into the pool," 5:7; "Have you caught anything to eat?..." 21:5).[5]

Even more surprising, the Father participates in some way in this situation of need. Jesus will say of him that he is "searching" ("... indeed the Father seeks such people to worship him," Jn 4:23), and in the parable of the Good Samaritan, which does not name or make any reference to him, his presence "is of no account."

However, just as God the Creator acted on the chaos and dust of the earth, the storytellers of the two scenes "work" with the inadequacies of their characters more than their positive traits. Neither the initial wariness of the woman with her "five husbands" nor the scribe's desire to justify himself will get in the way of their encounter with Jesus; neither will the different beliefs of the Samaritan people nor the ingrained ethnic prejudices of his own disciples. The woman's testimony will lead her fellow Samaritans to faith, and Jesus will reveal to his disciples that their food is to carry out the will of his Father and that his encounter with the Samaritan woman and the townspeople is now part of the desired harvest.

In contrast, the people who seem comfortable with the existing order and take their superior status for granted remain on the periphery of any change or transformation: the Pharisees at the beginning of John's text, so smug in their views about the rivalry between Jesus and John the Baptizer; and the priest and the Levite in the parable, convinced that they have avoided impurity by steering clear of a probable corpse. Other representatives of orthodoxy also cast their shadow over both scenes. Immediately preceding Jesus' encounter with the Samaritan woman, Nicodemus is introduced as a "Pharisee and master of the law" (Jn 3:1), but it is the Samaritan woman of a different creed who ends up accepting Jesus.[6] (Nicodemus will only do so at the end of the Gospel, cf. Jn 19:39.) It is precisely before the dialogue with the scribe that Luke includes the scene in which Jesus praises the Father for having hidden these things from the wise and the learned and revealed them to the childlike (Lk 10:21). Thus, the one who behaves appropriately is an "uneducated" Samaritan and not a "learned" jurist.

But the parable turns out to be even more controversial, because of its unusual perspective: a half-dead man is at the center and all the characters are distributed around him; it doesn't begin from above, from heady discussions revolving around the identity of one's neighbor, but from below, from the roadside ditch where the wounded man lies.[7]

With all these elements of violated norms, broken-down thinking, and changes in the way of doing things, the narrators seem intent on tricking or knocking the reader off balance, in the sense of getting him or her out of a rut. The unforeseen replaces what is expected, surprise what is normal. The habitual gives way to novelty and the reader, who first came across the woman's point of view and valued the concern of the scribe, is later confronted with some very unexpected reactions from Jesus. The "surprise effect" calls established values, judgments, customs, and roles into question.[8]

Ultimately, these mistaken ideas and initial false impressions reveal their truth. The profane and unsheltered places of the two scenes (a well in the middle of the countryside, a highway fraught with danger...), outside the protection of the safe zones such as in cities and temples, appear as places for encountering God. Of the three people in the parable of the Good Samaritan, it is not those known for being dignified (the priest and the Levite) who behave in a suitable way, but precisely he who belongs to a people considered heretical and schismatics. And at the well, the parched and forlorn traveler in hostile territory is revealed as the Son of God, who gives living water and who reveals how to inherit eternal life.

2. "And God said: 'Let us make man in our image, after our likeness (...)'

"And the Lord God formed man out of the clay of the ground and blew into his nostrils the breath of life." (Gen 1:26; 2:7)

Throughout these two stories, we listen to the words Jesus addresses to the people, and we observe his creative and re-creative action in them. He is the one with the leading role in both scenes, and the one who "authors" the strategies of the encounter:

As a skillful potter, Jesus repeats the very action that the narrator of Genesis attributes to God. The Samaritan woman, like the original clay, is being formed patiently, and just as the first "Adam" received the breath of God that brought him to life (Gen 2:7), she receives the water of life. The Samaritan man in the parable, made "in the image and likeness" of God, is proposed as a model for the scribe: "Go and become the image and likeness of that Samaritan because he is now the icon of the very heart of God's mercy."[9] Just as in the garden one of the created beings receives a name, those who came on the scene without a name of their own take on a new identity that is offered to all: "searched for by the Father," "graced by his gift," "called to do what the Samaritan did...."

As a skilled fisherman, Jesus casts his nets and weighs anchor to draw out those with whom he is conversing—the Samaritan woman and the Scribe—from the treacherous waters of trivial pursuits and the desire for self-justification in which they are drowning.

As a good shepherd who knows his sheep, Jesus leads them out of the desert of superficiality and intellectualism. Jesus guides them toward personal well-being and authenticity, "whistles" to them to leave behind the dark ravines where they are content to hide, and leads them to the land of Gift: what is received (the gift of living water) and what must be given (saving the life of one on the verge of losing it). Doing "honor to his name,"[10] his word communicates his conviction that whatever the negative conditions in which they find themselves, he has the power to find a way out for them: "If you knew the gift of God...," "But a Samaritan saw him and drew near...." In that consists the "fountain of peaceful waters" and the "fresh green pastures" in which he makes them lie.

As a master of wisdom and a skilled conversationalist, Jesus uses all the resources of the spoken word and devises strategies to win people over: he questions, dialogues, argues, proposes, persuades, narrates, suggests, affirms, values the viewpoints of others, provokes reactions of identification or rejection, and dares to extend invitations. He goes along with the evasive tactics of the woman and the scribe, and he uses these to bring them to a place they cannot escape;

they must face up to their truth or their ignorance: "I don't have a husband...," "Who is my neighbor?" First, Jesus enters into their points of view in order to lead them where he wants them to go. He doesn't retreat when the woman puts up her defenses or when the scribe attempts to take refuge in the realm of the theoretical. At first "tired," or aware that the scribe is attempting "to put him to the test," Jesus is not overcome by the scribe's efforts to resist and pull the wool over his eyes. He keeps on trying different tactics to maintain their interest. Throughout his conversation with the woman, he is intent on getting to the bottom of her mistaken notions. She thinks of him merely as someone who receives the water she offers, but he reveals to her his role as the giver. When she closes up and defends herself, he does not question her about what she does, but about who she is. The provocative and enigmatic responses she provides are leading her directly to him, and in the final analysis, to the Father.

As a friend interested in building personal relationships, at no time does Jesus render moral judgments of disapproval or reproach. Instead of accusing, he prefers to dialogue and propose. He uses a language aimed at the heart of those with whom he is speaking and utilizes an "open space" strategy:[11]

— In the conversation with the woman, the expression, "if you knew who it is who is telling you...," serves as "an opening" and creates a space between Jesus and the woman. She feels appreciated there and can ask questions about the identity of Jesus ("a Jew"), so clear for her when the dialogue began but that comes into question. And in working with the opening he has given her, Jesus acts slowly. He does not rush to put himself front and center, but he advances "in a spiraling way," to slowly awaken the woman's interest in accessing a fountain of an "other" life.

— In the dialogue with the scribe, Jesus does not respond to the man's question by teaching him a lesson or arguing with him on his own terms. Again, he looks for an "opening" between them to provide the man with an opportunity to discover, on his own, the answer to his question. By means of the parable, Jesus manages to turn around the scribe's concept of "neighbor," rooted in the soil of long and subtle theological studies and a facility for questioning, arguing, and discussing based on the theoretical. None of this ensnares or distracts Jesus; rather it leads him to another sphere in which the expert is not "the one who knows" but the "one who does." [12]

As a consummate artist and painter, Jesus traces the outlines of the Samaritan man, creating (does he realize it?) his own self-portrait. In the image of the compassionate man who approaches the wounded man, we see reflected the values, convictions, and preferences of Jesus: his theology, catechesis, image of the Kingdom, and prophetic criticism; what he considers important and not important (cult, temple, observance...); what he considers sin, omission, or virtue; and the code of conduct he proposes. Thus, the icon of the Good Samaritan becomes an illustration of the Beatitudes.

As an expert on humanity, Jesus shows himself to be profoundly attentive and interested in the interior life of those who question him. He reads in the heart of the scribe the intention to put him to the test and later to justify himself. He stresses that compassion was the basis for the Samaritan's behavior toward the wounded man. In the woman's heart, he uncovers a wellspring capable of bursting from the depths of her soul in contrast with the ancient law and external commandments. He also reveals to her the inner life of the Father and the search within him.

As a prophet possessed by the fire of the Absolute in God, and impassioned by his justice, Jesus questions, shakes up, and strips his opponents of whatever excuses or compromises distance or distract them from unavoidable and original truth: God is our Father and men and women are our neighbors.

3. "God blessed them..."(Gen 1:28)

"...And so man became a living being" (Gen 2:7)

In these two scenes, the Samaritan woman and the scribe are summoned to a "new creation" and given a choice. They can hang on to their old knowledge and beliefs, searching for living water and justification in the dried-up wells of shrines, laws, and customs, or they can choose "eternal life" and allow themselves to be taken in by Jesus' offer to transform and "transfigure" their lives.

A Paschal Process

In both texts there is a transition from one way of thinking and judging to another, from various customs, structures, and convictions to others, and in this "paschal process" we witness a "death." What seemed to be definitive turns out to be provisional, and the main supports and assurances in effect at the beginning of each text display their inability to transmit "living water" and "eternal life." They are overcome by the newness of the behavior and words of Jesus:

— The letter of the law, to which the scribe clings for justification, appears to be a means incapable of granting him life and answering his question about who is his neighbor. If the Samaritan woman represents those who try to quench their thirst in the traditions of their ancestors, the scribe knows his neighbor only in terms of erudition. By way of contrast, Jesus does not propose any external ideal but invites his interlocutors to welcome a gratuitous gift and not to concentrate on themselves and their own perfection but on how they relate to their peers.[13] He puts aside dissertations and scholastic academic casuistry and appeals to what is basic: the human being in need, which includes everyone regardless of ideology or religion, and the person recognized as neighbor by implication. The old institutions are replaced by the "new way" of his flesh (cf. Heb 10:20), and his own fragile humanity becomes a meeting place. His initial weariness and thirst make an exchange and reciprocity possible. His storytelling ability enables the person steering in the realm of the theoretical to come into contact with real people who act in real ways, and teaches him or her that true wisdom consists in showing one's humanness.

— Simply "to know" is sterile: Both the Samaritan woman and the scribe question Jesus with a hope of increasing their knowledge ("How is it you ask me...?" "Where do you get...?" "You mean you're older...?" "What should I do?" "Who is my neighbor...?"). The woman's words, which reflect the convictions of her people, affirm the differences among ethnic groups and theologies; they divide people and preclude the possibility of entering into a relationship, reducing people's expectations regarding the Messiah to what they can get to know ("he will teach us everything").[14]In regard to the scribe, what "he knows" hasn't secured "eternal life" for him either, and even though he has a thorough grasp of the Law, he pays no attention to the neighbor he is supposed to love. Jesus offers both the Samaritan woman and the scribe an "alternative knowledge," and invites them to go beyond "a multiplicity of knowledge" in order to enter into a truth that cannot be attained along the path of generalities, but only through tangible and concrete reality. Jesus' words are not meant to expand their knowledge, but to provoke in them a change of life. "Jacob's well," a symbol of the wisdom given by the law (Gen 54:5),[15] as well as "what is written in it" (Lk 10:26) lose their validity, replaced by "living water" and the call not to read about but to observe real people and behaviors and to act like the Good Samaritan. It is by doing and not by knowing that one attains life. A definitive knowledge replaces provisional knowledge, and it is not in the future but now, thanks to the word of Jesus, that one gains access to the newness of such knowledge.

— Gender roles and stereotypes appear to be overcome, too. Surprisingly, the Samaritan woman speaks up and becomes a witness and evangelizer for her fellow townspeople, taking on roles reserved for men. With regard to the Good Samaritan, Jesus describes him as someone who takes care of the half-dead man and through his actions generates life. He approaches the man, comforts him, bandages his wounds, lifts him up, takes charge of his affairs, looks for shelter and lodging for him, and sees to it that people continue to care for and feed him. The actions described are usually considered feminine and maternal.

People Transfigured

The woman enters the scene as "a woman from Samaria" and leaves as someone very knowledgeable about the spring of "living water," aware that the Father is looking for her to worship him. Her transformed identity turns her into an evangelizer who, by means of her testimony, persuades many people to approach Jesus and believe in him. She who was talking about "drawing water" as a task requiring great effort now abandons her jug: Jesus has uncovered a gift for her, one that doesn't require anything in exchange and is freely bestowed upon her.

The Good Samaritan, who also entered the scene anonymously and is identified only by his ethnic background, reveals his true identity at the end. The mercy dwelling in his heart leads him to act as a neighbor for the one who depends on him for survival. Jesus gives him a new name: "the one who had compassion." The scribe, who expressed his desire for eternal life in terms of possessing ("inheriting..."), is challenged to change that desire into an act of selflessness similar to that of the Good Samaritan.

Like water "that bursts into eternal life," a gratuitous current flows through both texts and transfigures the people involved. The woman, after her attempt to lead Jesus to her village and people, stands back and lets them discover him and believe in him on their own and not just because of her testimony. She has been led to her own inner self by means of a patient process that brought her from a dissipated to a unified life. Then, as a disciple of that Master, she attracts and leads the people of her village to him. Likewise the Good

Samaritan stands back and leaves the other man free, in an act of "genital sublimation,"[16] similar to a mother who gives birth and cuts the umbilical cord of her child to make it independent of her.

The "neighbor," whom the scribe talked about in a vague and ambiguous way and as a faceless figure without any defining characteristics, goes from being a complicated legal concept to a specific flesh-and-blood person. Neighbors cannot be defined by how close or far they are from others. Now they "reside" in the heart of every human being who relates to others as a "you," and in all who take responsibility for others in a disinterested way and enable them to move on with their lives.

At the outset we see Jesus as a tired and thirsty itinerant Jew. In the end he reveals himself as the spring of living water, as Lord, Prophet, Messiah, Savior of the world, and the Son nourished by his Father's will. He defines himself by his capacity for interpersonal relationships: "the one who is speaking with you." And just as God in the Jewish Testament, he brings the woman to a new "desert" to "speak to her heart," and in her he fulfills the promise made to Israel: "And you shall know the Lord" (Hos 2:22). In his conversations, Jesus seems to possess an authority that allows him to express himself in the forceful language of the divine commandments. "Believe me, woman," he says, "do this and you will live...." He admonishes the scribe, "Do likewise."

The image of God also seems transformed. He is not a distant and impassive deity dwelling in shrines made by human hands; nor is he a dictator of laws, an eternal recipient demanding tribute, gifts, or sacrifices in the Temple. In Jesus, God reveals himself as the One who generates life, who gives and searches out, who can be called "Father," and who does not let himself be confined or possessed because he is Spirit. If he searches for us, it is because he desires to broaden our experience and communicate joy and fullness to us. We don't have to gaze upward to find him, because he who came down to a bush in the desert flows as a fountain in the depths of every heart and reveals his presence in wounded people left for dead by roadside ditches. According to the best prophetic tradition, the "worship in spirit and in truth" he is looking for is within the reach of anyone who approaches another to lend a helping hand. While the priest and the Levite went out of their way to avoid getting their hands dirty and so be ready to offer sacrifices, the Samaritan, an outsider to the world of sacrifice, did not need to look for his offering elsewhere; he had within himself the only thing that God asks for: mercy and compassion (cf. Mi 6:8).

We do not see the "normal" or typical ending one might expect (the woman returning to her village with a jug filled with water from the well; the scribe pleased with himself for having spelled out the Law and receiving a response in the context of theory...). Rather, Jesus offers the scribe and the Samaritan woman another view of things that challenges them, a surprising and unforeseen development leading to a life-giving relationship ("water that bursts into eternal life..."; "do this and you shall live..."). In both cases, a breaking point from the former way of doing things (drawing water, finding answers to questions, or continuing a planned journey in the case of the people in the parable...) is the condition for accessing a greater event (receiving "living water," becoming a "neighbor," and practicing "mercy"). The jug, empty and left by the wayside, and the deeds of the Good Samaritan, who generously gives of his own belongings (oil, wine, money...), testify that it is through loss and generous service that one gains life (cf. Mk 8:35).

An Open-Ended Outcome

The outcome, however, is different in the two texts. The path taken by the woman leads to a new relationship and, spurred on by Jesus, she widens the circle of her involvement with others. The scribe, however, faces a fork in the road. We do not know if he will remain imprisoned in his legalistic world, if "he will try to avoid going near the robbery victim," or if, like the Samaritan, he will look for eternal life where it is found: in those deprived of life. The work of profound conversion that Jesus undertakes with this scribe remains open-ended. As in his conversation with the blind man, Bartimeus, Jesus asks the scribe in a subliminal way: "What do you want me to do for you?" And he offers him another perspective, a place of security other than his own ego: the other person. Unable to see, the scribe presumes that the notion of neighbor is defined in relation to himself, and he tries to pinpoint the boundary between those who are his neighbors and those who are not. But the perspective that Jesus proposes to him is totally different: "It is not for you to decide who your neighbor is; rather you should demonstrate your neighborliness for every human being in need. The person who, made in the image and likeness of God himself, needs your help is at the center, not you. Think about that Samaritan man: he is an icon in his willingness to change plans and give freely. Learn from him that justice opens out to eternal life: when a man was incapable of saving his own life, the Samaritan chose life for him, and the only evidence he left behind was that very life."

Having taken this contemplative walk through the two Gospel texts, we can go a step further and ask ourselves in what direction the protagonists seem "to be drawing us." Where are they leading us?

4. In the hand of the Samaritan woman

If the Samaritan woman took us by the hand, what would she say to us, and where would she bring us?

Surely she would invite us to accompany her to Jacob's well and tell us how she came there with the empty jug of her needs and distracting cares, all of which proved to be no problem at all for the man who was waiting to accomplish his work in her. And she would tell us that if she learned anything from Jesus at that time, it is that he is not put off by our defensiveness and the things we cling to. Rather, as the Son who always acts according to his Father's example (cf. Jn 5:19), he searches for the "fracture" in our makeup from which emerges our deepest yearnings, as if he were convinced that only a greater desire could put lesser ones in their place. That may be why

Jesus let the Samaritan woman go on telling him about her prejudices, wariness, and misgivings, until the thirst for life that she was
hiding in her heart revealed itself. Then he "pounced" on that desire:
"If you only knew the gift of God... ." Without his zeroing in on her
"fracture," she would not have recognized her unsatisfied needs;
without his focusing on it, she would have returned home with her
jug filled with water that was not quenching her thirst.[b]

If we asked her about how her desire was transformed, she
would encourage us never to let anyone or anything suffocate or hinder the desires we experienced when we first chose to follow Jesus
in the consecrated life. Rather, she would have us always keep them
vivid and unsatisfied, because in them are hidden the best of our "humanness" and all that allows us to remain open and filled with expectation of that Gift that we never fully comprehend.

Concerning her experience as a missionary for the people in her
village, the Samaritan woman might tell us of her strategy for leading others to Jesus. From him she also learned how to be an expert
in humanity, how to connect with dormant desires in the depth of
each soul and to look for those "fractures" that allow grace to pass
through, because that is where the Lord is already at work. For such
a mission it is better to put aside "individuality-realized-profession-
ally and busy-about-spiritually-inconsequential-commitments."[17]
Only "those who search for wells," who are capable of approaching and "getting in touch," of spending time and of being able to go
beyond appearances, can help others shed light on the spring of living water within themselves.

The Samaritan woman would try to convince us of the importance of our accompanying and sustaining each other in faith, learning how to reread life together and making it possible for each one
to share the water of his or her experience. She might reveal how cu-
rious she is to know where we channel the torrent of our emotions,
and whether or not our vows give to our energy a profound apostolic
orientation as Jesus had in his life.[c] She might even ask us to name
our "husbands," those realities with which we make pacts and which
separate us from our Center:

— The husband of the "stupidity of disinformation and conformism," that would have us believe that there is no hope for the world ("that's the way a market economy works...," "that's the price to pay for technological progress..."), and that the most sensible thing we can do is to go along with the way things are ("go with the flow").

— The "neoliberal, consumerist husband," that deceptively lures us toward "keeping up with the Joneses." The one that creates an ever-growing need for creature comforts and makes us think it is normal to find ourselves in the lap of luxury far removed from any risk-taking, and that camouflages our resistance to whatever threatens to take us out of our rut by labeling it "prudence."[18] When we live this way, the "spark of madness" that first motivated us to follow Jesus is snuffed out, our outlook becomes clouded, and we lose sight of the places of the poor that call for our involvement.

— The "individualist husband," that blinds us to the fountains which bring change, that seduces us with the easy-going ways of a trivial and distracted life in which the pain of others, the importance of God's presence, or the disturbing reminders of his Gospel fail to touch our hearts.

— The "pseudo-therapist husband," that relies on psychology as the ultimate explanation for everything, that is always suspicious of desires, invariably denying that they come from a transcendent source. This places us on a level of a seemingly indisputable positivism that claims everything stems from the innermost recesses of our psyche and all else is illusion, thus denying the possibility that our freedom extends beyond ourselves.

— The "secularist husband," that leads us away from the well, from the deeply moving encounter with the Lord and mystical experience. This "husband" would have us base our lives on solely ethical standards, and "secularizes" our hearts, taking from us the ability to express spiritual experiences. Out of this is born the inability to find the words to speak of the sublime, fear in the presence of mystery and symbol, fossilized liturgies, and an apostolic activism in which there is neither time nor space for substantial, silent, "leisure-ly," and constant prayer.[19]

— The "spiritualist husband," that strives to continue erecting shrines and to escape through the heights of new rites and reformist agendas with vague new age characteristics unrelated to everyday life.

— The "idolizer husband," that gets us to worship the media and its instruments, institutions, rites, and laws, which have nothing to do with a "return" to what is religious, making it more and more difficult for us to give the Father the adoration that he seeks from us.

— The "thousand-things-to-do husband," that hides behind the old dynamic of seeking justification through works; the one that sees us more as givers than receivers and converts apostolic failures or advancing age into traumatic situations, because that is when work loses its absolute claim on us.[d]

The Samaritan woman, whom Jesus freed from all her idolatries, would tell us above all:

"Be patient with the length of the process when you break off your ties with those husbands. Be assured that in each of your lives there is a well and that the Master is waiting for you there, seated at its ledge. Trust in his power to allure, his patience as he breaks down your defenses, his desire to lead you to the depths of your lives and your interior and secret fountains, because he knows how to accompany this descent without rushing or losing patience. When I heard him say twice, 'The water that I want to give,' I knew he was filled with a fierce desire to submerge all of us in its current.

"Don't be satisfied with what you already know about him: run along on this journey of intimacy to which you too have had the blessing to be invited. At first I thought of him as nothing more than a Jew, but he was leading me to the point of discovering him as Lord, Prophet, and Messiah, the One I had always waited for without knowing it. Have the courage to call him by new names that will never appear in the dull manuals lining your library shelves.

"Don't be afraid to acknowledge your thirst, and don't deceive yourselves into believing that your life as a consecrated man and woman exempts you from the uncertainties and vulnerability that throb in the heart of every human being. Change your attitude of being never-ending 'donors' and see yourselves as travelers with those who travel and seekers with those who seek. Only then will you experience the joyful surprise of being evangelized by the very people to whom you wish to announce the Gospel. Learn how to listen better and, instead of preaching and directing so much, become experts in asking questions, conversing, and sharing with others that human poverty that renders us all equals. Only if you experience your thirst will you be able to fathom what I learned by the well: the thirsty man who asked me for water turned out to be the one who quenched my thirst and later made me decide to tell everyone in my town about him. Precisely because I knew I needed salvation was I able to tell others that I had met someone who welcomed me without judgment or condemnation. Come celebrate that poverty with me, by the edge of the well. This poverty, when acknowledged and related to Jesus, is not an obstacle to receiving the gift of living water but the best chance we have to receive it and let it flow into eternal Life.

"But I caution you: be ready. He may be waiting for you anywhere and at anytime in your daily life—just when you're engrossed in trivial concerns, petty quarrels, or stale traditions bound up with status or rules. If you stop to listen to him, you are lost forever. At first he will ask you for something simple ('Please give me some water,' 'Call your husband...'), but in the end you will return home without water, without a jug, and with a thirst you have never known before to attract your whole town to him.

"Welcome the astounding news that the Father is searching for you and wants your adoration. Don't be afraid of that message, so strange to the world's ears, because it is the 'other land' to which you, like Abraham, have been summoned. Leave behind the old familiar places that sustained you and enter into a passionate relationship with the Lord and into his Kingdom where, as Benedict of Nursia used to say, nothing interferes with his love. This relationship becomes a way of life, as the psalmist proclaimed: 'Your love is better than life!' (Ps 63:4)."

5. In the hand of the Samaritan man

If the Samaritan man were to take us by the hand, what would he say and where would he take us?

Rather than listening to him (he seems to be a man of few words), we take time to contemplate the scene described by Jesus. We keep in mind that an icon is not a reflection of the life we already live; rather, it manifests the Other to us, the ideal we have yet to reach, the distance we have yet to travel for conversion. It places us before that gaze that penetrates our hearts and enables us to encounter the true face of our neighbor.

Will this icon find in us what dwelt in the heart and soul of Jesus, the one who told this story and who, without trying, "painted" his own features into it? Perhaps this is his masterpiece, the painting through which he was able to take his place in history and to be remembered even if there are now other reasons for doing so.

We begin looking at this scene as if we are already a part of it:

Above all, we are surprised by the stark realism of the artist, who spares us none of the bleak details. Robbers assault a man, strip him, beat him, and leave him half-dead. Two "qualified" passersby hurry on their way (and we can't help remembering the abuse in our world today, its forgotten victims pushed to the edge of society, our indifference or that of others as we pass them by, wrapped up in our own affairs...).

When the story insists on convincing us that evil has the last word in everything and that the situation is hopeless, the narrator brings another figure on the horizon, using a small grammatical device that leaves us in suspense: "But a Samaritan...." Where does the man come from and what does he intend in his introduction, that "but"? What opposing power can he represent in a world that seems to send out signals of frenzied possessiveness, with an obsession

for looking no further than one's own interests and a blissful ignorance while entire populations collapse in silence? Does not that
small "but..." tell us something about how Jesus views history and
of his unyielding hope that envisions a powerful though seemingly
weak force of resistance emerging from it?[e]

In the midst of so many signs of death, the Samaritan who enters this scene does not seem to possess many resources. He does not
belong to any center of power that backs him and assures him of prestige or influence; he is a foreigner traveling alone, with nothing but
a knapsack and his saddle. He turns his gaze to the place where the
man has been ambushed and, there, his heart is in rhythm with
Another.

Then he takes a minimal and immense step of walking over to
the fallen man. Where others have gone out of their way to avoid
him, not paying the slightest attention to his needs, the Samaritan
is moved by the wounded man and feels responsible for him. The urgency of caring for the man in need interrupts his travel plans and
puts all his projects on hold. His deep concern for the man's endangered life takes precedence over his own plans and brings out the
best of his humanity: an ego unencumbered by self. He is a foreigner
and thus no kinship or ethnic solidarity obliges him to take care of
the man, yet he stops and comes to the man's aid. He is a traveler
who dismounts, changes his itinerary, and kneels down beside the
man. He holds different religious beliefs, yet acts as his brother's
keeper. He interprets the commandment "You will not kill" to mean
"You will do whatever it takes for the other to live."[f]

What if this gesture of total readiness to change our plans contained the secret of our deepest identity and showed us where the
adoration that the Samaritan woman was calling us to leads? What
if this gesture were a sign in the midst of the world in response to
growing consumerism, a sign as poor as the manger or the empty
tomb, a presence affirming the value and dignity of the smallest
ones?[g] What if it were a tiny stumbling block in a field of neoliberal logic,[20] dreamers with their feet on the ground busy maintaining

a faithful relationship and not resigned to the status quo, able to discover viable possibilities for transformation and to imagine "other possible worlds"? In the time of the Good Samaritan, as now, there was a prevailing logic: "If you stop to take care of an unknown, half-dead man, you risk ruining your plans, your composure, time, oil, wine, and money." The Good Samaritan's reaction reveals the persistent logic of Jesus: "Don't measure, don't calculate, give into love. Others will give you back your identity just when you thought you were going to lose your life."[h]

We stop to contemplate the half-dead man. The person at the center of the scene leads us to think it was natural for Jesus to see the world with the eyes of those who live in the direst of circumstances. Jesus, the One born on the outskirts of Bethlehem, the One who dies outside the walls of Jerusalem, "pulls up stakes" and pitches his tent where nobody expects: with the dispossessed, with those who are cast down and excluded and for whom all hope seems lost. We will always find Jesus on the outside, with those whom the world has hurled far from itself.[21]

In the text, we read that the Good Samaritan "took care of him." Later, he will say to the innkeeper: "Take care of him." This shows a feminine deliberation and tenderness, which contrasts with our fast-paced lives and impatience for immediate results. The human dimension of "caring" can soothe our communitarian relationships with its warmth, break down our defenses, overcome the coldness that can make our celibacy gloomy, and allow us to show kindness, warmth, and tenderness.[i]

Again, we contemplate the half-dead man, facing the question that sometimes jumps out at us: whether or not consecrated life is at times responsible for some of its members being "half-dead." Honesty obliges us to recognize lives "half-lived" that seem to lack fulfillment and happiness, lives subordinated to the smooth running of institutions, smothered by the inertia of inflexible routines and unquestioned traditions; disembodied souls with their initiative and spontaneity snuffed out, rarely invited to think for themselves, to freely express their opinions, disagreements, desires, and dreams. Certainly one would have to define what is born of its sterile womb as "neither religious nor life" but "deadened subjects" that entered looking for the abundant life promised by the living God.

We continue looking at the half-dead man, relieved that someone is going to choose life in his name and do what he can for him. We realize with amazement that this suffering soul, because he is so helpless, has the power to reveal to the Samaritan his capacity for showing compassion, which makes him like God.

Suppose we felt that what was half-dead in us, both as individuals and as institutions, was meant to reveal dimensions of our existence of which we were not aware? What if the "messengers" charged with proclaiming something new in our lives were our very situations of increasing uncertainties, declining numbers, and losses? We would never have chosen such harbingers and, in fact, we continue to lament not being more numerous, strong, youthful, and influential. In many places we find ourselves in the opposite situation, and our resistance to impoverishment has become a source of a corporate spiritual depression that blocks our projects and prevents us from living happy and creative lives. We have a "half-dead" hope with respect to God's future in consecrated life, and we have signed on to an "emotional heresy"[22] far more dangerous than any other heresy: God can no longer do anything in this world, this Church, this apostolic Body; we shouldn't expect anything new from him. Perhaps we don't put it in these words, but that's how we feel, and that feeling enters subtly within and removes encouragement and hope. When there is a crisis of hope, faith and love begin to agonize.[j]

Do we not need Jesus, the great Samaritan, to come to us, to heal our wounds and pour out the oil of his consolation and the wine of his power on them? Is there not perhaps before us the *kairós* of discovering in our fragility "a new road" along which strength is manifested in weakness and life in death? Is it not perhaps the time to wholeheartedly trust that God is doing something new with our poverty and even our losses, and to accept being "bearers of the marks of Jesus" in the Church,[23] a weakness that is always fragile and never ending?[24]

Unless we decide to live to the full the deaths to which we are being led, unless we are able to "appreciate them," the life that is asking to be born from them will not come forth. It is a call to center ourselves on the essential, to a different way of relating to each other, of supporting each other intercongregationally, making room for the laity, and having a better understanding of the meaning of reciprocity and collaboration.

Can we imagine what would happen in congregations (and we are already beginning to see valuable examples of this) that abandoned all anxiety to control their future and instead left their charism, the pearl of great price, in God's hands? This abandonment does not mean we are disinterested, nor does it mean we stop offering the charism to others; rather it is abandonment in order to exercise the charism in seeking the Kingdom rather than assuring its survival at all costs. Can we imagine how much energy such confidence would unleash, and how novel it would be to stop blaming or beating up on ourselves over our diminishing numbers and precarious existence? Then would not these Congregations show us their radiant faces and reveal themselves not in terms of misfortune or drama, but as opportunities, painful yet pregnant with possibilities, for us to trust in the wisdom of the Gospel that speaks of losing and letting go?[k]

Don't we have the best chance today to live all of this to the full? As an immediate consequence, where the aging of consecrated life is experienced we could help one another to widen our view and be filled with joy that other Congregations at home and abroad are enjoying times of growth and expansion. This "vicarious consolation," this gesture of gratuitousness and detachment, would surely be in the best tradition of our Founders and would constitute one of those signs of newness we are looking for. This sign would be nothing less than the abandonment of our narrow views and letting our hearts beat to the rhythm of the universality of the Church!

Is it difficult to go forward on such faith? Certainly it is. But when we first decided to follow Jesus in a radical way, did people guarantee us that the future would be easy?

At last we arrive at the inn. Once again the place is characterized with the face of care, but now everything happens "inside" a house, within walls (of an institution, let us say).

How do we make the structures we have created become "inns" at the service of life, places where we feel welcome, places that offer us stability and permanence and that prepare us to return to our roads? How do we make sure that we do not forget that the reason for their existence is to generate (another feminine verb) "meaningful relationships" and to provide convenient structures and meeting places? How do we keep alive the memory of why they were born when the creative whirlwind of their imaginative Founders gave them built-in flexibility, so that they would not become stuck but might remain open to ongoing dreams?[25]

Inside the inn, it doesn't matter whether we are "on the front lines," or if we devote ourselves to making sandals for others who go out to meet those who need us, or if we produce the oil and wine used in dressing wounds. Some will have to devote themselves to denouncing the robbers who prey on the weak, creating "Samaritan communication networks" that raise awareness, protest, and work with "fellow dissidents" throughout the world who are already grappling against economic fatalism, inventing alternative economic models to promote solidarity, and using their full potential and resources to create a human order in which everyone's voice can be heard.[26] Others will feel the urgent need to spend time caring for this "half-dead" planet and to defend it from those who plunder it. Some will offer their time and attention to young people and those who knock at our doors in search of meaning. Some will feel called to engage in dialogue with other religions, and others to proclaim Jesus' name from the housetops.

The mission of our inn is to not only preserve the memory of our inheritance and strengthen our bonds, but also, above all, to make it easier for the human cause to resonate within us as God's cause, and to help us become a coordinated and well-conditioned body at the service of a wounded world.

6. From the hand of the scribe

If the scribe were to take us by the hand, what would he say to us and where would he lead us?

Maybe he would sit us beside his desk, covered with old, rolled-up manuscripts and commentaries on the Torah, and tell us how from his childhood he became used to scrupulously observing the Law, never knowingly breaking even one of its precepts. His constant concern was to find out how to reach "eternal" (i.e., "true") life, an abundant, profound, overflowing life beyond the limits of time, human weakness, and the dissolution of relationships.... In pursuit of this goal, he consecrated his life to reading and research, holding discussions with other scribes and then writing his findings on parchments, which he zealously preserved.

A teacher of knowledge with influence and prestige, he had spent the best years of his youth scrutinizing the Scriptures, but the teachings he mastered had become a tiresome burden, suffocating and trapping him in a tangled web of complicated propositions and subtle treatises.

People told him about an itinerant Galilean, with a band of disciples, who left behind an air of joy and freedom wherever he went. The scribe decided to go to see this man. Perhaps there was some text in the Torah with which he was not familiar, but which scholars at some Galilean synagogue had commented on. Maybe that might help him expand his knowledge of true life. With a mixture of curiosity and arrogance ("Can anything good come out of Nazareth?") he posed his question to Jesus. To his dismay, Jesus simply referred him back to the well-known answer found in the Law. The scribe quoted the *Shema* with the tone of someone who had repeated it by heart a thousand times: "You shall love the Lord your God with your whole heart...and your neighbor as yourself." Then, irked at the simplicity of the answer, he decided to test the Galilean's knowledge and asked, "And who is my neighbor?"

"And then came the shock," he confesses to us. "Instead of going through the laws and directives familiar to me, that puzzling teacher began telling me a surprising story that had nothing to do with what I had learned. This story turned everything upside down: the figures I respected and admired, the priest and the Levite, didn't measure up and were disqualified. The name of God was never mentioned, and the only remote reference to his Law (the prohibition concerning touching a dead body) was flagrantly violated. Above all, it was the story's conclusion that I found insufferable. Jesus proposed that I follow the example of a heretical Samaritan schismatic in order to become a neighbor!

"I tried to run away, but the hand of that stranger grabbed mine and took hold of me, leaving me at the crossroads where I now find myself. He is inviting me to leave behind all the roads I am used to and to set out on an entirely unfamiliar one, full of unknowns. He didn't demand that I renounce the inheritance I had received, but from there to create something new and very unexpected.

"My former knowledge and assurance are beginning to look worthless and I am getting dizzy. I am alarmed because without wanting to I am comparing the Samaritan with the priest and Levite, who for years symbolized the behaviors that nurtured my convictions. I am amazed that they are beginning to take on new meaning in my life: their lives seem sterile and obsolete to me, they express themselves in a dead language that I no longer speak. I see them as victims of cold, dead customs, satisfied with the opinions and conventional thinking of others, purveyors of empty words, godless professionals talking about God. Now I understand why in Jesus' story they gave the half-dead man a wide berth: their hearts were numb and atrophied, incapable of reacting to the unexpected and of freeing themselves from their routine, habitual ways of doing things.

Those men, just as I, knew by heart the commandment to love your neighbor. But their heads were not connected to their hearts and they fled from their true neighbor, who challenged them with his flesh-and-blood presence.[1]

"It's slowly dawning on me that the life I am looking for is not linked to laws, temples, rites, buildings, or customs, but on that word Jesus placed at the center of his story: compassion. The imperative he addressed to me, 'Do likewise,' is weighing on me, and I am debating whether to return to my world of certainties based on books, or to enter into contact with flesh-and-blood human beings to discover that in the company of the most downtrodden one gets to know eternal life."

What if we dared to see ourselves in the scribe? What if his words defined our habit of taking refuge in the sterile world of theories; the satisfaction we receive from stirring declarations; the calm of orderly, predictable lives; the security of rigid schedules and the sometimes invisible walls that keep us safe from the din of life; and the tears, cries, hopes, and laughter of those living and dying on the far-flung corners of our world?

How do we avoid having the adventure we undertook, born of a passionate love for the Lord and his Kingdom, from degenerating into a lukewarm existence, a boring adherence to customs, rules, and regulations?[m]

We are experiencing the frustration at not having hit the mark in our search for the full and overflowing life upon which we wanted to set our hearts. We are tired of meaningless words and are hungry to see, touch, and feel. We have reached a saturation point in terms of statements, documents, and theories about the specifics of our identity when what matters is not what we proclaim but how we live. Won't we be wasting our energy by preserving and holding on to a type of consecrated life and historical forms that had controversial and provisional beginnings?[27] Has the time perhaps not arrived to stop repeating what we have always done and to open ourselves to what lies before us, to the new realities the Spirit is creating?

We probably need to take the scribe's advice:

"Abandon your world of virtual reality, just as I shake the dust off my manuscripts. Even if only for a moment or two, turn off your computers that contain all the organizational charts, regulations, social projects, and pastoral plans you so zealously save and go out into the streets and town squares to listen to the noise of real people. Broaden your contacts with them. Don't avoid dangerous roads, because new things always emerge off the beaten path, away from safe, protected, everyday places.

"Be open to a spirituality that can deal with inclement and perplexing times without becoming defensive. Risk letting go of old practices and relearning the silent practice of tangible love—that is what will make your life shine, not your monotonous proclamations. Place greater interest in uncovering others' needs rather than in preserving hardware, in coming up with answers rather than in repeating formulas. Zero in on the basic issues that people are wrestling with: life, death, love, truth, peace, and the earth's future. Don't keep dispensing the trite answers that have outlived their time or let yourselves be paralyzed by discouragement. 'Precisely because things have gotten so bad, it's okay to hope.'[28]

"Don't grieve over the insufficiency of your strength to 'transfigure' your life: I didn't reach the life I was looking for on my own either. Rejoice if you have not words to define yourself. The Samaritan didn't use any words when he walked over to the wounded man and healed him. He simply did what had to be done.

"Don't try to run away when you experience situations of crisis and instability, when things break and come apart, when the theological privileges that sustained you are suspended. Only when you cease defining yourself by comparing yourself with others will the most authentic part of yourself be revealed.

"The life you have embraced is neither a code of ethics nor a founding story, but a passion, an adventure, a risk, a journey to accomplish with your eyes and ears wide open. On this journey the only guiding compass to your destination is mercy and tenderness.

"Let the imperative, 'Go and do likewise,' shake you up as it did me. Before you are open great avenues of worship and compassion that lead to 'eternal life.' Happy are you if you choose to travel on them."

7. In the hands of the first potter

As can be seen on the column in the museum at Nazareth, today Someone is taking us by the hand to draw us closer to himself, to make us his disciples passionate about him and his world.

He comes to us with the irresistible surge of spring water that bursts into eternal life and tries to lead us to the adoration the Father is seeking from us, until our whole life basks in his love and the primacy of his Kingdom puts everything else into perspective.

He comes to each one of us to heal our wounds and remove our burdens. He invites us to accompany him to the places where life is most endangered and to trust in the secret power of compassion and unflinching hope. In fact, he who already contemplates the head of wheat in the tiny seed buried in the earth, and hears the cries of the infant when the woman is still screaming out in labor pains (Jn 16:21), reveals life's hidden possibilities just when it seems that death has had the last word.

He is the giver of living water, the Samaritan who heals our wounds, the conqueror of death, the potter of the new creation.

Happy are we when we allow ourselves to be captivated and led to him.

Notes

Alphabetical

a. Two types of notes appear throughout this text: numerical to indicate quotes and references, and alphabetical to offer suggestions for personal reflection and dialogue in community.

b. We can recall the "wells" where we have enjoyed profound encounters with the Lord and received "living water" from him and get in touch with our thirst and with our own "fractures" as well as those of others, recognizing them as times of grace.

c. The two icons shed new light on our vows: we see them as the *over-flowing* of a living water that puts every other thirst in its place, a *compassion* that urges us to do everything we can to minister to people who lay wounded along the roadside, and the grace to be *counter-cultural,* creating alternative ways of living in a world ruled by possessiveness, self-indulgence, and the seductiveness of power.

d. In the words of St. John of the Cross, recognizing the "little things that the will sends our way" (*Subida,* Book I, Chap. 10, 1), and the "tiny thread that ensnares the bird" (*Subida,* Book I, Chap. 11, 4). Also our experience of a God who "will not allow anything else to dwell with him in our hearts" (*Subida,* Book I, Chap. 5, 8), naming the countless tiresome activities that distract us, the rushing about that dulls our senses, the hidden acquisitions that satisfy us, and the little certainties that tranquilize us.

Yet, since we are not serious and spiritual all the time, we can remember the story of "the seven little goats" from our childhood. When the wolf knocked at their door and said, "Let me in, my little children, this is your mother," the goats replied: "Show us your paw..." And the perverse wolf poured flour all over it to fool them. The moral being: You have to be wide awake and vigilant because those "would-be husbands" are constantly coming to our door to court us, and we need to help each other see their tricks and disguises for what they are.

e. We must animate each other to favor small accomplishments over grandiose projects; if anyone accuses us of tearing down utopias, we should tell him or her of the startling fact that this statement was made by none other than Blessed John XXIII, of happy memory. And taking heart from this text: "The fabric of hope is made from material taken from the sufferings of victims and can be universally applied, because if they have been able to hope and know how to hope then all of us can. Our particular work probably won't put an end to poverty, draw people out of the spiral of violence, or nationalize the means of production and change...but perhaps it has had the ability to unleash the joy that comes from taking action and getting things done. Acting on reality and changing things, even a little, is the only way to prove that reality is transformable" (Roca García, Joaquín and Aranível Said Rovira Ortiz, *Paisaje después de la catastrophe: Códigos de la esperanza* [Santander: 2003]), p. 146.

f. "There is a stirring up of holiness that secretly sustains the world," affirms Levinas, evoking the Jewish tradition of the thirty-six hidden just men, thanks to whom the world stays alive (*Sukká,* 45b). "As if the humility and kindness of a few could still, astonishingly, counterbalance the brutal and selfish pride of those who profess to be totally self-sufficient in life. As if they and only they are the source of that sweet, life-giving stimulus that restores the power to *'choose life'* (Dt 30:20) when evil strikes" (Catherine Chalier, *Levinas: La utopía de lo humano* [Madrid: 1995]), pp. 88 and 123.

We can bring to mind experiences of recognizing the power to "make vibrate the secret cord that ties us to goodness" (*ibid.* 121) when we have tenderly poured out oil and wine on the wounds of our brothers and sisters.

g. Calling to mind some of our chapter declarations about a "Preferential Option for the Poor" (usually capitalized) and trying to reduce such a magnificent decision to small letters, a holy water font, and comfortable time limits that might turn the proclamation into an albeit modest reality. That Option passes through our "communitarian body": through our eyes (what we read, the sources of information we turn to, the kind of people we notice, the TV programs we prefer...); through our ears (the voices, opinions, and judgments that have the greatest influence on us; the social media from which they come; the experience from which they speak...); our feet (the places we frequent, the people we visit, the places we stop, and from which we escape...); our hands (the people for whom we work, those we serve, the situations we get involved in...); our heart (the people to whom we are inclined, by whom we are moved, the causes we are passionate about...). And, on completing this journey, rather than drowning in a sea of guilt, we could work together on our living map to find out how to become people who search for roads, moving outside the walls that shelter us, and placing ourselves at a crossroads, within reach of marginalized people who have been made invisible, unrecognized, and voiceless in society, and recognizing these as privileged places for entering into communion with the Compassionate One and *"taking part with him"* (cf. Jn 13:8).

h. In the Samaritan's gesture of *pouring out* there appears the "mark" of the customs and the recommendations or Jesus himself (v. 24); *selling* (12:38; 18:22); *giving* (12:33; 18:22; 19:8); *contributing* (21:3); *letting things go* (18:29); *breaking and sharing* (9:16; 22:19); *not holding back* (9:24); *not storing up* (12:21)....We can welcome the countercultural obligations underlying these words, letting them accomplish their formative work in accordance with the Gospel.

i. Imagine a community life in which each member tries to put that "care" into practice, and where we give one another permission to exist as we are; permission to experience in our daily life together that the first thing of interest to each one of us is not what a person does or whether or not that person does it well or poorly, but what is each person's story, what he or she feels, what he or she is searching for, and what makes him or her tick. After a time of prayer, let us dare to express what we learn from one another in community and warmheartedly thank each other. We are accustomed to a peculiar ability to create "lists of rebukes," and the therapeutic effect of looking on others with an attitude of gratitude and admiration and our being able to express this would surprise us.

j. Let us recognize the "emotional heresies" that may exist in us and identify and own our ways of clinging to the past and our fear of letting it go that causes us to live defensively. Try to view new situations as the fissures or fractures through which the Lord is approaching us to "refound," and pledge to one another that we will "bite our tongues" when we find ourselves glorifying the past, speaking of how difficult the present is, and how woeful the future. Let us remind ourselves of the conviction that "creative times in the history of consecrated life have not been without their deep divisions. And this may be one of those critical times in history when consecrated life can be recreated in its entirety" (cf. Carlos Palacio, "El sacrificio de Isaac como parábola de la Vida Religiosa" [CLAR 3, March 1993]), pp. 19–20.

k. Thomas Merton tells this story: "Trungpa Rimpoche, a Tibetan Dahli Lama, had to flee to India. The monk who accompanied him wanted to bring a caravan of about twenty-five yaks loaded with all kinds of provisions. The Dalai Lama said to him, "We won't be able to take all those yaks with us; we'll have to wade and swim across rivers and we need to travel light." The monk replied, "We have to take them; we have to eat." They set out on the journey, and when the Chinese Communists saw the caravan of yaks along the road, they laid claim to them and all they carried. But the Dalai Lama was nowhere to be found. He had gone on ahead of the caravan, swam across a river, and escaped" (*Diario de Asia* [Madrid: 2000]), p. 300.

We could *role play* in community. One group could represent the "Dalai Lama," and another the "monk," giving specific names to what "we have to preserve," to our "yak caravans," and the actions that allow us to swim in freedom today.

l. *Vita Consecrata* contains expressions such as *sign, witness, testimony,* and *visibility,* together with verbs such as *to express, to make visible, to make recognizable, to manifest....* John Paul II presses consecrated life to eloquently proclaim its splendor and beauty, because it is "a mirror of divine beauty" in a disfigured world, one that is hypersensitive to the language of signs and symbols. Become aware whether or not the initial formation programs in our Congregation are designed to give us a "Samaritan look" (with the accent on our ability to handle the unforeseen, letting it affect us, and getting involved, warmly relating and coming near...), or a "Levitical look" (insistence on external signs of separateness, protected interests, keeping one's distance, and ritual observances...).

m. In a story about the Desert Fathers, a disciple said to Abbot Joseph, "Father, I fast a little, I pray, and I meditate. As much as possible I try to live in peace. I work at purifying my thoughts. What more can I do?" Abbot Joseph stood up and stretched out his hands toward the heavens. His fingers became as ten flames and he said, "If you want, you can be on fire."

Recall the times in our lives when our passion for the Lord and his Kingdom has made us "incandescent" and taken us out of our half-hearted measures and everyday concerns. Reflect together on how to "feed" this way of life....

Numerical

1. In addition, the contrast between these two figures is expressed by their heads: while the person "leading" is taller, is wearing a royal diadem that confirms her preeminence, the one "being led" wears a halo of holiness that comes from being bound by faith and adherence to it. Nevertheless, in contrast with the upright and resolute posture of the one who is leading, he appears reluctant and to be holding back.

Around both figures, we can see two other people. Enemies lying in ambush, they aim bows at the central figures. Their demonic presence expresses the temptations faced by those who are open to faith and discipleship. Though they are on the periphery, their attitude of watchfulness reminds us that the road of discipleship is always in sharp contrast to the world that surrounds it.

2. "The more time a man spends conversing with a woman, the worse things become for him; he distances himself from the word of the Law and is destined to be cast into *Gehenna*" (Abbot 15).

3. *Vita Consecrata,* no. 14.

4. "In the beginning, when God created the heavens and the earth, the earth was a formless wasteland and darkness covered the abyss..." (Gen 1:1–2). "At the time when the Lord GOD made the earth and the heavens, while as yet there was no field shrub and no grass of the field had sprouted, for the Lord GOD had sent no rain upon the earth and there was no man to till the soil..." (Gen 2:4).

5. Cf. Roberto Vignolo, *Personaggi del Quarto Vangelo: Figure della fede in San Giovanni* (Milan: Glossa, 1994), p. 161.

6. Cf. Dorothy Lee, *Flesh and Glory: Symbolism, Gender and Theology in the Gospel of John* (New York: Crossroad, 2002), pp. 71–87.

7. John Nolland, *Word Biblical Commentary,* Vol. 35, B, Luke 9:21–18:34, (Dallas: Word Books, 1993), pp. 586ff.

8. Cf. Roberto Vignolo, op. cit., p. 138.

9. God or Jesus is always the subject of the verb *splaxnizomai,* "to be moved with compassion" (cf. OT: Ex 34:6; Hos 11:8; Jer 31:20; NT: Lk 1:50, 54, 58, 72, 78; 7:13; 15:20...).

10. The Hebrew root *YS'* (to save) has to do with *"being spacious, ample,"* and can mean *"bringing to a spacious place."* If anyone feels besieged and filled with anxiety and comes across an opening, a fissure, that is where he or she experiences the saving action of God:

"Answer when I call, my saving God.

In my troubles you cleared a way..." (Ps 4:2).

11. Cf. Soon-Ja Park, "L'entretien avec la Samaritaine," *Sémiotique et Bible,* 96, pp. 26–55.

12. Alessandro Pronzato, *Las parábolas de Jesús* II (Salamanca: 2000), pp. 38–89.

13. Cf. J. Mateo and J. Barreto, *El Evangelio de Juan: Análisis linguístico y comentario exegético* (Madrid: 1979), pp. 222–248.

14. Soon-Ja Park, op. cit., p. 37.

15. Cf. Annie Jaubert, "La symbolique du puits de Jacob" in *L'homme devant Dieu, Mélanges offerts au Père Henri de Lubac I* (Paris: Éditions du Seuil, 1963), pp. 63ff.

16. Cf. Françoise Dolto, *L'Evangile au risque du psychanalyse,* Vol. I (Paris: Éditions du Seuil, 1977), pp. 37–57.

17. This is from Miguel Matos, SJ, in unedited notes on formation.

18. Cf. Jon Sobrino, *Resurrección de la verdadera Iglesia: Los pobres, lugar teológico de la eclesiología* (Santander: 1981), pp. 334–335.

19. Cf. Miguel Matos, SJ, op. cit.

20. Cf. Thirteenth General Assembly of CLAR, 1997 (Lima, June 12–21, 1997).

21. Cf. C. Duquoc, "El desplazamiento de la cuestión de la identidad de Dios a la de su localización," *Concilium* 4, 1992, p. 578.

22. Cf. Jose Antonio García and Dolores Aleixandre, *Seis imperativos, un aviso y un deseo: Releer el Cantar de los Cantares desde la Vida Religiosa* (Madrid: 2000), p. 21.

23. Cf. Gabino Uríbarri, *Portar las marcas de Jesús: teología y espiritualidad de la vida consagrada* (Madrid-Bilbao: Editorial Desclee, 2001).

24. J. C. Guy, *La Vie Religieuse, mémoire évangelique de l'Eglise* (Paris: 1987), p. 154.

25. D. O'Murchu refers to that return home and to ourselves as cosmic, planetary creatures who owe everything to creation, as the "vow of mutual sustainability." And being home creatively, with all the other beings with whom we share this homeland ("La Vida Religiosa: un llamado a la liminalidad," *Con-spirando,* n. 31/00).

26. Cf. Maurice Bellet, *Un trajet vers l'essentiel* (Paris: 2004), pp. 11–31.

27. Cf. José Arregi, "Ante el futuro de la Vida religiosa," *Lumen* 50 (2001), pp. 201–213.

28. Cf. Maurice Bellet, *Invitation: Plaidoyer pour la gratuité et l'abstinence* (Paris: 2004), p. 81.

THE IMPACT OF SOCIO-CULTURAL AND RELIGIOUS REALITIES ON CONSECRATED LIFE FROM A LATIN-AMERICAN PERSPECTIVE: A SEARCH FOR ANSWERS

João Batista Libânio, SJ

Introduction: Defining the Ideas

At the beginning of this new millennium, the sturdy ships of modernity that cross rough seas are being shaken by violent squalls. A culture is emerging that is eroding modern myths, traditional economic and political forms, the solid foundations of rationality, and time-honored religious institutions. The institution of consecrated life is being shaken in this whirlwind.

Consecrated life

In this text, consecrated life is understood as having three structural elements—a founding experience of God, community life, and mission—and not based only on the vows. The latter have significance in relation to these three elements. Other types of consecrated life are being born and displacing the characteristics and shaping new experiences, above all communitarian.

The Present Context

The contemporary world is analyzed through its cultural aspects, which are extremely complex. We discuss the culture of life from infancy to the ethics of elderly care, the anti-culture of death from abortion to mass extermination through endemic disease, weapons of mass destruction, and the plague of hunger. Pluralism embraces varieties of ethnicities, cultures, languages, values, and religions. However, it also results in the opposite: a globalized uniformity through information technology in English, fanaticism and intolerant fundamentalism, and canonical and dogmatic orthodoxies.

Things become more complicated because of the postmodern mentality, which paradoxically unites an ardent thirst for the sacred with an invasive secularization, the allure of transcendence with coarse sexual education, a thirst for love and affective intimacy with an uncontrolled disorder in the affective life.

These cultural expressions are not floating in an empty superstructure. Rather, they are produced and nourished by economic and political spheres, whose major effects are neoliberalism in its worst form of financial globalization, the decadence of formal democracy, and the migratory movements of the poor, the excluded, and the unemployed. Consistent cultural change is not possible without radical economic and political transformation. Therefore, the principle role of consecrated life unfolds in the cultural atmosphere, with one eye on the economy as a basic factor. There is no need for Marxism to affirm this; we need only look at the role of the economic administration in institutions, even religious institutes, to see the aberrations the economic aspect can produce in flagrant contradiction to the ethical principles that regulate it.

Inserted in this contemporary context, consecrated life participates in the culture of life and the anti-culture of death. Since consecrated life is not ours but is a gift of God to the Church and the
world, we have the responsibility, in the midst of this turbulent global economic situation, to strive to watch over it with zeal and the
greatest possible lucidity.

Latin America

Latin America enters into this reflection not as a geographical location of consecrated life to be studied, but rather as a perspective from
which to understand the totality of consecrated life. From this location one sees the totality of its reality, a totality coming from a par-
ticularity.

The location we call South America is a "metaphor for the human suffering caused by capitalism," indicates resistance to the do-
minion of the North, and in its authenticity speaks of not having been
totally disfigured and destroyed by this domination. According to the
sharp expression of the Portuguese political scientist, Boaventura
Santos, it has not been transformed by the relationship with capitalist colonialism.[1] And from the periphery the power structures of
the North become even more visible.

The religious stage of Latin America is distinguished from the
European by its dominant syncretism, a fundamental religiosity in
a phase of fragmentation, subjection of conscience, and a growing
number of religious agencies involved in services, while religion in
Europe seems to be enduring a violent process of secularization, as
well as suffering from the "revenge of the sacred"[2] and the presence of the "sacred savage."[3]

The Congress has put together its reflection in an intercultural
context—region, gender, age, diversity of responsibilities—entrusted with a four-fold fidelity: to today's humanity, to Jesus Christ and
the Gospel, to the Church and her mission in the world, to consecrated life and to the charism of the institutes.

The Approach of Our Current Reflection

Ours is an analytic rather than moralistic approach through which emerges restrictive and intentional aspects. The aim is to lead to a discernment of reality in its ambiguity, perplexity, and paradox. It seeks to come closer to reality and to understanding it in its complexity so as to master its specific historical and structural elements in the search for paths and answers. It makes its own the four indicative verbs in the basic text of the Congress: to welcome, to allow oneself to be transformed, to begin a new praxis, and to celebrate. And attentive to the new already coming forth as a gift from God, to that which will spring forth in the continuing present or in the unforeseen.

Aspects of the Contemporary World

1. Fear of Freedom and of Responsibility

Description

Actually, we are living a paradox with regard to freedom. It is important to make a distinction between freedom of choice and theological freedom. The first is practiced with regard to material and symbolic possessions. The more we enter modern society, the freer we are to choose alternatives and opportunities. Persons from the rural world, who plunge into large urban centers with bids for their attention on all sides to the point where they are exhausted, feel intoxicated by such a freedom. The illusory quality of such freedom is clear because people become slaves of consumerism. We will put this type of freedom aside.

Fundamental freedom, or theological freedom, refers to the true self because it is interpreted in the light of revelation. This freedom encounters its most important, profound, and radical moment when the self is before God and must make the profound choice to accept or to reject him.[4] Since such an act defines us for all eternity, we have a great dread of such freedom.[5] This freedom is the fundamental question of consecrated life. The fear of taking this freedom into our own hands makes it accept the gravity of consecrated life and its definitiveness, because it involves the totality of the human person, for life and for death. A great fear flows from this, because everything is at stake. In a culture of the temporary and the throwaway, freedom lived in its fullest sense, as the giving of oneself to the Transcendent, is frightening because of its definitive nature. This freedom is not realized in the world of things, but in confronting other liberties that express and make concrete the freedom of the God who calls us.

The Search for Answers

The path to confronting the fear of decisions is found in the formation to freedom. There are two fundamental perspectives in understanding freedom: conquest and gift. In the political realm, freedom is presented as the great flag of the French Revolution, written in the Charter of Human Rights in various forms. It was a conquest at the price of much blood. In the economic domain, capitalism proclaims free initiative as a fundamental dogma. Workers celebrate a series of social rights linked to freedom, gained through incredible struggle, symbolized in May Day celebrations. Certain existentialist philosophies set the overriding affirmation of human freedom against the existence of God. Psychoanalysis leads the fight for freedom for the unconscious. In this perspective, formation for freedom is defined as an incessant struggle against forces that block freedom. We must not neglect this aspect, because all human freedom confronts internal and external adversaries. And consecrated life is not exempt from this.

From a theological perspective, freedom is a gift in the order of creation and grace. God creates free human beings and sustains them in their existence of freedom before him.[6] This freedom is wounded by sin, but not wholly destroyed through the victorious grace of Christ. Pauline theology confirms this.

Freedom as grace brings salutary consequences to formation, inspiring attitudes of gratitude and responsibility. It removes the

harshness of belligerent claims or attitudes of independence and total autonomy, placing itself instead on the path of fundamental relationship with God and with other freedoms, which are also gifts.
Thus one understands how freedom comes precisely from confronting God's freedom and that of one's brothers and sisters and
how religious commitments are not a negation but rather the fullness
of realization.

2. Loss of Historical and Ethical Consciousness

Description

The loss of a consciousness of history characterizes this predom-
inantly postmodern time. The past is fading away, the future becomes
more obscure, and the present remains without a history. The chief factor at play here in the loss of awareness is information technology,
transmitting data without context, orientation, causality or end, purely immediate and continually "on line." Everything is present without a distinction between the real and the virtual, in a real world of
"simulation" (J. Baudrillard). There is no tomorrow nor is there an
accounting for it. Various terms describe this situation: the end of history[7] and meta-narratives,[8] the end of utopia,[9] the deconstruction of
history, etc. Ultimately, there is a generalized suspicion with regard
to reality, concepts, ideologies, and theologies that unravel the transitory present. Consecrated life is submerged in this wave.

With the end of history, responsibility disappears, as do the unconditional dimensions of ethics. No one commits him or herself definitively to anything or to anyone. Each decision is only for the
present and may be revoked for another that is also present.
Superficiality prevents people from taking on definitive commitments. One can ask if the weak historical consciousness of our young
people is a cultural given or a defect in formation. It is probably the
result of both.

History is a fundamental dimension of our human and
Christian identity, and consequently, of consecrated life. For this

reason, it is difficult to form a consistent identity in consecrated life without it.

The Search for Answers

In the 1970s, in Latin America, consecrated life seriously took on the formation of a critical conscience, according to the steps of liberating education provided by Paulo Freire.[10]

We created small tools to help to form critical conscience in different situations.[11] This was a necessary consideration in assemblies, in the revision of activities, and in studying communities. Unfortunately, it seems it is necessary to once again rethink this problem in this time of postmodernism with its extreme subjectivity and insubordination before reality.[12] It is not a question of provoking criticism of institutions and social realities outside ourselves, but of taking a critical look at ourselves in a movement of insertion and emersion, of proximity and of distance.

It is necessary that education develop within people the capacity for judging and appreciating their own experiences, thoughts, actions, and situations with self-awareness within a determined context. There are three fundamental aspects to the formation of a critical conscience: awareness of a definite character, possible awareness, and awareness of the myths of the times. Through definite character, one avoids the universalizing ideology of the particular; the limits of possible awareness allow the boundaries of thought and action to expand in a determined time and space; and the relief of myths breaks the obvious deception of current culture.

In order to educate a critical and historical conscience, studies must track the route of concepts and theories. But there is a certain ambiguity in the understanding of the historical. This allows for a process of liberation when one unmasks concepts and positions that have been arrogated direct and universal powers as relative, arbitrary, and contextual. However, one runs the double risk of generating relativism and historicism. Relativism destroys the possibility of building anything substantial, since "all projects for social transformation are equally valid or invalid."[13] The opposite danger comes from historicism, which imagines history as a linear development, judging all cultural moments and stages, especially those of peripheral countries, from the viewpoint of the development of central countries. The latter claim to be the prototype of development and determine for those who are behind the stages to be covered in the way of human growth. This historical model will never be able to understand or imagine that a peripheral region can be far more developed in some aspect than a country that is considered "developed."

The creation and development of a critical and historical conscience is helped through dialogue. And referring to the metaphor of the text of the Samaritan woman, and adding the scene of Peter's confession of faith, reveals the nature of this dialogue: to be moved by love. Only love rebuilds the person from the inside, opening greater horizons of courage, responsibility, and commitment. St. Augustine sums it up well when he says: "We are what we love."[14] The consecrated religious knows that the first Samaritan is God the Father. He sends us the Samaritan Jesus and comes close to us through other innumerable Samaritans who cure the postmodern sores of superficiality, banality, and empty decision-making.

3. The Neoliberal and Media Context

Description

Without going into the political and economic question of neoliberalism and the implications in the world of media, I will pause on the ideological and cultural aspect.

The strong impact of the media is dismantling fixed and universal points of reference, multiplying the models and views of life. Propaganda bombards motivations, creating the logic of stimulus-seeking, going well beyond the simple rules of capitalist supply and demand.[15] A nihilistic spirit is invading society. This means a deterioration of the supreme values; the question "why" has no answer and lacks finality. "Nihilism is atheism not in attitude, but in spirit. It is the dissolution of the ethical foundations of life and of their age-old foundation in the sacred. Nihilism is fundamentally illogical: it accepts nothing as the principle and end of all values"[16]—a traumatic experience that has provoked unforeseeable resistance in postmodernism.

Neoliberal ideology, sustained by the media culture, diffuses the values of health, a cult of the beauty of the body, and the decisive character of appearance. It is the reign of the physical and of marketing. This triumph of media culture reaches fully the world of consecrated life. It occupies the external and internal time of religious, and it influences the way they perceive themselves. It unravels the social fabric. It creates virtual identities, leading to confusion between the real and the virtual. More serious still is that it forms needy and egocentric communities,[17] with a clear loss of the social dimension. The liberal context facilitates the creation of narcissistic identities principally given over to the cult of the self, to one's appearance, and to groups that reinforce this existential dimension. All of this is fed by the media.

Globalization is tied to neoliberalism in a circular relationship of cause and effect. Globalization reinforces neoliberalism, which in turn prompts globalization. This brings with it a growing poverty and multiple forms of social injustice along with collective discrimination.

In psychocultural terms, globalization depersonalizes, uproots, and distorts above all poor and simple people, who have less possibility to react and resist. Meanwhile, in many places it provokes reactive positions of racism, xenophobia, nationalism, and social classes.

The Search for Answers

One superior general of a large religious congregation, when taking stock, found an obvious regression with regard to the commitment of solidarity with the poor, and the necessity to "seek the path of the poor" and to create a "style of personal and community life in solidarity with the poor." Only nine percent of the community's members were devoted to specific social works recognizing, with a hopeful outlook, that an option for the poor imbued these ministries.

A survey of new generations reveals that the option for the poor still carries great weight in vocational choice, though finding at other times a loss of this enthusiasm. There is probably ambiguity with regard to motivation. It is one thing to say one is motivated by the "cause of the poor," and quite another to desire to live and remain close to the poor as "an evangelical way" of life that can only be sustained through the mystique of identification with Jesus Christ.[18]

In other words, the incentive to realize solidarity with the poor allows for three different scenarios. In the first case, one can be content with isolated and sometimes only sporadic actions on behalf of the poor. One's heart is consoled with these. In the second and higher case, one seeks to be a loyal presence beside the poor in defense of their rights in an intermittent way and perhaps even inserted among them. A greater demand lies in developing a culture of solidarity. By culture is meant the creation of a real symbolic universe, in which the gestures, thoughts, and actions of persons are only comprehensible in terms of solidarity. This would be the highest ideal of the option for the poor.

Globalization can be interpreted through the metaphor of the story of the Tower of Babel. An attentive reading of this text shows that the confusion of tongues is the work of God, and the desire for one language in order to create external unity and uniformity as a means of control by the dominating force is the product of hubris. Globalization is the work of power and the imposition of the "lords" of the world who want to erect a great tower, and from its height, impose one market language. God comes and creates the confusion of the poor, the periphery that does accept this domination. God is the confusion of unifying power.

Continuing with the parable, for centuries consecrated life had created a uniform language, then along came postmodernism disseminating confusion with new forms and expressions. Perhaps this is God's new way of acting.

We could consider another biblical metaphor: Pentecost. It seems that everything happens in contradictions. The Spirit unifies, and such a reading presumes a lot. If one looks closely at the text, it does not state that the apostles spoke one language and that everyone understood, but that each understood in his own language, therefore in diversity.

Putting the two metaphors together, globalization seems an imposition that the Spirit of God destroys through a confusion of reactions (Babel) or through the different ways of receiving it (Pentecost). Uniformity comes from outside, interpretive perception from within, from experience, freedom, and awareness.

In terms of an answer, there is the necessity for inculturation and institutional flexibility, which opens enormous hope and expectation. We have truly only begun to take the first steps toward real inculturation, though the topic has been amply treated, especially in the sphere of interreligious dialogue.

4. Confusion Between Vocation and Career

Description

Modernism has muddled the idea of vocation and career, with consequences to the identity of consecrated religious. Career means competence, efficiency, productivity, and social recognition. It requires that one be involved in preparation for exercising that chosen career. One enters into a furor of courses and degrees in order to be always more credible and thus to obtain success and remuneration. A career does not allow for failure. A person's career ends when he or she no longer exercises it due to age, illness, or retirement. Time rules and everyone is subject to external forces.

Vocation, instead, exists in a world of gratuitousness. The motivation comes from within. Whatever activity the person engages in, a "more" is revealed. In the most adverse situations, such as illness and advancing age, the vocation continues, even if it is exercised only in prayer and in giving one's life. Vocation is characterized by its perennial nature, specific to giving oneself to God.

In theological terms, vocation belongs first to the charism rather than to the institution. Its finds its ultimate source in the call of God, both in the secular as well as the consecrated life.

The Search for Answers

Vocation and career are not two separate entities, but two different dimensions of human activity with specific distinctions. The identity of the consecrated religious relies on an appropriate relationship between these two entities, and it is threatened when a career overwhelms a vocation.

Vocation is foundational. It gives meaning and inspiration to one's work and not vice-versa. Consecrated life views professional competence as coming from and as a function of vocation and not as an autonomous reality.

Career and vocation are distinct, although joined. Today's society values career in such a way that it becomes a criterion for assessing vocation. Crises flow from this continually. The formative path seems to be the contrary: to look at a career in terms of vocation according to the Ignatian criterion of *tantum quantum*. The career is greater the more it helps vocation and mission.

The principle of the solution lies in the theological understanding of vocation as a call from God, which gives meaning to a career. The latter enters into consecrated life as a concrete expression of a greater vocation, a gift from God. There is no purely secular career in consecrated life.

5. *The Fallibility of Institutions: The Loss of the Source of Security*

Description

Consecrated life has received and continues to receive enormous incentive from the institutional Church, especially with new forms of consecrated life born from movements of renewal and new experiences of community. Besides this, the dicasteries continue to regulate their norms.

The institutional Catholic Church, even in its supreme form, feels as threatened as any institution in a postmodern world by an increasing loss of credibility. In the past, attacks against the Church came from enemies. These helped to reinforce the institution. The novelty of the present situation is that the Church recognizes its own fragility. After the holiness of Christ, the Second Vatican Council called the Church holy, but also sinful, in need of purification, and unceasingly in search of penance and renewal.[19] In a very visible and concrete way, John Paul II publicly asked for forgiveness for the sins and historical errors of the Church, some of which were grave and which violated fundamental human rights.[20] Elsewhere, he wrote: "Although she is holy because of her incorporation into Christ,[21] the Church does not tire of doing penance: before God and man *she always acknowledges as her own her sinful sons and daughters*."[22]

If this act was on the one hand an act of greatness of spirit, on the other hand it produced some insecurity. If the Church erred gravely in the past, could she not err in the present? Thus, the authoritative affirmations of the past that absolutely guaranteed truth and credibility now cast a shadow of suspicion: "who knows...?" The work of González Faus alerts us to this.

The Search for Answers

The difficulties faced in countering such suspicions are larger the greater is the generalized disaffection with all institutions. The crisis with regard to trust affects all institutions. The May 1968 movement in France was the epicenter of this crisis. From then until now, political, social, and cultural institutions have not recovered. The Church is not exempt from this avalanche in the loss of prestige, though it continues to have some reasonable respectability in Brazil. In other countries, especially following the media revelation of sexual scandals, the lack of credibility has increased. The press as a whole frequently portrays the Church in caricature, negatively exploiting its positions, especially with regard to family and moral questions.

It is difficult to *"sentire in et cum Ecclesia,"* which "not only expresses a favorable feeling toward the Church, but also thinking with and an interior communion with the Church, with one's head and heart."[23] Here we touch upon the problem of the incarnation of grace. If, in the time of Jesus, his being flesh was a scandal for many who could not go beyond it and recognize in him the Messiah, the One sent by God, today the Church provokes the same scandal. To believe in the saving sacramentality of the Church at a cultural moment when its fragility and sinful condition are exposed to the maximum implies a deep dimension of faith. Mistrust, suspicion, and above all parallel behavior are becoming very common in the Church, not to mention in consecrated life.

It is time to deepen the relationship between the Church and the Reign of God from the perspective of the parables of the Kingdom. The metaphors of the yeast, of the grain, and of the hidden pearl allow us to comprehend the Church's dimension of inner mystery, despite all the external difficulties. Only a mystical experience of love makes such a reading possible, avoiding the two extremes of iconoclastic rebelliousness and of obsequious subservience.

6. Fluid Postmodernism in Consecrated Life

Description

Consecrated life is currently experiencing the impact of postmodernism. A discussion of this and its characteristics would be too long, so I will examine some elements.

The term, postmodernism, reveals some ambiguity. We have a "post" that is not only "after" but "with." There is, therefore, a "post-with-modern" in which elements of these two moments coexist; and a "post-pre-modern" that jumps over aspects of Western modernism and finds some of its fundamental values in other cultural avenues.

Postmodernism did not come about after the death of modernism. The latter is very much alive and advances under various aspects, for example, in the techno-sciences, triumphant in the areas of bio-genetics and information technology.

Liberation theology compares a second reading of the critical social break, inspired by Marx, with the first that had promoted bourgeois ideology. In talking about postmodernism, it is also fitting to propose a reading of "opposition," critically positioned with regard to dominant postmodernism, also having many points in common. This synthetic description has as many traces of dominant ideas[24] as those that propose an opposing position in the form of post-colonialism.[25]

A Philosophical-Scientific and Psycho-Sociocultural Break

The dominant postmodernism questions and undermines the prevailing scientific and philosophical dogmas of modernism, and it proposes alternatives. On the logical-scientific level: plurality of reasoning and complex thinking; a constructive, relative, syncretistic view of reality, approximate truth reinforced by quantum theory; inter-, multi-, and trans-disciplines; little relations and the plurality of sources of knowledge; and the principle of reflexivity.[26] In the ethical area: the need for building a global ethic; placing greater value on the idea that the ends justify the means. On the social level: the family's variety of forms; emphasis on fragmentation on the margins and peripheries; heterogeneity and plurality of differences, agents, subjectivities; reconstruction of multiple, realistic, and critical utopias arising from the poor.[27]

Another fundamental aspect of postmodernism is the new subjective pattern of the individual,[28] in which feelings and emotions are the basis of self-understanding and relationships. The "I" is at the center. It feeds on pleasure, on subjective and emotional experience, reuniting, as our primary text indicated, a thirst for love along with affective disorder. It establishes a new relationship with the body, through exaggerated care of oneself and experiencing it as the source of joy and the fundamental way of entering into relationships.

In community life, this has the consequence of creating a desire for emotional communities, replete with affection and kinship. I would go so far as to say that community meetings with fewer people are preferred and mega-events rather than routine community life. Routine undermines emotion, interior satisfaction, and perhaps even pleasure, and these are behind new forms of community. Our primary text refers to the major search for meetings of various types among ourselves and with lay persons. Choices are directed toward democratic, interpersonal relationships that are characterized by the openness and tolerance one finds among friends.

Mixed in with this are recent achievements with regard to pain medications: the alleviation of physical pain through anesthetics and psychic pain through psychotropic drugs that promise chemical bliss. Prozac has been greeted as the "perfect drug." G. Sissa speaks of the "happiness of the wallet."[29] In addition there is the pedagogy of solace, which aims at avoiding any type of suffering, seeking to minimize or abolish pain entirely. Imagine a society without pain or suffering, swimming in the happiness of medications and solace, and therefore incapable of any sacrifice, renunciation, or suffering, living in a state of pacifying the soul with good humor and positive thoughts.

The centrality of the individual as the source of values in contemporary society necessarily leads to a relativizing of values and places emphasis on the choice of experience without absolute criteria, stressing flexibility, spontaneity, and a *carpe diem* mentality.[30] Modern and postmodern individualism "is characterized by the emergence of individual value at the center of the social, the symbolic, and the organizational systems of society."[31]

A painful fragmentation is pervading culture and individuals. Intellectual, spiritual, cultural, and professional activities, as well as pleasure, leisure, and entertainment are experienced separately and in a dissociated way. We are very far from the desire of the Council Fathers who dreamed of an integrated formation for the clergy![32]

Psychoanalysis favors a fragmentation of identity when it considers the individual's psychic structure as conscious (ego) and unconscious (id, superego). People confuse their self-image, now seeking anonymity, now fleeing from stable relationships, now taking pride in appearance, and now hiding in virtual relationships.[33]

Living in a culture marked by hedonism, immediate consumerism, the preferential option for pleasure through media, computers, and high-speed Internet on one hand, and on the other the suffering of enormous psychic vulnerability, there is tremendous difficulty in working out frustration, anguish, expectation, and taking a position on macro-politics. Small transformations and short-term projects are preferred.

Consecrated life is verifying the separation of the new generation of religious from the social body of congregations. A "third man" is entering consecrated life, one who knows the rules and doesn't object, but follows them only as he wills.[34] There is a true schism[35] that creates a dual language, frequently in conflict and even in contradiction. There is a language for the public: superiors, colleagues, and social expectations; and there is another real language of internal experience and individual conscience. Not all of this is conscious. According to studies, formators have doubts about the declared motivations of those in formation in terms of their giving themselves to the poor like Jesus, their desire to be humanitarian, and their search for God. They doubt the depth of their conscious and unconscious motivations, which vacillates around self-promotion, self-recognition, and the veiling of affective-sexual problems.

Spiritual Character

In postmodern times, religiosity and spirituality are another world. Its most significant expression is called New Age. This is a universe of religious expressions, characterized by enormous syncretism and freedom, autonomy and subjectivism in religious forms with minimal or no links to institutions, formal religions, or authority. Fundamental to this is the post-traditional concept of God, the person of Jesus, salvation, religion, and the institutional Church with a new religious awareness that tends toward Gnostic monism, esoteric mysticism, humanistic psychologizing, sacred wholism, profound ecologic preoccupations, cosmic energy, and so many other "isms." There is a passage from "hard" faith to "soft" spirituality and religiosity. In a word, there is a weakening of the personal concept of God and a return to a more fluid understanding of the divine as energy, as an adjective rather than a noun, ending in the death of God.

In the footsteps of K. Hervieu-Léger, B. Carranza observes how the postmodern religious climate is invading all spheres and styles of life with a diffused spirituality. This deinstitutionalized, anarchic, drifting, consoling spirituality is closer to the universe of New Age on one hand, and on the other hand to fundamentalism, offering speeches and practices that reach the sacred, guarantee salvation, and testify to miracles and divine blessings.[36] Both types offer consolation and identity to the faithful.

In the realm of charismatic Catholicism, which is participating in this wave, an inner experience of revival, rebirth, and baptism in the Spirit is found. Frequently, the word "mystical" comes up, which conveys the original sense of a transcendent form as well as the most barbaric form in the sea of media jargon.[37]

In this climate there exist authentic initiatives, such as the spiritual exercises in daily life, contributing to the deepening of the spiritual experience. Such practices have been led by religious and lay persons and are directed toward faithful Christians as well as the general population.

This spiritual movement has adopted two diverse forms of reading Scripture. In some cases, there is the search for almost magical answers to personal problems through an uncertain, subjective reading of Scripture. In other cases, the reading of Scripture nourishes religious and secular communities through Bible-study groups.

Socioeconomic and Sociopolitical Characteristics

In the wake of the fall of socialism and the crisis of neocapitalism, postmodernism is also present in the economic arena in the form of neoliberal finance with an awareness of the limits of growth and progress through globalization in the various stages of production and commercialization. In the political realm, it points to the failure of formal democracy and national States, and organizes the theme of the World Social Forum: "Another world is possible," with a plurality of collective projects articulated in a non-hierarchical manner. An ecological mentality is spread as well as the struggle for the humanization of bureaucracies.

Postmodernism is linked to an extremely pluralistic society in all areas. Thus is expands the breadth of choices, the complexity of relationships from various social groupings, making understanding more difficult and paralyzing social action. Processes of inclusion and exclusion in large cities are changing, increasing the level of permissiveness.

One can observe a distance and gap between the language of consecrated life and the experiences of religious men and women in this society. In a violent, unjust, and aggressive reality, one can read idealistic documents almost empty of real beauty. The political and social consciousness of religious is declining.

In comparing a survey of seminarians taken in the 1980s with one in the 1990s, the analyst affirms that "the number of seminarians who are involved (or inclined to be) with base Christian communities, pastoral work among the landless, the urban poor, worker movements, human rights, indigenous peoples, and immigrants has declined about fifty percent.... The current generation of seminarians (apparently also contemporary youth) do not show clear plans for changing, and care more for their own personal realization."[38]

Hence, one sees a loss in commitment, ardor in free reasoning, and a withdrawal from the inserted community, with a shift from pastoral social work toward liturgical-sacramental activities.

The Search for Answers

Let us imagine consecrated life inserted in this broad context of postmodernism, participating in all these realities, sometimes without reflection and out of routine, sometimes reflectively and critically. Postmodernism raises great doubt with regard to the formidable nexus of modernism that reaches even consecrated life, and the South has misgivings about the melancholy celebration of postmodernism in the North.

The answer to this must consider the exhaustion of Western modernism. Therefore, it is a question of thinking of economy beyond capitalism and socialism, of politics beyond representative democracy, of culture beyond instrumental and scientific rationality, and, analogously, challenging ourselves to imagine a new paradigm for religion, for the Church, and for consecrated life. Religion is moving in the direction of surpassing a social function and of rediscovering a mystagogy. The Church is called to go beyond its triple centrality—Rome, diocese, parish—and (in the language of H. Kung) the medieval Roman Catholic paradigm[39] and the colonialist mentality, of which Bonaventura Santos speaks, to find true ecumenism. Consecrated life, in its search for greater inculturation, is confronted with surmounting Tridentine canonicity still in existence after Vatican II and the centralization of general governments.

In broader terms, at stake is the perspective of a greater rationality that surpasses the superiority of rational, instrumental, or scientific-empirical knowledge. It is also a question of rethinking modern social emancipation "from the perspective of the victims' experiences, from the perspective of social groups that have suffered from the epistemological exclusivity of modern science and the reduction of possibilities for emancipation in Western modernism, and the possible restitution from modern capitalism."[40]

In this process, we confront the paradox of a modern culture that is at once indispensable and inadequate. In part, we also run the risk of embarking on a celebratory, festive postmodernism that impedes a postmodernism of opposition that is born out of the plight of victims and not only of those who feast at banquets with the great lords.

Consecrated life will only rise from the ashes of the fire of postmodernism if it recovers the founding experience of God, true mystagogy, introducing consecrated religious to the Sacred Mystery.[41] This is an absolutely irrefutable element for a consecrated life that seeks to go beyond emotional fervor and charismatic trends. This task becomes ever more important the more weakened becomes the concept of God, until it dilutes it into a kind of transcendence or immanence[42] or the fluidity of a nebulous esoteric mystique.[43]

The Conference of Latin American Religious has, for five years, offered a deep, existential, and prayerful reading of Scripture through the *Palavra-Vida* project,[44] an excellent way of deepening the Word of God in consecrated life. A prayerful reading of Scripture leads to true faith, according to the classic theological adage: *lex orandi est lex credendi*. Besides articulating faith and Scripture, prayer and faith, contemplation must be in intimate resonance with action and vice-versa: *in actione contemplativus*. We are not speaking of a material measurement, dedicating more or less time to action or contemplation, but of living these in an intimate harmony.

Postmodernism suffers from the contradiction we have referred to on two occasions and stressed in the primary text: thirst for love and affective disorder. The answer to this is in the practical sense of the dialectic of love and establishing pedagogy for this. Inverting some expressions introduces possibilities. Instead of seeking self-realization *through* the other, one finds self-realization *in* the other. This is the profound paschal Christian dialectic in which we find true life and ourselves when we lose ourselves by going out of ourselves to give to others (Mk 8:35). The renewal of consecrated life travels this road. To achieve this, it is necessary to build a true pedagogy that begins in postulancy and ends with the Anointing of the Sick.

At the beginning of St. Ignatius's "Contemplation to gain love," two simple and almost transparent principles are established. They always bear repeating: "Love should be put more in deeds than in words," and, "Love consists in reciprocal communication."[45]

In the field of pedagogy, an extremely fluid postmodernism calls for a greater balance between motivation and support structures. It does not have great confidence in people's intentions and desires, because they are part of the fluidity of this culture and, therefore, cannot endure. These motivations are lacking in objective reality, situated in time and space that guarantee constancy. In my class orientations, I have the habit of telling my students, "What is not on the schedule doesn't exist." The problem is to understand how to give discipline and schedules worth in the eyes of young people as a school of life, reflecting a normal human condition that realistically draws us closer to other's lives. It is the dose of existential realism demanded by human life. Motivation, interior energy, and utopian strength run the motor and the concrete, historical, and practical meditation, which makes this flow possible. A sociologist, speaking to base Christian communities, said that small, successful practices change consciences. Small because they fit into the horizon of the feasible; practical because they are actions realized with intelligence in order to change reality; and successful because they permit verification of the facts, thus avoiding distrust and desistance.

Confronted with the newness of this postmodern condition, the primary text allows us to ask if this is not a case of recognizing the difficulties of perpetual and definitive commitment and envisioning a consecrated life *ad tempus*.[46]

7. Return of Exteriority

Description

Opposite the subjective and interior character of postmodernism there is, paradoxically, the overemphasis of the external. Pope Paul VI, following in the footsteps of such existentialist philosophers as Gabriel Marcel, criticized a society of possessing rather than being.

Today the emphasis has moved from being and possessing to that of appearing. We find ourselves in a marketing society. Appearance governs people's lives. To be and to have are not important as such, but to appear and to shine, even if beneath it all there is an existential emptiness and illusory possession of goods. Beauty, in its twofold positive value as the ultimate manifestation of God's beauty and as a seductive force, greatly preoccupies the younger generation.

There are new forms of consecrated life being born that highlight the distinctive exterior aspect that seeks social recognition, personal security, and self-validation, which serves the purpose of saying to others: Know who I am! And to oneself: I know who I am! And to everyone else: Respect me!

Importance is placed on religious symbols, especially symbols of power and customs, to habits in the dual meaning of clothes and habitual external practices.[47] Members of these religious groups create their own codes of language and behavior, which identify and distinguish them from others. They use expressions and rituals that only they understand. In some cases, they go even further. They adopt ways of smiling, a tone of voice, and a way of carrying themselves when relating to others that give them certain characteristics that make them recognizable even from a distance, to the point that these communities and their members are easily identifiable.

They create for themselves and their group an imaginary social sphere in which the person of the Founder, as well as dignitaries and of associates, occupy a unique place and have varying degrees of moral authority over the members of that social body. For these groups consecrated life is distinguished externally even by the type of works and activities that they carry out in a particular way.

When these groups are international, they normally receive handouts and uniform directives from their central quarters through letters, videos, and videoconferencing, in most cases using modern technologies of communication. Uniformity in formation is guaranteed and reinforced by giving emphasis to the exteriorization of laws, norms, and canonical rules that are common to all.

The community creates a protective barrier that is the more necessary and desired the greater the modern and postmodern bombardments of extraneous elements to this type of life. What sociologists call the "total institution" is realized, in which lodging, work, and leisure all take place under one roof and under one authority.[48] And they exercise in this way a better protection and even control over consciences. The major interest of the members is within the community itself and not the world outside. A dual effect is established: inward and outward.

In these circumstances, one easily runs the risk of fanaticism, of Manichaeism, dividing the world between the pure and the impure, between those who assume the exteriority of consecrated life and those who are outside. Instead of having religious forms in a spirit of openness and ecumenism, we have a repetition, along with the signs of postmodern exteriority, of archaic behaviors and practices.

The Search for Answers

It is necessary to guide such a seeking of the external through a deep spiritual experience of God, cultivating it through prayer and through the practice of faith, hope, and charity. This is not possible without cultivating silence and without encountering one's interiority.

There is a pedagogy of solitude that is not isolation, nor the incapacity to communicate. Rather, it is a withdrawing in order to be sent, a return to the sources of the spirit before the mystery of God. To enter into mystery is the ultimate need of human nature and of profound self-fulfillment. Only in this does one find life's meaning amid suffering and disasters.

Reflection on symbols also sheds light on this point. The mystery of interiority, as we have seen, becomes a real symbol when it produces something other than itself, but which is true for oneself and for others. The symbol, for its part, leads to mystery. It is not an empty sign, but it is full of the mystery of which it is a manifestation. All the exteriority of consecrated life does not come from nothing or from superficiality and absence, but rather springs from the founding mystical experience.

Consecrated life is unthinkable outside of the experience of mystery. Karl Rahner has contributed immeasurably to the understanding, valuing, and living of mystery. He touches the heart of the problem when he indicates to us the true and unique mystery of our faith: "The truly absolute mysteries are realized only in the very communication of God in the depth of existence, called grace, and in history, called Jesus Christ, and this already includes the Trinity—economic, salvific, and immanent. And this one mystery can very well be brought close to man if we understand it to refer to the mystery that we call God."[49]

The beauty, depth, and actuality of his reflection is found in relating the mystery of God to the mystery of the human being, who is always open above all to the totality of incomprehensible reality and within it to its foundation, who is God, absolute Mystery. There is a historical link between human nature and the only Savior and the meaning of God, who, as much as he is absolute and holy Mystery, kindles reality and draws it toward himself. The human person has the capacity of accepting or repelling God: this is his mystery. Through this, the human being is structurally correlated to mystery, because his nature is related to the Mystery.[50] The transcendence of the human person appears as "transcendence open to the absolute mystery of God, who is the absolute nearness to forgiveness." God means the silent, absolute, unconditional, incomprehensible Mystery. This infinite distance evokes that horizon toward which is directed—completely and permanently, in an incomprehensible and immutable way—the understanding of private realities, their reciprocal relationships, and our relationship with them. This horizon remains forever silent, always at an immense distance when every understanding and action bound to him ends and is extinguished.[51] Human nature is indefinable, empty, and its limit is its unlimited relationship to infinite Mystery in its fullness.[52]

These brief quotes from Karl Rahner point out the mystery of God, who is infinite and absolute and who is in relationship with us, who are also mystery, drawing us out of narcissism and the exterior superficiality of postmodernism.

Liturgy, in its pedagogy of mystery as true mystagogy, offers an excellent contribution so that consecrated life may not lose itself in pure exteriority. It does this in an excellent way by uniting visible symbol with the reality of grace in the liturgy. Such a lesson is all the more important as we live the loud invasion of exteriority coming through the world of media. It is necessary to cultivate the experience of God in depth, to cultivate silence, and to live a liturgy, which celebrates the interiority of mystery through the exteriority of symbols.

8. The Erosion of the Classic Form of Consecrated Life and the Comparison with New Forms

Description

Briefly, I will indicate the phenomenon of the erosion of the classic form of consecrated life through a series of key concepts: the canonical leveling of charisms; invasive secularism in community life with the growing distance between religious life and the simple poor; the loss of the life-blood of contemplation in favor of routine spiritual practices, external charismatic fervor, disincarnated spiritualism, or even of an uncontrolled, purely secular activism; the weakening of the concept of God; the dualism of prayer life and apostolic activity; the gigantic weight of works at the expense of missionary creativity; the aging of members without the needed influx of new generations; a patronizing adaptation to consumeristic and hedonistic modernism even in poor countries; and a growing individualism in a narcissistic and virtual connotation.

New forms of consecrated life present the vigor of opposition, first in life and practice, then in speaking and indictment, against this dark side of classic consecrated life.

The Search for Answers

The first answer comes from the Spirit, who gives rise to a marvelous flowering of buds on the old wood of traditional consecrated life—new, vigorous buds, and others infected by pests. In order to understand this phenomenon, we return to the metaphors of Babel and Pentecost, which helped us to understand globalization. A single speech prevailed in consecrated life, a single canonical language imposed itself in its monotonous uniformity, and God comes to sow confusion among the tower builders. Now we find ourselves before a proliferation of new religious forms. This does not mean that all the effects of confusion caused by God are willed or desired by him, but it goes back to his initiative, if we understand the message of Babel.

Pentecost adds to or even corrects the experience of Babel, when many people hear the same message in their own language (cf. Acts 2:7–13). Thus, each new form [of consecrated life], in its originality, brings with it a sign of a certain unity. Where do we find it? In the Johannine intuition, for whom the Spirit leads everyone to Jesus Christ, in the understanding of that same Gospel. Unity is built from within and not from without, as happens with canonical and legislative leveling.

These new forms reveal the freedom of the Spirit. Cardinal Ratzinger considers as marvelous, "the energy and enthusiasm with which the new ecclesial movements live faith and feel the need to share with others the joy of this faith received as a gift."[53] These movements are characterized by a birth through a charismatic leader, configuring themselves into concrete communities, trying to live the Gospel in its entirety and its exigencies, and recognizing in the Church, without which they would not exist, their reason for living. They enter into the apostolic mission of the Church in a spirit of social service, based on a personal encounter with the Lord, and nourished by a faith rooted in the Church, uniting the

Christological, pneumatological, ecclesial, and existential dimensions of a personal following of Christ and an experience of the Spirit in the Church.[54] This fact shows us the pooling together of the new expressions of consecrated life that are born of these movements. They naturally partake in history's ambiguity and lack discernment, especially in terms of the various pedagogies used by these new forms.

The pedagogy of breaking away, of disruption, unites old and contemporary dimensions; the Gospels and St. Paul insist on the "breaking away" that means following Jesus Christ and embracing the Christian faith. Sin, blindness, and the "old man" come before the newness of grace and light and the "new man." This is an element of the most ancient and most genuine Christian tradition. Meanwhile, there is something new in the pedagogy of certain new religious forms. They deal with a generation of youth who have very little sense of guilt. Without entering into an interpretative discourse, every day confessors notice always more on the part of the young a certain silence about those actions that used to be the principal and repetitive matter of confessions. Without a doubt, psychology has had an enormous role in the loss of a sense of culpability and responsibility with regard to sinful acts.

Faced with this fact, some ecclesial movements of renewal, from which are born many new religious forms, have inverted their pedagogy. They have returned to beating on the subject of sin, especially in the area of sexuality, producing a new type of guilt, and reawakening a sense of unease. To be free of this, they propose the path of conversion, especially by joining and participating in these movements. So we have the before and the after: before we were immersed in sin and spiritual mediocrity, now we are full of fervor and action. In these conversion movements, there is also a festive and celebratory side to entering into the movement or new form of consecrated life. And this is one of the aspects that attracts!

Without doubt, this whole process is facilitated through contact with the significant and extraordinary personalities of the various founders, who reinforce the pervading strength of the call to conversion. Moreover, this gesture is imbued with external signs that are even more impressive. In one of these religious forms begun in Brazil, the members show, in all purity and simplicity, their new way of living. People from their neighborhoods come into their houses, become acquainted with their way of life, and participate intensely in their lives. They bring the poor into their houses as well as beggars, who end up sleeping in their beds while the members sleep on the floor. All of this is done under the admiring gaze of visitors. They live a new type of the option for the poor that is closest to a medieval style and they repeat, almost literally, the religious epic of Francis of Assisi.

To this experience of separation is joined the experience of being at home, offering members a strong sense of belonging and identity. In a fragmented society characterized by painful anonymity, they feel they are among family. Consecrated life fills an existential vacuum, giving the sensation of having something precious and joyful. This reminds us of Jesus' metaphors to describe the reality of the Kingdom of God: yeast, grain, pearl, banquet, and wedding.

Classic consecrated life is called to be in dialogue with these new forms, avoiding the either/or dilemma. We are moving toward an ever more pluralistic Church, and consecrated life will have a role to play in this pluralism. Both forms can and should mutually nourish each other. The new forms have much to learn from the history of consecrated life, and the classic form feels challenged to look at itself in the mirror and see its wrinkles and defects. And concretely, on a daily basis it is necessary to collaborate on three levels: the experience of God, community life, and apostolic mission.

Another way of thinking of consecrated life is in terms of a sacramental model, an expression that needs to be explained. Behind consecrated life there is the experience of the Church in the Second Vatican Council. The Church found itself faced with a painful dilemma. On one hand, there was the traditional Tridentine ecclesiology and the ecclesiology of Vatican I, which strongly emphasized the external elements of belonging to the Church. On the other hand, there was the tradition of the Reformation that stressed the opposite. In a desire to be ecumenical and, therefore, to draw as close as possible to the reformers on the one hand, and on the other hand to remain faithful to the fundamental and non-negotiable elements of Catholic tradition, the Second Vatican Council overcame this impasse through the *sacramentum,* a bridge between the two traditions.

The external dimension of Catholic tradition is maintained. There is no sacrament if there is no visible sign, and the visible sign indicates the invisible interiority of grace communicated and received, reinforced further by the evangelical précis.

The fundamental point of this model is to ask questions regarding the sense, meaning, and interior reality of the rules, signs, symbols, and practices of consecrated life. If they do not promote any spiritual or interior personal experience, they have no reason for being. In turn, if interiority is not exteriorized in signs and practices, there is the danger that consecrated life may become pure arbitrary subjectivity. This sacramental structure becomes a criterion for discernment. Consecrated life withdraws from pure interiority when it affirms the incarnation of grace and rejects pharisaism, legalism, and the externalization of religious rites with no corresponding interior experience.

The sacramental model, therefore, tries to articulate internal convictions, the conversion of the heart, and the commitment of conscience in terms of the social and external demands of consecrated life within society.

What can be done so that consecrated life may give life to this model?

The reinforcement of the external in some new forms of consecrated life does not respond to an awareness of modernism and postmodernism that values the inner person and his or her autonomy. On the other hand, capitulation before fluid postmodernism runs the risk of degenerating into the subjectivism and arbitrariness that would spell the death of consecrated life. A commitment to reinforcing the external signs of consecrated life, much appreciated by an insecure generation, formed by the media culture of appearances, can have immediate amazing and statistical success. But it does not fulfill the deepest part of consecrated life and is a dangerous disfigurement of it.

If the path of the external seems at first glance to have greater success, the choice of the opposite path clearly promises no future. The path of privacy cannot be controlled and loses itself in unhealthy deterioration.

The best path, therefore, seems to be that of the sacramental model. There is a dual task at hand: when facing the lack of substance of postmodernism, offer sufficiently stable and well-grounded parameters; when facing exteriority that is reinforced by means of authority, go to the sources of consecrated life.

Let us deepen this proposal.

The lack of substance

As we have already mentioned, classic consecrated life shows clear signs of depletion. Given this fact, consecrated life is called to a movement of returning to its sources. This means looking at its phases of development and discovering moments of regression, to analyze and critique them according to actual data, to single out those that appear to be deviations, and to recover the original evangelical inspiration.

This is a monumental task. Each congregation can do this with regard to its development, from the initial founding event up to the present day, singling out the points of regression and of eventual deviation in order to return to the original inspiration.

It would be a lengthy task beyond the limits of this discussion, in the face of the birth of new intuitions, to look for those things that have constricted classic consecrated life and the reasons for the sense of exhaustion in these last years. At the end of the Second Vatican Council, Pope Paul VI indicated to consecrated life the path of returning to the initial charism. In what is particular to each congregation, there is a common and fundamental point: the following of Jesus Christ. From this all inspiration is drawn. This theme has merited detailed and deep study. We are referring, in a particular way, to the texts of Jon Sobrino, restructured in a personal and original way in the work of Sister Vera.[55]

It is not a case of belaboring points of dogmatic Christology, although this is important, but of emphasizing the figure of Jesus of Palestine, discovered always anew through modern exegesis within the context of the original *kerygma*. What is at stake here is the Christian sense of a passionate following of the person of Jesus and his style of life as a life choice and a foundational experience of consecrated life.

In the life of Jesus, we see the centrality of the Kingdom of God and the God of the Kingdom. Here we find ourselves in the unique and singular role of the poor, the excluded, and the sinner as the primary receivers of the Kingdom and those whom God loves with a preferential love. In following Jesus, the religious meets once again the poor in all their reality and needs. Jesus Christ is the door that gives access to the experience of God, in which there is no separation between God and the world of others. The evangelical model of living consecrated life necessarily includes this openness to the poor, thus rendering this form of life significant for religious and others. However, at various cultural moments the poor do not always have the same historical expression.

Forms of poverty follow one another throughout history, but in all of them there remains the basic deprivation of the good things of life. Today the neoliberal system brings them even closer to death. Given this vision of the poor, prematurely and unjustly condemned to nonexistence and non-acceptance by society, religious must live their following of Jesus in a way that is close to the poor.

It seems obvious that any refounding, renewal, or reinvigoration of consecrated life must go through relationship with the poor. The option for the poor is and will be the most credible sign of consecrated life. We are not dealing with a theoretical question about poverty, which preoccupied practically every founder of religious congregations, but the relationship with the person of the poor in a physical sense, in past and present forms of poverty. In today's world, we find millions and millions of exiles and those who have fled their countries for a myriad of reasons: economic (poverty and unemployment), ethnic and religious conflicts, and internal wars and those conducted by the great powers. This happens in plain sight of all. These masses of people seek to go to rich countries, which, in turn, increasingly tend to close their borders. A consecrated life that is blind to this worldwide phenomenon passes by the wounded man like the priest and the Levite. This is a consecrated life that does not understand the parable of the Good Samaritan, the icon of this World Congress of Consecrated Life.

A number of factors has moved consecrated life to a new and promising relationship with lay persons: the dearth of new members, the rapid aging of persons, the weight of apostolic work, and a new theology of laity.

At one time, a closer collaboration with lay persons was sought in order to pursue educational and social works, which would have been left undone due to the scarcity of religious. In this way, more lay persons became associated with religious, even holding directive positions, while the religious congregations maintained the ultimate authority. In a deeper way, some congregations share life with lay persons on the level of charism, spirituality, and community life, even with some juridical expressions of belonging. This phenomenon is occurring in traditional consecrated life and is becoming common in newer forms of consecrated life. In these, original modalities go beyond current canon law, causing paradoxical reactions of support and suspicion on the part of ecclesiastical institutions. Within the same movement, and sometimes even under the same roof, there are priests, consecrated lay persons with a definitive commitment, and lay persons considering marriage or who are already married.[56]

A general movement in society has opened up new perspectives for consecrated life in the field of works and actions, since for economic reasons many institutions have sought out partnerships and/or third parties. Although there are ambiguities and uncertainties in this type of economic relationship, they can produce excellent apostolic fruit in the pastoral sense. Recently an editorial appeared in a theological journal in Brazil in which the author asked if this was not the time to avoid multiplication of theological magazines produced by various faculties and institutions and to join together to produce one journal. In a parallel way, consecrated life has unexplored possibilities to form partnerships and collaborate with similar religious, Church, and secular institutions.

The "new social movements" present challenges on a regional and worldwide level for each congregation to move out of the little world of their own works. What will be consecrated life's participation in ecology, pacifism, anti-armament activities, questions of ethnicity, gender, the defense of human rights, the struggle for land for indigenous peoples and the landless and homeless, those without a country, in other words, with regard to innumerable movements?

Consecrated life is established fully in a growing postmodernism. One of the characteristics of this cultural moment is skepticism, boredom, emptiness, and existential nausea with regard to the future. Nothing seems to mobilize people. All energy is expended in an attitude of *carpe diem,* seeking the enjoyment of the present moment. And thus, we close ourselves in sad narcissism and materialism.

This narcissistic materialism is supported by the pillars of chemical happiness and an exaggerated care of the body. When faced with the least amount of physical pain and the smallest psychic unease, we take easily accessible antidepressants, and so live in a permanent Prozac euphoria. People cannot bear the mystery of the self, affective loneliness, failure, or any suffering. At the same time, the body receives the care once devoted to the spirit. Where once libraries and bookstores abounded, today fitness centers are multiplying.

And young people are particularly susceptible to this climate of the double cult of induced happiness and the well-sculpted body. If consecrated life does not want to disappear, it must find followers among them. What is to be done? A twofold announcement is expected of consecrated life, not only in words, but especially in lifestyle.

The first message is one of hope: *spes contra spem* (hoping against all hope). The joy of religious, their enthusiasm for their lifestyle, their happy abandonment in mission spread hope among young people who have aged too soon, have emptied life of its meaning, and so lose themselves in idleness without significant commitments.

The relationships that many young people have established among themselves have withered and they have lost the freshness of love and end up merely using the body of the other. They have learned a great deal about sex and have forgotten love. Young members in consecrated life have much to tell us about this. The newness of pure love found in many groups of consecrated young people, who share the same charism and who live or work close together, shows the miracle of purity just when this seems bitterly condemned to being forgotten.

We are, however, neither ingenuous nor romantic. There are dangers in both extremes: either a return to the moralizing and repressive refrains of the past or ambiguous relationships disguised under verbal purity. A mature balance in relationships and encounters will be a permanent challenge, especially for the young generations with their open and youthful affectivity, which sometimes can be invaded by dark expressions of fear or vague lyricism.

Renewed hope and love are signs of a new dawn breaking, said J. Delumeau.[57] In times of greater crisis, we return to the fundamental and original elements. When everything seems to be in turmoil, we concentrate our efforts on fixed points of existence. Hope and love are two of the most important realities for human existence. It is important to remember once again the great figure of Karl Rahner. In his first public lecture in Munich after the Second Vatican Council, he said: "All that is done in the Church, all that is institutional, juridical, sacramental, every word, every action, every reform of whatever ecclesial element, in the last analysis—if correctly

understood and without traces of self-worship—is all service, pure
service, a simple offering of help for something entirely different,
something totally simple, and, therefore, ineffably difficult and sacred. This something is Faith, Hope, and Love, to be instilled in the
hearts of men. To use an example from secular science, we can say
that something similar happens in the process of extracting uranium.
We know that a ton of uranium ore must be mined to obtain 0.14
grams of radium. Nevertheless, it is worth the effort. A Council also seeks the hearts of men, the believing, hoping, and loving hearts
that yield to the mystery of God. If this were not true, then the
Council would have only been a terrible theatrical presentation of
man's and the Church's self-idolatry."[58] What St. Paul says in the
hymn of charity applies to the Council: "If I have the gift of prophecy, understanding all the mysteries there are, and knowing everything, and if I have faith in all its fullness, to move mountains, but
without love, then I am nothing at all" (1 Cor 13:2).

The *agape* dimension of consecrated life is its greatest sign of
credibility. Hans Urs von Balthasar wrote, "Only love is worthy of
faith."[59] The rejuvenation of consecrated life will depend on the signs
of love it can radiate inwardly and outwardly. In an extremely com-
mercialized world, based on interest, profit, and gain, gratitude breaks
through like the luminous dawn of another society. Gratitude is present at the beginnings of every genuine religious branch. Wherever
economic interests infiltrate, then the original waters lose their transparency. Today's economic systems and mentalities make it very difficult for religious to live and witness gratitude, which is demonstrated
rarely and with great difficulty. It is necessary to invent new forms.

Strictly connected to gratitude is the spirit of service and poverty. Both of these—service and poverty—offer a visual angle to see
in a new way the relationship between profession and vocation. The
spirit of service is a quality that any professional work or activity
of a religious should show. It is the vocation that provides the elements of grace and spiritual beauty to any profession.

The spirit of poverty and of simplicity is consecrated life's answer to consumerism. When Father Arrupe would go through a shopping center, he would say, "How many things I don't need!"

Moreover, consecrated life maintains an ineluctable eschatological dimension. At the same time, it offers the religious an astounding freedom in terms of the present and an unlimited commitment in this same present, because in each person there exists the ultimate beyond history. The definitive and eternal are not dimensions attached to the real and to the present, but they cut through and overcome time. The definitive begins in the present. It will only be that which it was.

Paraphrasing Karl Rahner, who said, "I believe because I pray,"[60] we are religious because we pray. The experience of prayer nourishes consecrated life; without it, the spring dries up. Every return to the origins of consecrated life implies a new and fresh visit to the pure waters of prayer.

Conclusion: The Problem of Vocations

The road has been long. What about the future of consecrated life? It evidently depends, according to the obvious biological law, on the arrival of new generations. Therefore, the vocational problem is crucial.

The new movements have created an interesting strategy in the form of "concentric circles." It is not a new strategy, but these groups use it with great success. It consists in dividing young people into groups with different levels of participation, formation, and needs, and then to manage these groups in different ways. There is a more restrictive, smaller group that chooses full-time religious life in its consecrated form, establishing close juridical bonds with the religious institute. Obviously, within this group there will always be those who take more advantage and receive more. This is a smaller circle made up of yet smaller circles that have greater needs and receive more formation. Then we have a larger circle of those participating in the movement. They are attracted to it, but without binding themselves to the institute. Naturally, in this case it is possible to have different levels of closeness. There are those who maintain written contact, or who give contributions, or who receive news bulletins, and who, in general, establish a relationship that is more distant but nonetheless real. In practice, many move toward the smaller circles and greater commitment.

This pedagogical construct offers innumerable possibilities based on the circumstances. The key here is the particular intuition of working with the new generation in a way that is differentiated and progressive. Not all begin with the enthusiasm and generosity that characterizes those in the inner nucleus. No possible link should be lost, however tenuous. Thus, other circles of people, always more involved, will revolve around the smaller nucleus of more committed members. Through the resource of information technology, it is possible to establish virtual circles of those who contact the movement and are reached by it.

The risk in a sea with few fish is to be happy with whatever fish we catch, lowering the level of requirements with regard to the spiritual and intellectual capacities of candidates. A passage from John provides an expressive parable for vocations: "Hearing this, the two disciples followed Jesus. Jesus turned round, saw them following and said, 'What do you want?' They answered, 'Rabbi'—which means Teacher—'where do you live?' 'Come and see,' he replied; so they went and saw where he lived, and stayed with him the rest of the day. It was about the tenth hour" (Jn 1:37–39).

The point is whether or not we have the courage to ask Jesus' question and to give his answer. What do we have to show? Do we have zeal in missionary activity, faith flowing from a contemplative life, a sense of the Church, prayerful discernment, and simple and fraternal community life?

Statistical studies help to give us an idea of the population that comes to us. Regarding Brazil, vocations make a journey that reveals contradictions that test their authenticity. These vocations come from the poorest social classes into a middle-class life of abundance, from a rural to an urban world, from labor to study, from public schools to the private schools, from a lack of social status to a place in society, and with an affective transference from the father/mother structure to that of the institution/formator.[61] Besides this, formators have had increasing difficulty in discovering conflicts in those being formed and in a timely manner and with competence.

Postmodernism is forging a different generation that also offers hopeful aspects to configure new forms of consecrated life. It can experience enjoyment while being sensitive to playfulness and feasting; it values the body and its sensibility without letting it dominate; it develops self-esteem along with self-care and intimacy as a way to defend against a dangerous, violent, and fragmented society; it can see its own limits, but with strong self-affirmation in response to the insecurity regarding self-realization; it is rebellious regarding regressive institutions and impatient with despotic authority; it manifests a sense of belonging with regard to motivation and horizontal and democratic experiences; it cultivates bonds of friendship between groups with the desire for a fraternal community life, shared prayer, personal life, and mission, and is also open to friendships outside the community; it prolongs the time for important decisions so as not to risk an uncertain vocation; it is more tolerant, has fewer preconceptions and prejudices with regard to race and deviant behavior; it has greater sensitivity toward new forms of life; it finds relevance in everydayness, in what is small, in the individual, in participation, in the transformation of micro-institutions pointing to institutional flexibility of consecrated life; it seeks transparency in the field of economics and in social relationships and work relationships; it stresses communitarian management, and it reveals a growing ecological, pacifist, and liberating mentality.[62]

A young woman in formation summarized well the postmodern conviction of vocation: "A God who is so generous that he gives one, two, three vocations through which we can find fulfillment. For a God who is so close to us, and a culture as relativistic as ours, the perpetual nature of the vocation is as important as its happiness. Vocation goes from being eternal—I was chosen from my mother's womb!—to being relative and temporary—I was called for freedom. Can it be that a vocation is less than it was in former times? Has God perhaps changed his opinion? He has not, but what about us?"[63]

Dynamics

1. In terms of theoretical intellectual exercise, how can the culture of the joyful present of the younger generation grasp the existential exigencies of a consecrated life lived through definitive commitments?

2. In terms of experience, how do I see the twofold movement: the tension between the search for religious externals and a narcissistic, individualistic focus?

3. In terms of action, what concrete, visible practices do we have to form young people according to the sacramental model?

Notes

1. B. de Sousa Santos, *Do Pós-moderno ao Pós-colonial e para Além de Um e o Outro: Conferência de abertura do VIII Congresso Luso-Afro-Brasileiro de Ciências Sociais* (Coimbra: September 16–18, 2004, tirado de http://www.ces.uc.pt/misc/Do_pos-moderno_ao_pos-colonial.pdf).

2. L. Kolakowski, *A revanche do sagrado na cultura profana, in Religião e Sociedade* (1977), no. 1, pp. 153–162.

3. R. Bastide, *Le sacré sauvage et autres essais* (Paris: Stock, 1997).

4. Karl Rahner, *Hörer des Wortes: zur Grundlegung einer Religionsphilosophie* (Munchen: Kosel, 1963), p. 209.

5. E. Fromm, *O medo a liberdade* (Rio de Janeiro: Zahar, 1960).

6. Rahner, *Teologia da Liberdade* (Caxias do Sul: Paulinas, 1970).

7. F. Fukuyama, *O fim da história e o último Homem* (Rio de Janeiro: Rocco, 1992).

8. "Simplifying to the utmost, incredulity with regard to the meta-narratives is considered 'postmodern'": J.- F. Lyotard, *O pós-moderno* (Rio de Janeiro: José Olympio, 1986), p. xvi.

9. H. Marcuse, *O fim da utopia* (Rio de Janeiro: Paz e Terra, 1969).

10. J. B. Libãnio, *A consciência crítica dos religiosos* (Rio de Janeiro: Conferência dos Religiosos do Brasil, 1974); H. Cl. de Lima Vaz, "A Igreja e o problema da Conscientização," in *Vozes* 62 (1968), pp. 483–493; P. Freire, *Pedagogia do oprimido,* 3rd ed. (Rio de Janeiro: Paz e Terra, 1975).

11. Formação da consciência crítica 1: subsídios filosófico-culturais. Petrópolis: Vozes; Rio de Janeiro: Conferência dos Religiosos do Brasil, 1978; Formação da consciência crítica 2: subsídios sócio-analíticos. Petrópolis: Vozes; Rio de Janeiro: Conferência dos Religiosos do Brasil, 1979; com colaboração de L. A. Monnerat Celes. Formação da consciência crítica 3: subsídios psicopedagógicos, Petrópolis: Vozes; Rio de Janeiro: Conferência dos Religiosos do Brasil, 1979.

12. A 1998 study states that religious (78.4 percent men and 88.0 percent women) admit to "not having a good political education": CERIS/CRB, *Vida Religiosa no Brasil. Pesquisa e primeiros resultados* (Rio de Janeiro: CRB, 1988), p. 75.

13. B. Santos, op. cit.

14. *"Talis est quisque, qualis eius dilectio est,"* St. Augustine, com. 1, ep. Johan, II, 14.

15. E. Cardieri, *Juventude e vida religiosa. Enfoques educacionais,* in M. Fabri dos Anjos, Novas Gerações e Vida Religiosa. Pesquisa e análises prospectivas sobre Vida Religiosa no Brasil, Aparecida/São Paulo, Santuário, 2nd ed., 2004, p. 117.

16. H. Vaz, *Religião e Sociedade nos últimos Vinte anos (1965–1985),* in Síntese 15 (1988), p. 29.

17. L. W. Storch, J. R. Cozac, *Relações virtuais: o lado humano da comunicação eletrônica* (Petrópolis: Vozes, 1995).

18. Father Palacio notes that there is an identity between a commitment to the cause of the poor and serving them in the name of Jesus and the Gospel. However, motivations in these two areas might not be the same. The evangelical aspect appears when, even in the case of a lost cause, the struggle continues. "Continuing against all hope, when all the rest leave off, is, perhaps, the Christian way of excellence in serving the poor. To 'stay' and make oneself poor with the poor, affirming with one's life the absolute value of the person of the poor, with his sacred and inviolate human dignity, even though disfigured. Identifying one's own life with the life and destiny of the poor is more than a 'cause,' and this cannot be confused with doing. It is 'an evangelical way of living' whose justification is Jesus himself: because he identified and lived in solidarity with the little ones. To achieve this identification with the little ones and the excluded is more than a question of altruism. It can only be sustained if it is nourished by identifying with Jesus Christ—this is meaning of the Christian journey—as an expression of the solidarity of God with human life.

He continues by asking if service to brothers and sisters, as a primary motivation, might not be a platform for a religious life of 'doing' rather than a form of evangelical life. One of the greatest contradictions of religious life today is a dislocation between religious life that 'does' and its 'way of living.'"
C. Palácio, *Novas Gerações e o Futuro da Vida Religiosa: Primeiras reflexões sobre a pesquisa* "Novas Gerações e Vida Religiosa," in M. Fabri dos Anjos, Novas Gerações e Vida Religiosa. Pesquisa e análises prospectivas sobre Vida Religiosa no Brasil, Aparecida/São Paulo, Santuário, 2nd ed., 2004, p. 145f.

19. Vatican II, *Lumen Gentium,* n. 8; Rahner, *O Pecado na Igreja, in G. Baraúna, A Igreja do Vaticano II* (Petrópolis: Vozes, 1965), pp. 453–469.

20. John Paul II celebrated on the First Sunday of Lent (March 12, 2000) a penitential act in St. Peter's Basilica with the words: "We forgive and we seek forgiveness!" Various concelebrating cardinals and archbishops and members of the Roman curia also asked pardon for the historical sins of the Church.

21. John Paul II, *Carta Apostólica Tertio millennio adveniente* (São Paulo: Loyola, 1994), no. 33f.

22. "The authority and the ordinary magisterium of the Church has been mistaken many times. Moreover, it was mistaken about important matters in which the contrary positions appear evident today. On other occasions, it was mistaken with very solemn language and words with which it tried to express its conviction or the force of its teaching. And, finally, it was mistaken with and greatest solemnity and most frequently in the past two centuries. Even though this last conclusion may be scarcely evident in the texts presented, it seems to me that it goes along with the whole, as routinely occurs in research." This last statement is in relation to another made by the same author that in the last centuries there has been a magisterial "inflation": J. I. González Faus, *A autoridade da verdade: momentos obscuros do magistério Eclesi·stico* (São Paulo: Loyola, 1998), pp. 197–278.

23. H.-P. Kolvenbach, *Alocução final, in 69ª Congregação de Procuradores* (São Paulo: Loyola, 2004), p. 45.

24. Among the most well-known are: Rorty, Lyotard, Baudrillard, Vattimo, Jameson, and others.

25. B. Santos, in the quoted text and in other comments we are making.

26. A. D'Andrea, *O self perfeito e a nova era: individualismo e reflexividade em religiosidades pós-tradicionais* (São Paulo: Loyola, 2000), p. 24ff.

27. B. de Sousa Santos, *Do Pós-moderno ao Pós-Colonial e para Além de Um e o Outro, Conferência de abertura do VIII Congresso Luso-Afro-Brasileiro de Ciências Sociais* (Coimbra: September 16–18, 2004, http://www.ces.uc.pt/misc/Do_pos-moderno_ao_pos-colonial.pdf).

28. B. Carranza, *Lógicas e desafios do contexto religioso contemporâneo, in Palestras da XX AGO* (Rio de Janeiro: CRB, 2004), pp. 29–53.

29. G. Sissa, *O prazer e o mal: filosofia da droga* (Rio de Janeiro: Civilização Brasileira, 1999), p. 21.

30. W. C. Castilho Pereira, *A formação religiosa em questão* (Petrópolis: Vozes, 2004), pp. 127–129.

31. A. Renault, *O indivíduo. Reflexão acerca da filosofia do sujeito* (São Paulo: Difel, 1998), p. 30.

32. A proposal of the Decree, *Optatam totius,* called for greater integration of the spiritual, intellectual, communitarian, and pastoral life of seminarians.

33. Boaventura Santos calls our attention to the plurality of subjectivities: "We live in a world of multiple subjects. My proposal in general terms is that each of us is a network of subjects in whom various subjectivities correspond to the various basic forms of power circulating in society. We are an archipelago of subjects that are combined differently according to various personal and collective circumstances. Early in the morning, we are mostly members of families, during the day of our workplace. We are no longer exclusive subjectivities, but we give each other, according to conditions, the privilege to organize that joining with the rest. As the collectivism of the group disappears, the collectivity of subjectivity evolves even more": B. Santos, *Pela mão de Alice* (São Paulo: Cortez, 1996), p. 107.

34. F. Roustang, *Le troisième homme, in Christus* 13 (1966), n. 52, pp. 561–567.

35. C. James, *Análise de conjuntura religioso-eclesial: Por onde andam as forças, in Perspectiva teológica,* 28 (1996), pp. 157–182.

36. B. Carranza, *Lógicas e desafios do contexto religioso contemporâneo, in Palestras da XX AGO* (Rio de Janeiro: CRB, 2004), pp. 40–49.

37. H. Cl. de Lima Vaz, *Experiência mística e filosofia na tradição occidental* (São Paulo: Loyola, 2000), p. 9.

38. L. R. Benedetti, O "Novo Clero": Arcaico ou moderno? In REB 59 (1999), p. 112, citando CNBB, Situação de vida dos seminaristas maiores no Brasil (São Paulo: Paulinas, 1995), p. 36ff.

39. H. Küng, *Christianity: The Religious Situation of Our Time* (London: SCM Press Ldt, 1995).

40. B. Santos, *Do Pós-moderno ao Pós-Colonial e para Além de Um e o Outro, e J. Sobrino, A fé em Jesus Cristo. Ensaio a partir das vítimas* (Petrópolis: Vozes, 2000).

41. J. B. Libanio, *O discernimento espiritual revisitado* (São Paulo: Loyola, 2000), pp. 19–34.

42. L. Ferry, *L'homme-Dieu ou le sens de la vie* (Paris: Bernard Grasset, 1996).

43. F. Champion, *La nébuleuse mystique-ésotérique. Orientations psychoreligieuses des courants mystiques et ésotériques contemporains*, in *De l'émotion en religion: Renouveaux et traditions* (Paris: Centurion, 1990), pp. 17–69.

44. CLAR, *Projeto palavra-vida: 1988–1993* (Rio de Janeiro, CRB, 1988).

45. St. Ignatius of Loyola, *Spiritual Exercises*, nos. 230–231.

46. It is interesting that eighty-five percent of the answers in a survey among religious express the conviction that religious life is splendid and that perpetual vows are for life. The median age of the male religious questioned was 54.8 years and that of women religious 52.23 years (CERIS/CRB, *Vida Religiosa no Brasil: Pesquisa e primeiros resultados* [Rio de Janeiro: CRB, 1988], pp. 68f., 72).

47. "What draws our attention [...] is that newer priests appreciate the distinctive signs of their state—celebrations, vestments, power...there is an absence of concern for the destiny of society (and of the Church), little love (or none) for study, no ecumenical passion, or for social justice. The priests are more preoccupied with their own sacred character and power than with being a significant presence in the world, in dialogue with society, and in competent service to contemporary man" (L. R. Benedetti, op. cit., p. 89).

48. "A basic disposition of modern society is that the individual tends to sleep, play, and work at various locations and with various participants, under different authorities, and without a rational generalized plan. The centralizing aspect of total institutions can be described as a breaking of the barriers that usually separate these three spheres of life. Firstly, all aspects of life are realized under one unique authority. Secondly, each phase of the participant's daily activity is realized in the immediate company of a relatively large group of people, all treated in the same way and obliged to do the same things together. Thirdly, all the daily activities are rigorously scheduled; one activity leads to another in a determined time, and the entire sequence of activities is imposed from above, through a system of explicit formal rules and a group of functionaries. Finally, the various obligatory activities have a unique rational planning, supposedly assembled to see to the official objectives of the institution" (L. R. Benedetti, *O "Novo Clero": Arcaico ou moderno?* In REB 59 (1999), 123.

49. K. Rahner, *Curso fundamental sobre la fe. Introducción al concepto del cristianismo* (Barcelona: Herder, 1979), p. 29.

50. K. Rahner, op. cit., p. 258.

51. K. Rahner, *Gnade und Freiheit. Kleine theologische Beitrage* (Friburgo: 1968), p. 19, cited in H. Vorgrimler, *Karl Rahner, Experiencia de Dios en su vida y en su pensamiento* (Santander: Sal Terrae, 2004), p. 194f.

52. K. Rahner, *Corso fondamentale*, p. 259.

53. Cardinal Ratzinger, "Movimenti ecclesiali e loro posizione teologica, in Il regno" (43 81998/13), no. 818, p. 400.

54. *Ibid.,* 406ff.

55. V. I. Bombonatto, *Sequela di Gesù: un approccio secondo la cristologia di Jon Sobrino* (San Paolo: Paulinas, 2000).

56. A very clear canonical study is by G. Ghirlanda, "Carisma e Statuto dei movimenti ecclesiali" *(Regno,* 43 1998/13), no. 818, pp. 407–411.

57. J. Delumeau, *Guetter l'aurora* (Paris: Grasset, 2003).

58. K. Rahner, *Vaticano II; Un inizio di Rinnovamento* (San Paolo: Herder, 1966), pp. 45, 47f.

59. H. Urs von Balthasar, *Solo L'amore è degno di fede* (Paris: Aubier-Montaigne, 1966).

60. K. H. Weger, "Ich glaube,weil ich bete," Fur K. Rahner zum 80, geburtstag, in *Geist und Leben* 57 (1984), 48–52.

61. W. Castilho Pereira, *La formazione religiosa in questione* (Petropolis: Vozes, 2004), p. 11.

62. W. Castilho Pereira, op. cit. p. 130f.; M. Fabri dos Anjos, "Gioventù e crisi di valori morali," in *REB* 59 (1999), pp. 531–550; E. Valle, *La percezione della vita religiosa in religiosi/se giovani: Osservazioni psicosociali,* in *M. Fabri dos Anjos, Nuove Generazioni e Vita Religiosa: Ricerca e analisi prospettive sulla vita religiosa in Brasile* (Aparecida/San Paolo, Santuario, 2nd ed., 2004), pp. 75–97.

63. E. M. Braceras Gago, *"Vida religiosas a medo do fim,"* in *Journal de Opinao* 16 (2004), nos. 801, 807.

RELIGIOUS LIFE AFTER SEPTEMBER 11: WHAT SIGNS DOES RELIGIOUS LIFE OFFER?

Timothy Radcliffe, OP

We live in the shadow of September 11. We all remember where we were that day, but not just because it was a terrible event. People in many places have endured worse sufferings since, for example in Darfur. Rather it is symbolic of the world that we inhabit at the beginning of this new millennium. What has religious life to say to this new world?

It is a world that is marked by a paradox. We are ever more tightly bound together by instant communication. We live in the intimate little world of the global village. We are ever more marked by a single world culture. Young people everywhere wear the same clothes, listen to the same songs, and dream the same dreams. And even if they cannot afford the real designer label objects, they can buy cheap imitations. They are often more obviously marked by a generational identity than a local one. We all inhabit McWorld, the Pepsi-planet, or the Coca-culture.

On the other hand, it is a world that is ever more deeply divided by religious violence. All over the planet Christians, Jews, Muslims, Hindus, and Buddhists square up to each other aggressively. In Northern Ireland, the Balkans, the Middle East, India, Indonesia, Nigeria, and so many other places, communication seems to have broken down. It is precisely the intimacy of the global world that provokes violence. Most murders occur at home, by people who are close to each other, and in this global village, we are all neighbors. What has religious life to say to this intimate and violent world? And what does this world have to say to us?

I will focus on three aspects of our culture. First of all, there is a crisis of homelessness. We all inhabit the global village, but 9/11 disclosed its hidden violence. How can we religious be a sign of humanity's common home in God? Secondly, what future awaits us? September 11 symbolizes the beginning of an era that seems to offer only a future of violence. Thirdly, faced with this uncertainty, there is a growing culture of control, the struggle for hegemony. Faced with each of these, religious life embodies a word of hope. There is a fourth topic that is fundamental, but about which I will hardly speak, and that is the culture of consumerism and the vow of poverty. I will say nothing about it because it is so obvious. Many people have written much about our witness to poverty in the culture of the marketplace, so I have preferred to look at some other slightly less obvious topics.

The Crisis of Homelessness

Many of you are looking rather jet-lagged. You have flown in from all over the world. We are inhabitants of the global village. My family often says enviously, "Join the Dominicans and see the world." Every morning when we open our emails, there will be messages from around the planet. We are citizens of a new world in which, for many people, space has ceased to be of much importance. Fukuyama talked about the end of history, and Richard O'Brien has added, "the end of geography."[1] Zygmunt Bauman wrote that "in the world we inhabit, distance does not seem to matter much. Sometimes it seems that it exists solely in order to be cancelled; as if space was but a constant invitation to slight it, refute it, and de-ny it. Space stopped being an obstacle—one needs just a split second to conquer it."[2]

This may almost look like an anticipation of our eschatological hopes. When Jesus meets the Samaritan woman, he promises a time when God will be worshiped neither on the mountain of the Samaritans nor in Jerusalem, "but in spirit and in truth." The Good Samaritan in our other text walks away from the sacred space of Jerusalem. Sacrifice to God is offered by the roadside when he tends the wounded man who fell among robbers. Christianity liberates us from a religion of holy spaces into the life of the Trinity, "God, that center who is everywhere, and whose circumference is nowhere."[3] Cyberspace looks a little like the fulfillment of the Christian promise. Margaret Wertheim wrote that "while early Christians promulgated heaven as a realm in which the human soul would be freed from the frailties and failings of the flesh, so today's champions of cyberspace had it as a place where the self will be freed from the limitations of physical embodiment."[4]

September 11 is a symbol of how distant is our global village from the Kingdom in which all of humanity will be at home. On that day, the hidden violence of our world culture became visible. Our planet is in fact suffering from a crisis of homelessness. We are ill at ease in the global village. First of all, we who are at this Congress have been able to obtain visas and pass through immigration controls. But millions of people are attempting to travel, to flee from poverty or oppression, and cannot. There is a vast displacement of people searching for a new home. Europe is building walls to keep out the crowds who want to get in. Never in history have so many people lived in refugee camps and are, quite literally, homeless.

Even those who remain at home are, in a sense, displaced. The human community is fractured by escalating inequalities. And modern communication means that the poor can glimpse the paradise of the wealthy on their TV screens every day, and yet are shut out. The financial nomads who rule our world can move their money anywhere they wish. They have no commitment to the workers of any country. If labor becomes too expensive in England, then they can move to Mexico, and then to Indonesia. Bauman writes, "Brief encounters replace lasting engagements. One does not plant a citrus tree to squeeze a lemon."[5] This has produced a terrible uncertainty. Even the employed cannot be confident that they will have a job tomorrow. Some economists present us with the picture of a benign world of free trade. But our home is distorted by trade barriers, tariffs, and subsidies that exclude the poor nations. It is partly held together by vicious networks of laundered money, by criminal mafias, the drug trade, the sale of women and children for prostitution, the market of body parts and of weapons.

Finally, there is the imposition of a global culture that is in fact Western, and largely American. Johann Baptist Metz argued that "for a long time non-Western countries have been under siege from a 'second colonization': Through the invasion of the Western culture industry and its mass media, especially that of television, which holds people prisoner in an artificial world, a world of make-believe. It alienates them more and more from their own cultural images, from their original language, and from their own history. This colonization of the spirit is so much harder to resist because it appears as a sugar-coated poison and because the gentle terror of this Western-culture industry operates not as an alienation but as a narcotic drug."[6] We are "unanchored selves," whose comfortable old homes are being dismantled. On 9/11 the vast anger that this has generated exploded in the heart of the Western world.

So there is a crisis of homelessness, both literally and culturally. A widespread reaction to this is to build communities of like-minded people, with whom we may feel safe and at home. Mrs. Thatcher famously asked of a political rival, "But is he really one of us?" We have become afraid of differences. Richard Sennet wrote, "The image of the community is purified of all that may convey a feeling of difference, let alone conflict, in who 'we' are. In this way, the myth of community solidarity is a purification ritual.... What is distinctive about this mythic sharing in communities is that people feel they belong to each other, and share together, because they are the same."[7]

This search for those who are like us can be seen everywhere, from the Internet to religious groups. On the Internet people surf around searching for others who share their interests and tastes, whether political, sporting, or sexual. And if differences emerge, then one can simply break contact and change one's email address. Fundamentalist religious groups also gather the like-minded. I suspect that the polarization within the Catholic Church today is partly rooted in the pain of living with those who are different from ourselves. The Church has always been fractured by battles, from the time that Peter and Paul slogged it out in Antioch. What is new is our difficulty in reaching across these divisions in a common language. We cannot find words to share communion with those who are different, even within the Church.

Now, in this crisis of homelessness, religious life has surely an urgent vocation to be the sign of God's vast home, the wide openness of the Kingdom, in which all may belong and be at ease. If we are at home in the spaciousness of God, then we may be at home with anyone. We may do this in all sorts of ways. Thousands of religious brothers and sisters have simply left their homes to be at home with strangers. Small communities of sisters settle down in Muslim villages from Morocco to Indonesia, learning to inhabit foreign languages, eating foreign food, embedding themselves in the tissue of other ways of being human.

We also embrace cultural and ethnic differences within our own communities. I drove through Burundi when the whole country was on fire, to visit a monastery of our contemplative nuns in the north. Half the community was Tutsi and half Hutu. They had all lost their families, except one novice. And while I was there her parish priest rang to say that her parents had been murdered. And yet [the community] lived together in peace. This was only possible because of a deep life of prayer and the endless labor of making communion. Crucially they listened to the news on the radio together, and so shared each other's sorrows. In a country that was burnt and brown, and in which no one could sow crops, their hill was green since any-one could come and grow their food there in safety: a green hill in a brown land is a sign of hope.

The toughest difference for us to embrace in religious life is per-haps not ethnic or cultural; it is theological. I can live at ease with a brother from another continent. But can I be deeply at home with one who has another ecclesiology or Christology? Can we reach across the ideological fractures of our Church? It is only if we can do this that we may be a sign of the vastness of God. Communities of the like-minded are weak signs of the Kingdom.

This requires of us much more than mutual tolerance. Indeed, we must dare to speak our disagreement. It requires of us a mutual attentiveness that draws us beyond the narrow limits of our own sym-pathies and language. Do I dare to be touched by the imagination of the other and enter the land of their hopes and fears? We have to embark upon a stretching open of our hearts and minds, what Thomas Aquinas calls a *latitudo cordis,* which draws us into the capacious home that is God.

In *Larry's Party,* the Canadian novelist, Carol Shields, explores how language offers us a home to live in. Larry's first marriage breaks up because he and his young wife did not have a language that was large enough for them to find and love each other. Finally, when they are reconciled it is because their language has become spacious enough for them to be together for the first time. Larry asks, "Was that our problem? That we didn't know enough words?"[8] Being a sign of humanity's common home in God requires that we seek the words that are large enough for us to live in peace with strangers. These strangers may be people of another faith or ethnic group. But a vital preparation for this, and the test of its authenticity, is that we even look for the words that open bridges across the polarization within our own Church and congregations.

This is the obedience needed today, especially after 9/11. It is not an obedience of blind submission to the dictates of religious superiors. It is, rather, deep attentiveness to those who speak different languages and live by different sympathies and imaginations. It is that ascetic exposure to other geographies of mind and heart, even within our own communities, so that we may be drawn out from the narrow prisons that separate human beings from each other. It is a creative obedience, in which together we seek new and old words, which offer fresh air and mutual ease. Religious communities should be the crucibles of renewed language.

One evening in Rotterdam, I met some young people, and I asked them why they still came to church when their contemporaries did not. They found it hard to answer. And then at midnight a young man who had been struggling with this question came back with a letter for me. He explained that he came to our community because here he could use words that he could not use in his home anymore: words like, "Glory to God" and "Holy," words of praise and wisdom. He needed somewhere where he might share these words with other people and be at home in them.

Living Without a Story

A home is not only the sort of space that we occupy, with its mental walls and windows, exclusions and inclusions. We also need to be at home in time. We need to live within a story that embraces a past and looks to a future. We make a home within the stories of our ancestors, and are at ease in a shared hope for the future, before and after the grave. We may be at peace because we know roughly where we are in the plot. For example, in Hinduism there are four stages in the life of a man: being a student, a householder, becoming a forest dweller, and finally the stage of renunciation. One can be at home as one passes through this shared narrative of human life. September 11 changed the stories that we tell of ourselves and our world, and this has deepened our sense of homelessness. We have no story of the future in which to be at home.

To vastly oversimplify, this is the second major transformation of time that the West has lived through in recent years. In my childhood, we were sustained by a fundamental optimism. There was a shared confidence in the progress of humanity. For some, humanity might be moving toward a capitalist paradise, and for others it was a communist paradise. But East and West, left and right, shared the belief that there was a longer story to tell, and that humanity was on its way to a better world. This confidence in the future began to erode after the fall of the Berlin Wall. As Fukuyama famously said, and has been regretting ever since, history ended. The fall of Communism was proclaimed as humanity's arrival at its destiny. The future was here and it looked like America. We have the birth of the Now Generation, who ceased to dream of a future. There was also an increasing hopelessness for those shut out of this capitalist dream. The inequalities of the world went on escalating. Whole continents, especially Africa, were locked in a poverty that seemed beyond healing.

With 9/11 we enter a third moment, in which there is again a story to be told of the future, but it is one without any promise except of more violence. For some it is "the war on terrorism," and for others it is jihad against the corrupt West. This is not a story in which anyone can be at ease and at home. What sign of humanity's home can religious life offer?

First of all, what we do not do is offer an alternative story of the future. The twentieth century was crucified by those who claimed to know the road map of humanity. Millions of people died in Soviet gulags, killed by those who knew where humanity was heading. This year I went for the first time to Auschwitz. At the entrance to the camp there is a map that shows how it is at the center of a network of railway lines, from Norway to Greece, from France to the Ukraine, which carried people to their death. Here was literally the end of the line, imposed by those who efficiently planned the future of humanity. Pol Pot slaughtered a third of all Cambodians because he knew what story must be told of the future. Even capitalism's imposition of its road map impoverishes millions. We are rightly suspicious of those who claim to know the big design.

The foundational story of Christianity is precisely of that moment when we lost a story to tell of the future. No doubt the disciples went to Jerusalem buoyed up by some anticipation of what was to happen: Jesus would be revealed as Messiah; the Romans would be thrown out of the Holy Land, or whatever. As the disciples on the road to Emmaus confessed to Jesus: "We had hoped that he was the one to redeem Israel" (Lk 24:21). Whatever story they told now collapsed. Judas had sold Jesus; Peter was about to betray him. The other disciples would flee in fear. Faced with his passion and death, they had no story to tell. At the moment when this fragile community broke down, Jesus took bread, blessed it, and gave it to them saying, "This is my body, given for you."

The paradox of Christianity is that it offers us a home in time, but not by telling us a story of the future. We have no road map. We cannot open the Book of Revelation and say. "Hey, guys, five plagues down and one to go." We believe that we are on the way to the Kingdom of God, in which death will die and all wounds will be healed, but we have no idea how we shall get there. After 9/11, when some are seduced by the eternal present of the Now Generation and others tell tales that promise only violence, we offer good news. We have a hope that is not anchored in any particular story of the future. Jesus embodied this hope in a sign, bread broken and shared and a cup of wine passed around. How may we religious be signs of that hope?

One way is by daring to embrace our uncertain future with joy. Our vows are a public commitment to remain open to the God of surprises who subverts all our plans for the future and asks us to do things that we never imagined. We say that if you wish to make God laugh, then tell him your plans. Try telling your brothers and sisters, too! When I was examined for solemn profession, I said that I would be happy to do almost anything, except to be a superior. The brethren thought otherwise! But we embrace this uncertainty with the joyful freedom of the children of God. Václav Havel wrote that hope "is not the conviction that something will turn out well, but the certainty that something makes sense, regardless of how it turns out."[9] Our joy is the confidence that somehow our lives, with their triumphs and defeats, will be discovered to have meaning, however futile they may sometimes seem now. The meaning of our lives is the mystery of God, for which we have no words.

Once again, the vow of obedience is the clearest sign that we will let God go on surprising us. We place our lives in the hands of our brothers and sisters, to do with as they wish. This is not a regression to infantile passivity. We remain intelligent people who have a say in our future. Few religious today would be prepared to plant cabbages upside down! Rather it is a free acceptance that we are not the sole authors of our stories. It is a Eucharistic gesture, following Jesus who gave himself into the hands of the disciples saying, "This is my body and I give it to you." And the young will not be drawn to us unless they see that we are eager to accept the gift of their lives and use that gift courageously. Recently I met a sister at a conference in the United States who said that in thirty years of religious life, her congregation had never asked her to do anything. They did not dare to!

Our vow of chastity is also the promise to remain open to the surprises that God may have up his sleeve. We renounce a relationship that expresses a hope for a predictable plot, a stable love for better or for worse, until death does us part. Instead we promise to love and accept love, without any clear idea to whom we shall entrust our heart. When I came to solemn profession for me this was by far the most difficult act of trust. Would I end up a dried up and lonely old stick? Would my heart remain alive? By this vow, we trust that God will give us hearts of flesh, in ways that we cannot anticipate.

Alas, for most of us the vow of poverty hardly commits us to any uncertainty. In many parts of the world, one of the attractions of religious life is that it offers financial security and all the resources of sure wealth. At the Synod on Religious Life, Cardinal Etchegaray made an appeal for religious to embrace a more radical poverty. If people saw in our poverty a real precariousness, then what a sign of hope that would be!

Our vowed life will only be a sign if we live it with joy. Then we will be seen to be at home in this uncertainty, at ease in not knowing the pattern and story of our lives. We can happily rest in the confidence that our lives will be found to have meaning even if sometimes we cannot now say what it is, for it is God.

St. Augustine said, "Let us sing Alleluia here below while we are still anxious, so that we may sing it one day there above when we are free from care."[10] One of my close friends in the Order is a French Dominican called Jean Jacques. He was trained as an economist, went to Algeria to study irrigation, learned Arabic, and taught in the university there. It was hard but he was profoundly content. And then one day his provincial phoned to ask him to come back and teach economics in the University of Lyons. He was utterly thrown; he grieved, and then he remembered the joy of having given his life away without condition. So he went and bought a bottle of champagne to celebrate with his friends. A few years later I was elected to be Master of the Order, and I was desperate to have someone in the General Council whom I knew. I tracked down Jean Jacques and asked him to come. He asked if he could think about it. So I said yes. He asked if he could take a month. I asked him to take a day. He said yes. More champagne. This is the joy of being at home in God's unpredictability.

Charles de Foucauld went to visit a young cousin, François de Bondy, who was twenty-one years old and much given to the pursuit of pleasure. But his life was transformed by seeing the deep joy of this dried-up ascetic from the Sahara: "He entered the room and peace entered with him. The glow of his eyes and especially that very humble smile had taken over his whole person.... There was an incredible joy emanating from him.... Having tasted 'the pleasures of life' and able to entertain the hope of not having to leave the table for a while, I, upon seeing that my whole sum of satisfactions did not weigh more than a tiny fraction in comparison with the complete happiness of the ascetic, found rising within me a strange feeling not of envy but of respect."[11] Enzo Bianchi quotes a fourth-century Father who says that the young are like hounds in the hunt. If the hounds sniff the wolf, then they will carry on hunting to the end. If they never smell the wolf, then they will grow tired and stop.[12] If the young catch from us the whiff of the joy of the Kingdom, then they will carry on to the end.

It is intrinsic to this witness of hope that we dare to give the whole of our lives, *usque ad mortem.* We trust that the whole of our lives will be found to have meaning. In the end, the whole story of our lives will make sense, even the darkest moments. In the *Instrumentum Laboris* (no. 37), it is written, "Confronted with the newness of this postmodern condition, the primary text allows us to ask if this is not a case of recognizing the difficulties of perpetual and definitive commitment and envisioning a consecrated life *ad tempus*" (VC, no. 56, and *Propositio,* no. 33) which would avoid giving the sense that someone who has joined consecrated life for a time, has deserted or abandoned it. I agree. Religious Orders have always, for centuries, offered ways to belonging to those who do not wish to make a permanent commitment. Many of our congregations are now exploring new ways in which this may be developed. It is also the case that some people join us and make profession but one day leave. We do not wish them to be forever crippled by a sense of failure. But this should not put in question the centrality of a commitment *usque ad mortem.* It is often wondered whether today's young are capable of such a commitment. Perhaps the issue is rather whether we believe that they are and are ready to fight for their vocation.

The Subversion of the Culture of Control

The final topic I wish to address is the culture of control. Never has the planet been under such tight control by a few nations. Despite so much rhetoric of development, the national interests of a few countries call the shots. Above all, we live, as never before in the history of humanity, under the control of a single superpower, whose worldwide interests are always to be protected. As Bill Clinton said, there is no difference between domestic and foreign policy. September 11 was in part a protest again those who wish to take control of the planet and its resources. It struck at the symbols of Western economic and military power, the Twin Towers and the Pentagon. But 9/11 has also intensified this culture of control, an escalation in the gathering of information, the control of migration, the militarization of the world, and the loss of human rights.

At the same time, paradoxically, this is a time when the national state, and even the United States, seems always less able to control anything. We live in what Anthony Giddens has called "the runaway world,"[13] "a manufactured jungle." Bauman imagines our world as an airplane that has no pilot. The passengers "discover to their horror that the pilot's cabin is empty and that there is no way to extract from the mysterious black box labeled 'automatic pilot' any information about where the plane is flying, where it is going to land, who is to choose the airport, and whether there are any rules which would allow the passengers to contribute to the safety of the arrival."[14]

At the heart of modernity is this paradoxical combination of a culture of control and of our inability to take charge of our lives. It is powerfully symbolized by our modern technological wars, with their highly sophisticated weapons and yet the immense difficulty in achieving the stated goals. Just look at Vietnam, Afghanistan, and Iraq!

In part this is rooted in the fact that the multinational corporations are largely beyond national regulation. The economy is uncontrollable. The fluidity of modern capitalism generates insecurity and anxiety. All this anxiety becomes projected upon the strangers outside our frontiers and within them. Increasingly governments see law and order as their primary task. Fighting crime is the modern drama, locking up the strangers upon whom we project our fear. In virtually every country in the world, the number of people being locked in prisons is soaring. People who have agendas that are different from our own are increasingly seen as enemies, "terrorists," belonging to some "axis of evil." Poverty is becoming criminalized. Even humanitarian aid and development is being co-opted into the Western security agenda. Global security means Western security, and development agencies will only get grants if they accept its priorities. This is why it is so hard to raise support for the Sudan or the Congo or other disaster areas of Africa.

The culture of control enters the bloodstream of public life as management. Every form of institution must be managed, checked, measured; must meet targets and be assessed. Even the Church is becoming an institution that is ruled by the culture of control. We are watched, reported upon, and assessed. This is not some evil plot of the Vatican. It shows that the Church is living the crisis of modernity, just like everyone else! Even religious congregations often succumb to the culture of management. Those elected to government become "The Administration." Brothers and sisters are transformed into "personnel." I have met Superior Generals whose offices remind me of multinational corporations. The Superior General becomes the CEO. Chapters set targets and assess achievements. Everything must be measurable, and above all money is the measure.

But religious life should explode into this culture of control as a burst of crazy freedom. We can see hints of what this means in the story of Jesus and the Samaritan woman at the well. The apostles go away to do the shopping, and when they come back, there he is chatting with this lowly woman. "Turn your back and you never know what he will be up to!" Jesus is watched, checked up on, but he is our uncontrollable Lord.

Our congregations have different understandings of the nature of government. It may be paternal, democratic, or military. We have no single understanding of the nature of obedience. But we would surely all accept that leadership—to use a word that I detest—is not about control. It is at the service of God's unpredictable grace. No one owns grace and can bend its happening to his or her agenda, especially not the superior. The role of those in leadership is to make sure that no one takes possession of God's grace, neither the young nor the old, neither the left nor the right, neither the West nor any other group. God is among us as the One who is always doing something new, and those in leadership will usually be the last to know what this might be. They have the role of keeping all of us open to the unpredictable directions in which God might lead us, for as God says in Isaiah, "Behold, I am doing something new."

So leadership will be shown in helping our communities to take risks, to not always go for the safe option, to trust the young, to accept precariousness and vulnerability. It will be in keeping the windows open to God's unpredictable grace. So, in this culture of control, religious life should be an ecological niche of freedom. It is not the freedom of those who impose their will, but of surrender to the abiding novelty of God.

I was in the United State during the time that those few envelopes containing anthrax were distributed, and in Asia during the SARS crisis. In both cases, I was astonished by the climate of panic. In this fearful and anxious world, religious life should be an island of freedom and confidence. We may not necessarily be fearless, but we should not be ruled by fear. Christ has died, Christ is risen, Christ will come again. This is the only ultimate drama. Of what is there to be afraid?

When I was a student, our community in Oxford was subject to a couple of very small bomb attacks by a right wing political organization that deeply disliked us for some mysterious reason. I remember being woken in the night by the sound of explosions. I rushed down to the front of our priory and found all the brethren gathered in their different nightwear. But where was the prior? The police arrived, and the prior still slept on. I rushed to wake him. "There has been a bomb attack," I cried excitedly.

"Is anyone dead?" he asked.

"No."

"Is anyone wounded?"

"Well, no."

"Then why don't you let me sleep, and we can all think about it in the morning."

That is when I first glimpsed what leadership might mean! It undramatizes our small panics. If our vows are a promise to let God go on surprising us, then leadership keeps us faithful to this brave embrace of uncertainty.

So, to conclude, after 9/11 our little planet is suffering from a crisis of homelessness. This is literally true for the millions of refugees, asylum seekers, and illegal immigrants. We also suffer from a cultural homelessness, a sense of precariousness, and the subversion of the local cultures in which humanity has made its many homes. As religious we are called to be a sign of that large home which is the Father's home, "in which there are many rooms" (Jn 14:2). We may do this by making our home with the Samaritan and welcoming the Samaritan into our home. At this moment we also face a more subtle challenge, to make our home with the strangers in our own congregations and our Church. All of this requires of us a creative imagination. We need to let the Holy Spirit break down the little ideological discourses, whether of the left or the right, in which we find security. We need to find the words that open us to the vastness of God, and not shrink God into the pettiness of our hearts and minds.

Since 9/11, that sense of homelessness has been deepened by the loss of a story that we can tell of our future. Increasingly the story that dominates our lives is of a war against terrorism and jihad. We religious may be at home in this time of disorientation, not by offering an alternative story, but by joyfully and freely embracing uncertainty. We trust that our lives will ultimately be found to have meaning and so can happily let God go on springing surprises on us.

The insecurity of these present times generates anxiety, and this fosters the culture of control. This can even infect religious life, so that we may succumb to the model of management and administration. But leadership should wedge open the doors and windows of our homes, to let in the Spirit, of whom "no one knows whence it comes and whither it goes.... So it is of everyone born of the Spirit" (Jn 3:8).

Notes

1. *Global Financial Integration: The End of Geography* (London: 1992), quoted by Z. Bauman in *Globalization: the Human Consequences* (London: 1998), p.12.

2. *Globalization,* p. 77.

3. Allan de Lille, quoting St. Bonaventure in *The Soul's Journey into God,* trans. Ewart Cousins (New York: 1978), p. 100; cf. William Cavanagh, "The City: Beyond Secular Parodies" in *Radical Orthodoxy,* ed. J. Millbank, Catherine Pickstock, and Graham Ward (London: 1999), p. 200.

4. *Globalization,* p. 19.

5. *Liquid Modernity* (Cambridge: 2000), p. 122.

6. H. Regan and A. Torrance, *Christ and Context* (Edinburgh: 1993) p. 212, quoted by T. J. Gorringe, op. cit., p. 85.

7. "The Myth of Purified Community," *The Uses of Disorder: Personal Identity and City Style* (London: 1996), p. 36, quoted by Z. Bauman, op. cit., p. 180.

8. *Globalization,* p. 336.

9. Quoted by Seamus Heaney, *The Redress of Poetry,* p. 4.

10. Sermon 256.1, translation of the breviary.

11. Quoted by Fergus Fleming, *The Sword and the Cross* (London: 2003), p. 235f.

12. *Ricominciare nell' anima, nella Chiesa, nel Mondo* (Genova: 1999), p. 53.

13. *Runaway World: How Globalization Is Reshaping Our World* (London: 1999).

14. *Liquid Modernity,* p. 59.

RELIGIOUS LIFE IN THE FUTURE

Sandra M. Schneiders, IHM

I. Introduction

A. *Framing the Question*

My assignment, to talk about the future of religious life, is both the best and the worst of tasks. It is the best because no one can prove me wrong in the present. It is the worst because no one can safely speculate on what "the future" means in our multi-cultural, pluralistic, globalizing, nuclear-threatened, and environmentally compromised postmodern world that is changing kaleidoscopically at a blinding speed. In short, any attempt to describe the future in order to ground some kind of plausible prediction is impossible. So, instead of talking about the future of religious life, I will talk about religious life in the future, whatever that future may be.

The question I am asking, in other words, is not an empirical one about *what will be,* but an imaginative one about *what can be.* What understanding of this life can be humanly meaningful and evangelically effective no matter what the future holds for us, for the Church, for our world?[1] I will propose an imaginative construction of religious life which assumes that, no matter when or where it is lived, it must be Gospel-based and capable of being lived simultaneously and diversely in the vastly varied cultural, social, and ecclesial contexts which affect it profoundly and are affected by it.

B. My Hypothesis

The hypothesis I will offer rests on two assumptions. On the one hand, religious life is profoundly Christian—i.e., religious share in the identity and mission of all the baptized with whom they relate as equals. On the other hand, religious life is a distinctive lifestyle in the Church—i.e., a state of life that can be recognized and identified by its specific contribution to the life and mission of the Church. By way of prolepsis, I will suggest that religious life is an alternate lifestyle in the Church. Religious, by the vows they profess and live, create an alternate "world" in the midst of this world, the *saeculum.* Religious do not simply attempt to live differently in the world, which all Christians must do, but to create a different world that will offer a prophetic witness in, to, and sometimes against the world and even the institutional Church. At the end, I will connect this hypothesis to the theme of redemptive marginality evoked by our icon of the Samaritan woman in John 4 and the Samaritan man in Luke 10.

C. Presuppositions

Three presuppositions frame this hypothesis. The first concerns the meaning of the term "world," a concept that must be carefully parsed today lest Christians continue policies of domination and exploitation of nature or rejection of creation in the name of religion.[2] Perhaps our best New Testament source for a nuanced theology of the world is the Gospel of John, which uses the term more frequently than the rest of the New Testament combined.[3] Four meanings of the term *kosmos* can be distinguished in the Gospel. First, world can mean the *whole of creation,* which John's Gospel, echoing the first chapter of Genesis, declares came into existence through the Word of God (cf. Jn 1:9–11), and which the creator God declared very good (cf. Gen 1:31). Second, the world can be seen as the *theater of human history.* Jesus spoke of his own coming into the world as light to save all (cf. Jn 12:46) and prayed at the last supper not that God take his disciples out of the world—i.e., out of human history—but that God preserve them from evil as they lived and acted in the world (cf. Jn 17:15). Third, the world is the *human race* in its entirety. God "so loved the world" as to give the only Son, that all who believe in him may have eternal life (cf. Jn 3:16). All three of these meanings of "world" are essentially positive. The world created by God, especially the human race in its journey through and creation of history, is the handiwork of God, redeemed in Christ and destined to glory.

But the fourth meaning of "world" in the fourth Gospel, used much more frequently than the preceding three, is distinctly negative. Jesus refers to a world that is *a synonym for evil;* that is in the grip of Satan (cf. Jn 13:27), the devil, the "Prince of this world."[4] Jesus is not of this evil world nor are his disciples (cf. Jn 17:16). The minions of the Evil One will persecute and even kill them, but they are to have confidence because Jesus has overcome the world (cf. Jn 16:33). Against Jesus, the Prince of this world is powerless (cf. Jn 14:30) and will finally be judged (cf. Jn 16:11). But until the consummation, the struggle against the evil world and its Ruler continues.

This evil world, then, is not a place nor a group of people; it is a construction of reality according to principles or coordinates that are the polar opposite of the central values of the Gospel. These opposing realities, the Reign of God and the kingdom of Satan, are produced by the moral choices of human beings under the influence of the Spirit of God or of the Devil, and they come to expression not only in the personal behavior of individuals but in the political, economic, social, cultural, and religious institutions of society. The Gospel project of self-transcendence toward God in Christ for the sake of the world is directly opposed to the self-enclosed and divisive dynamics of oppression and domination inspired by Satan. All Christians at their Baptism are called to renounce "Satan and all his works," to disaffiliate themselves from the reality-construction of the Evil One. But some Christians—namely, religious—incarnate this world-renunciation in a particular way, which we will shortly discuss as the creation of the alternate world generated by the profession of the vows.

My second presupposition is that *the foundation of the Christian challenge to Satan's evil construction—i.e., the negative "world"— is the Resurrection of Jesus,* in which the victory of God over Satan is realized in the person of the crucified and risen One. His paschal mystery is the principle of the Christian enterprise. It establishes definitively that eternal life comes through death—not the death which is a natural biological process, but the death which results from the refusal to integrate one's life into the reality-construction of Satan. The followers of Jesus will risk and accept death in their effort to realize the Reign of God in this world. Until the will of God is realized on earth as it is in heaven—until all creation, and especially human beings, can experience the infinite *shalom* of God—the struggle between the Prince of this world and the true Prince of peace will be waged in and by the followers of Jesus in collaboration with all people of good will. Different members of the glorified Jesus will participate in this struggle in different ways. The question for us is: What is the distinctive way religious participate in this enterprise?

This brings us to the third presupposition, namely, that *religious participate in the struggle for the Reign of God by creating, living in, and ministering from an alternate world.* Again, "world" is not the natural universe, a geographical place, or a group of people. "World" is a reality-construction. When we say something like, "My world fell apart when my mother died," or, "I don't know where she is coming from," we use a material or spatial metaphor to reference a complex construction of reality within which we coordinate our thinking, feeling, choosing, and acting. Specifically, the imaginative construction of reality, "the world," is primarily a certain way of understanding, organizing, and operating within and upon the basic coordinates of all human life: material goods, power, and sexuality. Material goods which we relate to in terms of possession, power that we exercise through freedom, and sexuality that we construct and express through relationship are the raw material which humans shape into "world," either the Reign of God or the kingdom of Satan, as they work out their destinies, personal and corporate, in history.

The distinctiveness of religious life as a lifestyle arises from the public, lifelong commitment of the members, as individuals and as communities, to a characteristic approach to material goods, power, and sexuality that creates a particular concrete realization of the Reign of God, on a 24-hour-a-day, 7-days-a-week basis. Because of the overlapping and intertwining of the Reign of God and the kingdom of Satan in all human experience, religious, in order to undertake a pattern of life in which there are to be no exceptions to the dynamics of Gospel life and no compromise with the dynamics of the evil world, actually construct an alternative to life in this world, in the *saeculum*. We need to recognize the utopian character of this project which is particularly challenged in the postmodern context by the suspicion of all unitary projects and meta-narratives.[5]

Prior to the renewal inaugurated by Vatican II, religious often tried to handle the ambiguous environment in which the Reign of God and the kingdom of Satan are intimately intertwined by physical separation from the people and processes that surrounded their convents and monasteries. But as this "total institution" model of religious life was deconstructed,[6] as it had to be, in favor of the full involvement in the human enterprise that the Council recognized as the vocation of the Church and therefore of religious,[7] the full gravity, scope, and difficulty of religious life as an alternate lifestyle has become much clearer. Because this project is no longer protected by physical and social isolation nor legitimated by a blanket rejection, if not condemnation, of everything outside religious life as "worldly," religious are challenged to rearticulate the nature of their venture, and to commit themselves explicitly to pursuing it in the very midst of this ambiguous situation, within human history and in cultures and social settings which are structured to a large extent by the satanic dynamics of sexual exploitation, political domination, and economic oppression locked in mortal struggle with initiatives, religious and non-religious, which promote right relationships among all God's creatures.

Religious construct their alternate world by the profession of vows. Profession is the solemn and public act by which individuals integrate their life into the reality that began in the charismatic vision of a Founder or Foundress, and has been lived into reality by generations of religious within a particular community. By their personal and corporate living of the vows, they create the distinctive and characteristic lifestyle by which they participate in the Church's mission of witnessing to and realizing the Reign of God in this world.

It is therefore crucial to rescue our understanding of profession and the vows from the almost exclusively juridical framework in which they have been immured, especially since the 1917 revision of the *Code of Canon Law*.[8] Profession was seen as the assumption by vow of narrowly defined supererogatory obligations. In reality, profession is a global commitment, an orientation of one's whole person, life, and history toward the realization, by particular means, of the Reign of God. It is a specification of baptismal commitment that is courageously open-ended, not merely a restriction on specific behaviors. The vows, whichever ones are made in particular congregations,[9] are Gospel-based global metaphors for the stance religious take toward the fundamental coordinates of human existence, material goods, sexuality, and power. It is through these metaphors that we imagine and construct the living parable of religious life as an alternate world. Like Jesus' parables, the vows not only describe, but narratively generate a different world not just a different way of living in this world.[10] The world of Jesus' parables, the Reign of God he presents, is a world of endless forgiveness, of abundant refreshment at the wedding feast of eternal life where the last are first and the marginalized included, and of equality and dignity for all. In what follows, I will very briefly and inadequately explore how religious through two of the vows, poverty and obedience, try to tell this story into reality, to generate this al-

ternate world and offer it in and through the Church as a real possibility, a future full of hope, to the world in which they live. Time
will not permit dealing with the vow of consecrated celibacy (with
which I have dealt at length elsewhere),[11] but I hope the consideration of these two vows will spark our creativity to continue this
imaginative process in our discussions.

II. Evangelical Poverty:
The Economy of the Reign of God

Poverty is the focus of a great deal of ambiguity and guilt among
religious. We often feel uneasy, even hypocritical, as we enjoy adequate material well-being in a world of widespread want and even
destitution. Perhaps this malaise is an invitation from the Spirit to
probe more deeply into the meaning of the poverty we vow.

Poverty is, first and fundamentally, about material goods, the resources without which we cannot live at all, much less live well.
Thus, we naturally tend to think about poverty in quantitative terms.
How much property or economic leverage should we, individually
and corporately, have? By what standard should we measure our possessions? I suggest that our focus should be less on the quantity of
goods with which we deal, something that necessarily varies enormously from situation to situation, and more on the economic system within and according to which we deal with material goods. And
the standard for freely chosen evangelical poverty, which is very different from unsought deprivation, should be derived not from a comparison of our standard of living with that of any economic class, but
from the Gospel. The Gospel says much about material goods, about
our attitudes and behaviors in relation to them, and about the kind
of world these attitudes and behaviors generate. But it does not say
anything about actively seeking deprivation, much less destitution,
or about comparing standards of living. This might suggest where
we need to concentrate our attention.

Let me diverge from our theme to stop for a moment on the
thought of an American culture critic, Lewis Hyde, whose oft-

republished book, *The Gift,* is a profound reflection on our topic.[12] Hyde, studying the foundations of our superficial typology of economies under the form of trade, industry, technology, and so on, proposes that there are essentially two types of economy—i.e., two ways of organizing the use of material goods within a society— namely, commodity economy and gift economy.

In a commodity economy goods are seen as objects of owner- ship and the primary economic activity is acquisition.[13] The object of economic behavior is to take as much as possible of the avail- able goods out of circulation into private ownership. Social status and power accrue to the person who owns more, and, since materi- al goods are intrinsically limited, what one person has another can- not have. In such a zero-sum economy the desire for more than one actually needs, saving against a possible future need, display of one's possessions, and competition for goods always perceived as scarce simply because they are limited are considered natural behaviors required for survival. In other words, greed, covetousness, hoarding, conspicuous consumption, conflict, and even the defense of one's goods at the expense of another's life if necessary are virtues in a commodity economy.

By contrast, in a gift economy, which characterized many pri- mal societies and still characterizes some tribal communities, ma- terial goods are regarded first of all as that which we have received—from God, nature, family, community—and therefore as that which we, in turn, can give to others. The primary economic activity is keeping goods in circulation, contributing to the well-be- ing of the community through one's work, the use of one's talents, the sharing of one's material possessions. Ownership is relative to the needs of others and no one owns what all need, such as land, water, food, and air. The highest status in a gift economy accrues to the one who contributes the most. Real poverty consists not in hav- ing nothing but in having nothing to give. Scarcity may be, at times, a community concern, but it is not a personal disgrace. Greed and hoarding—even refusing to share what one actually needs, especially when other members of the community are in want—is dishonorable and ignoble. Conspicuous consumption is vulgar. Irresponsibility or refusal to work is disgraceful. The virtues that are admired in a gift economy are generosity, sharing, work, responsibility, simplicity, and compassion for the less fortunate.

Needless to say, these economies are not morally equal. From the Christian standpoint, one is clearly marked with the signature trait of the Evil One—namely, divisiveness; the other provides a fertile substrate for the Gospel values of right relationships in a community of shared life. Against this background, let us return to our consideration of the evangelical poverty that religious vow and by which they construct and live in the alternate world of the Reign of God.

In the Gospel story of the rich man who asks Jesus what he must do to inherit eternal life (Mk 10:17–22 and parallels), Jesus says that all are called to obey the commandments. But when the man persists, Jesus tells him that he lacks one thing. He should dispossess himself completely and join the itinerant band of disciples following the homeless Jesus. Notice that Jesus does not say he should become destitute and die of starvation, exposure, or disease. Nor is he proposing an ascetical ideal to the man. Jesus invites the man to join a community of disciples who are individually without possessions and who live simply, sharing a common purse and accepting the generosity of others even as they freely serve others through the preaching of the Gospel in word and deed.

Shortly before religious make a vow of poverty they cede the administration of anything they own (patrimony) and renounce ownership of everything they will ever acquire by work or gift.[14] Even if their patrimony is still legally owned by them, the religious renounce all the rights of ownership, the "use and usufruct" of the property, as well as independent control of anything she or he will acquire in the future. In other words, the religious becomes functionally *possessionless,* totally economically interdependent within the community. If the vow is lived seriously by all the members of the community, they are creating and living in a radically gift econ-

omy. All things used by any of the members are held in common—
i.e, everyone puts everything into the common fund, and all receive
from it according to need. They have accepted the condition the rich
young man refused because "he had many possessions." It was not
difficulty or hardship before which he faltered. After all, he had kept
all the commandments "since his youth." What he could not embrace
was being without personal, individual possessions. Jesus' band of
itinerant disciples lived a community of gift, of shared simplicity,
in which private commodities had no place. For modern people to
undertake this kind of economic life is to create an alternate economic world in the context of the globalization of market capitalism.

Another Gospel story, the parable of the eleventh hour laborers
(Mt 20:1–16), illustrates a second economic feature of the alternate
world that religious create. The vineyard owner, clearly a God-figure,
employs a series of workers beginning with a shift hired early in the
morning and ending with a group hired an hour before closing time.
He agrees to pay each what is just, and at the end of the day he pays
all an equal wage, making sure that the earliest shift sees what the
5:00 P.M. workers received. They indignantly object. Should not people who work longer and harder be paid more than people who work
less? Should not earnings be proportionate to labor?

The God-figure, however, claims to be operating according to
a different economic system. No one earned anything; all is gift!
Divine generosity, not personal effort, is the source of what each received. The vineyard owner asks, "Are you envious because I am
generous?" All we have we receive freely from God's largesse.
Without our very being, our strength and talents, and God's "employment" of us, we could do nothing. Our system of acquiring
through earning is a provisional human arrangement in a commodity economy. It does not express our true relationship to material
goods, which are always God's gift to us and ours to each other.

But even more significant is the vineyard owner's pay scale. He
agreed to give each worker "what is just" and that is "a day's wage";
in other words, what a person needs to live. The need met by "a

day's wage" varies enormously among individuals and is culturally conditioned.[15] But in any context, those who can work more do
not need more than the necessary resources for life and mission. And
those unable to work as much do not necessarily need less to live;
indeed, they may need more.[16] All should contribute what they can
to the common enterprise and receive what they need.[17] The vineyard owner does not want anyone standing around idle. But the right
to life and the resources needed to sustain it do not arise from what
we do. Rather, work is the overflow of life sustained at the appropriate level. This disconnecting of work from the right to life-sus-
taining resources is a fundamental subversion of our human illusion
that we "support ourselves" by our work and its logical conclusion
that those less able to work deserve to suffer want. Jesus says that
all should contribute as they are able, but all must receive what is
necessary for life.

This is the approach to work in the shared enterprise of ministry that characterizes a religious community that takes seriously its
economic common life. Each religious is to work as much and as
well as she or he is able. Religious, therefore, do not "retire" from
ministry at a certain age to live in leisure on the savings they have
amassed from their earnings. They have not gotten rich by working
and saving. Religious do not personally earn but act, and receive
compensation, as agents of their congregation. But when, because of
age or infirmity, they can no longer bear the "burden of the day's
heat," they continue to minister in whatever ways they can and to receive "the day's wage" within the community just as they did in the
prime of their work lives. In other words, in a gift economy, especially the radical version of such an economy that involves complete
possessionlessness and total economic interdependence, all things
are placed and held in common, everyone works as much and as well
as he or she is able, and everyone is sustained and cared for according
to need. There is no economically based social class, no status, power, or influence flowing from superior wealth, no dependence and
shame attached to poverty, no destitution as long as there are any

resources to be shared. The gift economy is the material basis for the
radically egalitarian community of disciples that Jesus founded.

Not only does such a community foster the right relation of
members with God (that is, the joyful poverty of spirit that is expressed in dependence on divine providence and openness to others)
and with one another (that is, a genuinely communitarian life of
Gospel friendship among equals), but it also enables the community to minister freely and generously not as paid service providers in
a consumer economy, but as sisters and brothers to fellow human
beings in need. Religious congregations have traditionally chosen
ministries to those who are underserved precisely because they cannot pay or pay well for the services they need. Religious can afford
to serve the needy because they are not trying to get rich by their
work. Thus, those they serve do not feel exploited on the one hand
or diminished and patronized on the other by religious who serve
them out of divine compassion. The needy in body, mind, and spirit are not beggars but brothers and sisters, first of Jesus and then of
those who serve them in Jesus' name. The salaries of religious whose
ministries pay well, the proceeds of prudent investments, the gifts of
generous partner-donors, can help support ministries that are not self-
supporting. However, it is easy for a congregation to get so caught
up in the dynamics of a commodity economy that it loses sight of the
real, indeed radical, difference between ministry and gainful employment even if the two coincide. Furthermore, religious can be co-
opted into ecclesiastical agendas that are foreign to their own
charismatic identity so that they become a cheap job corps rather than
ministerial agents within the self-determining congregation. But this
need not happen if the community is reflective in its ministerial
choices and decisions and understands the uniqueness of the economy created by the profession of evangelical poverty and its relation
to ministry.

Finally, the authentic living of a gift economy in the midst of a
commodity economy can offer a prophetic witness that challenges
the very foundational convictions of modern capitalism, as Jesus

challenged the rich man and the wage-earners in his audience. It says very effectively, and in a way that simply imitating the poor or practicing conspicuous deprivation cannot say, that material wealth is not the primary value in life, that all ownership is provisional and conditional, that all people have a right to what they need, that greed and hoarding and conspicuous consumption are not virtues but vices, and that violence against persons in defense of property is never justified. If the poverty that religious vow were lived seriously and consistently by every member of a congregation, no matter when or where that congregation found itself now or in the future, its spirituality, its community life, its ministry, and its witness would effectively challenge the world construction of the Evil One with the Gospel's vision of the Reign of God.

III. Prophetic Obedience: The Politics of the Reign of God

I turn now, necessarily more briefly, to the second vow, obedience, by which religious construct the alternate world that exposes and challenges the reign of Satan. This vow stands in need of massive reinterpretation today because the very concept of obedience has been seriously deformed and contaminated by the world's politics of violence and coercive domination. Although an adequate treatment of obedience requires a thorough discussion of the meanings of the correlative categories of freedom and authority, we cannot engage these topics here. So, let us stay focused on the contribution of prophetic obedience to the political organization of religious community understood as a particular realization of the alternate world of the Reign of God.

As poverty is about material goods and therefore about the economic order, so obedience is about power and therefore about the political order. As poverty is not about renouncing material goods but about establishing a Gospel relationship to them—namely, possessionlessness that helps constitute an alternate world of the gift economy—so obedience is not about renouncing power but developing a prophetic exercise of power as genuine freedom, which will make religious community life and mission an alternate political world—namely, a discipleship of equals in community and mission. Our question is: What does the Reign of God look like, politically?

Despite the fact that religious life through much of its history has organized itself and functioned in imitation of available secular political models, especially those of empire or divine right monarchy—and today to some extent in some countries quasi-democracy—one of the striking facts about religious life is that it is not a natural society and, therefore, organizing it politically according to such models does violence to its very being. The assumptions of all forms of hierarchical political organizations, especially those believed to rest on ontological inequalities, demand that some (e.g., royalty, whites, men, clerics, free people, etc.) rule others (e.g., commoners, people of color, women and children, the non-ordained, slaves, etc.) by divine necessity and decree. But the ontological inequalities which are thought to ground hierarchy and its governmental expressions in secular and even ecclesiastical societies do not, in fact, exist in religious community. Nor is the kind of equality underlying the democratic notion of majority rule established by "one person, one vote" verified in religious community. In other words, religious community by its very nature is neither hierarchical nor democratic.

Religious life is not a natural but a voluntary society. First, in the religious community there are no children to which parents have a natural, and perhaps the only genuine (though temporary), hierarchical relation of authority. Everyone enters religious life as a free adult.[18] Second, religious communities are generally single gender societies, and thus the fallaciously asserted hierarchy of male over female is not operative.[19] Third, the vow of poverty abolishes class, the hierarchy based on material wealth. Fourth, religious leave their families of origin so that nobility or lack thereof become irrelevant, even to the point, in times past, of suppressing family names. Finally, no one is born into religious life and no one is obliged to enter for the sake of salvation or sanctification, so the community has no non-negotiable hold on the members. The religious community, in short, is a society made up of equal, free adults who choose to come together, not primarily for each other (as in marriage), nor primarily to do something together (as in a business venture), but because their love of Christ and desire to live the Gospel in a particular way draws them together to pursue that ideal.[20] The relation of community members to each other and the ministries they undertake together flow from this particular commitment to Christ in response to a personal vocation over which no one has control.

But the horrors of the Holocaust pursued in blind obedience to state authority, and the feminist analysis of hierarchy as a fundamentally dysfunctional system of domination based on dichotomous dualisms, have illuminated our reflection on what kind of society, what kind of political order, the Gospel challenges Christians to imagine and effect. The community of disciples which Jesus gathered around him was not a revised version of either the religious establishment of institutional Judaism or the Roman empire. It was something radically new, a kinship of faith, not blood (cf. Lk 11:27–28), in which there are to be no fathers (cf. Mt 23:8–10), and all who hear and do the will of God are brothers, sisters, mothers of Jesus (cf. Mk 3:35). It is a community of believers in which there are to be no rabbis or teachers who bind impossible burdens upon people, for all are disciples of the one teacher, Christ (cf. Mt 23:6–11). It is to be a political entity in which there are no rulers lording it over others and styling themselves benefactors (Mt 20:24–28), for all are called to mutual service in imitation of Jesus who laid down his life for them. Jesus stated categorically that domination by the powerful is the way of the world, and "it shall not be so among you" (Mt 20:26; Mk 10:43). Jesus' community is, in the felicitous phrase of Elisabeth Schüssler Fiorenza, a discipleship of equals. The development in the institutional Church itself of a pervasively hierarchical structure that resorts to the use of coercive power as a normal mode of control often renders this Gospel version of Christian

community virtually invisible and creates an imperative for prophetic witness to the new kind of political order that Jesus called into
being, a witness not only to the world but to the institutional Church
itself.

Jesus' murder by the collusion of the state and the religious establishment testified to the subversive nature of what he proposed
and to the fundamental agreement about power of the two institutions. Jesus' vision of relations among his followers fundamentally
subverts the political systems, whether religious or secular, which
operate through coercion of the disempowered by the powerful.
Religious life, if it took seriously its own constitution as a purely voluntary society of those who hear the word of God and live it as a discipleship of equals united in mutual service, could become the
alternate political world which would announce to secular and ecclesiastical powers alike the possibility of a truly non-hierarchical
community of sisters and brothers united around Jesus, the Risen
Victim of the power structures of this world.

The recourse, in secular society, in the institutional Church, and
often in religious life, to worldly political structures of hierarchy and
coercion is based on a fear that any other political arrangement will
inevitably degenerate into a chaotic war of all against all for personal advantage. Only a hierarchical structure in which the powerful,
claiming to speak for God, assign control to themselves and their sur-
rogates, can prevent such a catastrophe. This is not a phantom fear
but it is a counsel of despair that nullifies resurrection hope. Human
nature is indeed deformed toward violence by what tradition calls
Original Sin, that is, the influence of the Evil One, the Prince of this
world. Even in Jesus' lifetime he had to intervene in the power dynamics among his disciples jockeying for prestige and power over
each other and trying to control the relation of others to him. But Jesus
did not accept these power dynamics as inevitable or invincible. He
refused to assign places of preference in the Reign of God (cf. Mt
20:20–28 and parallels), to command one disciple to restructure her
discipleship according to the pattern chosen by another (cf. Lk

10:38–42), to repulse children (cf. Mk 10:13–14 and parallels) or women or Samaritans or pagans or the ill or the handicapped as inferiors, to close his inclusive discipleship to society's (cf. Lk 19:1–10) or the religious establishment's outcasts (cf. Lk 7:36–50), or to let his disciples call down fire on those who did not have their permission to preach (cf. Lk 9:51–55). He insisted that the first be last and raised the last to first, and demanded that his disciples be servants of all. Jesus continued to his last breath to accept the condemned as fellow citizens in the Reign of the One he called his "father," refused to retaliate against his persecutors, or even to condemn the unrepentant (cf. Lk 23:32–43). He exercised no power over others, no coercion. But Jesus was not naïve. He did not say that this would "work" in the worldly sense of that term. The politics of domination has always been the way of the world. What Jesus did say is that it must be different among you who are called together by one who washed your feet (cf. Jn 13:1–15) and who refused recourse to power even to save his own life (cf. Mt 26:53; Jn 18:19–11).

Obviously, if religious life is to be a peaceful, orderly, and ministerially effective lifestyle that bears prophetic witness to the possibility of an alternate form of community in service of the Gospel, it must develop criteria and procedures by which to decide what to do and how to do it. Obedience, whose etymological root is "to hear," is the principle of this nonhierarchical Gospel organization. Religious vow to attend, always and first, to the voice of God, to seek explicitly for God's will in this world. Obedience is a vow not about submission to heteronomous control, but about listening to the intimate voice of the only One who truly commands our obedience. The practice of obedience in community is the specific and concrete way of attending that characterizes religious life.

In the past, religious tended to locate the voice of God exclusively in the Rule and the will of the superior. The working assumption was that, as long as one was not doing one's own will but the will of another, God's will was being done. Modern psychology, as well as the disasters resulting from blind obedience, make this approach highly questionable. At best such "obedience" is infantilizing; at worst it promotes real evil. Vatican II, especially in *Gaudium et Spes* and *Perfectae Caritatis,* urged all Christians, including religious, to widen our focus in the search for God's designs. We must attend to the "signs of the times,"[21] a fortunately imprecise notion that embraces historical and cultural developments, social changes, scientific advances, and the deepening awareness of the cosmic context of the human adventure. We may and must attend seriously to our own personal and corporate experience of what fosters and what hinders life in Christ and the coming of God's Reign. The Gospel is to be the ultimate norm of all Christian life, the perennial fount of spirituality, and the heart of all theological reflection and ecclesial practice.[22] The charism of Founders, the needs of the Church and world, and the gifts and initiative of members, as well as constitutions and legitimate traditions and the authority of leaders, are to be heard and heeded.

But how is such a welter of incoming information to be processed so that, rather than being paralyzed by a flood of incoherent data and polarized by numerous and conflicting agendas, the community can live peacefully and minister effectively? The answer, of course, is "discernment." Rather than evading the difficult work of discernment by passive abdication of personal authority to rule, tradition, or superior, religious must vigorously exercise discernment in an atmosphere of equality and freedom in the effort to hear the voice of God in the din of the world and in the still, small voice speaking in prayer. And this is the work of the whole community, not merely of the leaders, even though different members have different roles in the process at different points in time.

Over its long history religious life has developed a wisdom tradition, enshrined in foundational documents, in wholesome traditions and customs, and in valuable experience, that plays a privileged role in the work of discernment. That tradition must continually develop, because even the best human wisdom is not divine.[23] But we do not have to start from scratch each time we face decisions. Furthermore, religious have developed ways of selecting leaders who, while in office, exercise a privileged role in relation to the common good, including articulating the corporate vision and decisions. Leaders and members must be able to distinguish megalomania or ideological fixation, as well as external intimidation, from the genuine leadership that helps to keep the common good in focus as discernment proceeds, without ever assuming that concern for the common good is the exclusive charism or contribution of office-holders.

If, in the past, obedience has been understood as submission or compliance, perhaps today it is better understood as responsible participation and wholehearted cooperation. To cooperate is to work together. Religious life is a working together in the Spirit of all the members in the construction of their life and the effecting of their mission. By vowing obedience, every member commits her or himself to that enterprise, in season and out of season, when convenient and inconvenient, when one's own ideas and projects prevail and when they do not. To vow obedience is to commit oneself to participate in the process of discernment and in the work of embodying the fruits of discernment in life and mission. To stay at the table of discernment, to come back from temporary disillusionment, dismay, or even despair, to speak with courage and listen with vulnerability, to respond responsibly to decisions flowing from communal discernment and/or articulated by legitimate authority are all part of obedience.

To regard obedience not as an alienation of one's freedom and responsibility through submission but as an exercise of freedom through participation and cooperation is to recognize and affirm certain principles which have emerged in practice in renewing congregations in the wake of the Council. However, although many congregations have moved instinctively, in the spirit of the Council and the Gospel, toward a de-hierarchicalizing and de-militarizing of obedience, they have sometimes failed to articulate and fully appropriate the real Gospel valence of these principles. This can result in an uncertainty that is exacerbated by the rejection in theory and attempted suppression in practice of these principles in some hierarchical circles within the institutional Church. What I am describing as a contemporary understanding of obedience that is emerging in renewing congregations is not a rebellion against past dictatorship nor a rejection of legitimate authority. Nor is it the quiet withering away of authority and obedience as everyone does her or his own thing, occasionally informing superiors of one's decisions. Religious congregations have not adopted a sacralized democracy, where one casts one's vote (or does not bother to) and lives with the will of the majority. I am talking about a Gospel-based prophetic organization of the exercise of power within a community for the maximizing of freedom in the service of personal holiness and ministry. It remains to offer a partial list of these principles of obedience with an indication of their Gospel roots and their prophetic potential.

First, the foregoing description is based on the premise that religious life is a lifestyle bringing together in a voluntary community free, responsible, and committed adult Christians who are radically equal as human beings and especially as children of God, and whose equality is not abolished or compromised by the always provisional leadership arrangements which the community creates to foster its discernment and commitments.

Second, prophetic obedience involves a prodigious act of faith in the power of grace working in people of good will to overcome in an ongoing way the will to dominate, the quest for privilege, the recourse to coercion that are endemic to the human situation still under the influence of the Prince of this world.

Third, it affirms that human intelligence and goodness, when placed in the service of the common good and motivated by the urgent love of Christ, can and will discern the designs of God at least to the extent necessary for the decisions that must be made here and now, and that the community will have the courage to rectify its mistakes as well as execute its valid decisions.

Fourth, such a vision of obedience is based on a belief in the inalienability of freedom, the primacy of conscience, the acceptance of responsibility for oneself and the other(s), a humble realization of the intrinsic limitation of all human effort to know and do, and a commitment to the processes and the results of discernment.

Finally, it recognizes the full seriousness of making such a commitment by profession, of vowing in perpetuity to actively participate in this Gospel form of political life as a constitutive dimension of one's own growth in Christ and one's commitment to the Reign of God. Religious do not simply cooperate out of passivity or amiability when and if they have the time or inclination to do so. They take on, by vow, all that it means to participate fully in the life and ministry of the congregation. Living on the margins of the community and minimal participation are not a legitimate choice but a violation of vowed obedience. Participation includes the major requirements and annoying details of financial and ministerial accountability as well as the investment of time and energy in such things as committee work, consultations, and chapters, and sometimes even the major self-gift of holding office or undertaking some other full-time community service. It includes the sometimes onerous task of working out differences with other members and leaders. At times it will demand genuine self-abnegation for the sake of the common good. Like evangelical poverty and consecrated celibacy, prophetic obedience characterizes every moment of every day in the life of the vowed religious, not because one is fulfilling the rule or doing the superior's bidding at all times, but because one lives with one's ear ever attuned to the slightest indication of God's will and work in the world and a heart ever disposed to embody that will in one's life and ministry. It is my conviction that living the politics of the Reign of God can and will move religious life into a future that is full of hope.

IV. Conclusion

Let me conclude by returning to our premise, namely, that by their vows religious create an alternate world which, on the basis of the Gospel, prophetically challenges the power of the Prince of this world. This alternate world is not a place or even a group of people. It is a reality-construction, a way of imagining and handling the basic coordinates of human life (material goods, power, and relationships) that expresses and fosters the Gospel values of the Reign of God. Religious not only create this world as their own environment, but act out of it in their efforts to create a different future.

The conference icon, the Samaritan woman in John 4 and the Good Samaritan in Luke 10, is a powerful symbol of this new world. Samaritanism, a religious-ethnic identity marker in Jesus' time, was a principle of alienation, marginality, exclusion, and inferiority in relation to the Chosen People. Jews and Samaritans had nothing in common, used nothing in common, did not worship in the same place, did not accept the same canon of Scripture. But both Gospel vignettes are about crossing artificial boundaries, breaking down walls of separation, subverting power structures, dismantling privilege, putting the private and exclusive in common to build community in this world.

The dialogue between Jesus and the Samaritan woman starts with Jesus' *request for a gift* of water. And when the woman invokes the exclusivity that forbids her to respond to his request, *Jesus offers her a gift,* the wellspring of eternal life. This invitation to mutual gift giving, to an economy of gift rather than of possession, leads to a discussion of the theological basis of the divide between Jews and Samaritans over patriarchal origins, true worship, and the identity of the Messiah. Jesus' subversion of biological, geographical, historical, or even ritual criteria of true religion in favor of worship of God in Spirit and in Truth sets a new standard for inclusion. Jesus says all who believe are welcome in his new family of faith, in a discipleship of equals, not because of their patriarchal genealogy, their orthodoxy or *orthopraxis,* their Scriptural warrants, or their traditions. Jesus' proclamation, "neither on this mountain nor in Jerusalem" but "in Spirit and in Truth," relativizes all human litmus tests in favor of divine inclusivity and equality based on faith—i.e., on free receptivity to the free divine gift. And the image of this new dispensation is mutual gift between man and woman, Jew and Samaritan. In this scene that images the new dispensation there is no sexual exploitation, neither domination by the man nor manipulation by the woman, but mutual respect between equals. There is no economic brokering as Jesus freely shares his very identity and divine gifts (cf. Jn 4:26) with the woman who freely receives and then becomes the one who freely shares what she has received with her fellow towns-people (cf. Jn 4:29). There is no exercise of dominative power be-tween these two who relate as equals, discerning through dialogue God's will and work in this world in openness to a genuinely new possibility. In this tiny locale of Sichar, sexuality, material goods, and power have been integrated into a new creation. A new world, in which the Prince of this world has no part, is coming into being.

Verse 27 of the pericope reveals just how radical Jesus' revela-tion is. The male disciples, returning from town, are shocked that Jesus is talking to a woman, and even, as will soon become clear, includ-ing her in his mission. Neither discipleship nor mission, it appears, is exclusive to males, nor are these men in charge of it (cf. Jn 4:37–38). They are called to reap what others have sown and labored to raise, to enter into a work they did not originate and do not control.

The returning disciples are also disturbed that their role as ex-clusive providers for Jesus apparently has been usurped by some-one (the woman?) who apparently has "brought him something to eat" without their knowledge or permission (cf. Jn 4:31–33). But Jesus is looking beyond the physical hunger that preoccupies his dis-ciples toward the horizon of the new dispensation he is inaugurating, the time for which he hungers with God's desire, when the univer-sal salvific will of God will be realized well beyond Israel. The Savior of the world (Jn 4:42) sees the harbinger of this new day in the Samaritans, the despised outcasts, coming to him through the wit-ness of a woman (cf. Jn 4:39).

Luke's parable of the Good Samaritan carries a similar message of crossing artificial boundaries. Hierarchical boundaries of purity, prestige, and power are imaged by the two clerics who pass by the mugged man on the other side of the street. But the Samaritan, him-self a religious outcast in this Jewish environment even though he seems to be financially well off, reaches out in compassion, literally lowers himself to the level of the victim and treats him as an equal, a fellow human being. He freely shares with the victim all that he needs (cf. Lk 10:33–35). And Jesus says he does so precisely because he recognizes the less fortunate, even the enemy, as neighbor. Clearly, this Samaritan who ignores all the boundaries set up by society and religion to treat as an equal someone he had every reason to despise and hate, who neither rejoices in nor ignores the misfortune of this member of the oppressor class, is an image of the One who, being divine, did not consider divinity something to be clung to, but emptied himself to become one of us, our equal (cf. Phil 2:5–7).[24]

Jesus did not come to establish a new religion with new boundaries, new litmus tests, a new caste system based on gender, power, or wealth. He came to inaugurate a new world, to give the power to become children of God to all those who believe in him regardless of human origin, social status, gender, or any of the other markers humans have created to divide humanity into the dominant and the oppressed (cf. Jn 1:12–13). It is this new world, this discipleship of equals in which there is no Jew or gentile, slave or free, man or woman—and, we might add, no royal or common, rich or poor, cleric or lay, white or colored, straight or gay, and so on—that religious aspire to create by their way of life. By perpetual vows of consecrated celibacy, evangelical poverty, and prophetic obedience they establish an alternate world which they live into being on a 24-hour-a-day basis, witnessing against the Prince of this world's version of a hopelessly divided human race, and to a people whose hope springs from the resurrection, that universal *shalom* in the Reign of God is possible. They seek to announce in every culture and every age that the Savior of the world has come that all may have life and have it to the full (cf. Jn 10:10).

Notes

1. I am not suggesting here that religious life is a kind of immutable and uniform Platonic "essence," which is realized differently in diverse contexts, but is always essentially the same. Cultural and ecclesial contexts vary enormously and will vary in the future. Religious life is always a contextualized project in which context influences religious life and, in its turn, religious life influences the context. I am trying to discern the specifically religious "take" on the Gospel dynamics that religious will have to find a way of embodying in their lifestyle no matter where or how it is lived.

2. The pre-eminent promoter of the "story of the universe," an attempt to situate human beings within the larger cosmic context, is probably Thomas Berry. His influence among first-world religious, especially women, has been enormous. At times, religious have reacted strongly by calling for a virtual moratorium on the specifically Christian story while we immerse ourselves in the "world" we have so long ignored or rejected. The overreaction needs to be recognized, but the necessity of being attentive to the issue is not thereby abrogated.

3. The term *kosmos* occurs seventy-eight times in the Gospel of John and twenty-four times in the Johannine epistles (ninety-two times in total) in contrast to fourteen times in the Synoptic Gospels and forty-seven times in the Pauline letters.

4. I cannot enter here into the question of the nature of the devil, who John calls Satan. The Fourth Gospel assumes, indeed affirms, the existence of this evil power and clearly regards "him" as a personal agent. This captures the important point that moral evil is not simply "what happens" as nature and history take their course, but that personal volition in opposition to God's salvific will is at work in the world. Jesus is said to overcome both "the Prince of this world" and "the world." Thus, there is a meaning of "world" which is synonymous with the embodiment or symbolic expression of the principle of evil at work in human history.

5. We cannot go into a discussion of postmodernism, which is increasingly the context of first-world religious life and is making inroads, through globalization, into other cultural situations, but the fragmentation characteristic of this worldview poses special problems for any theory of religious life as a unitary project. A good introduction to the characteristics of postmodernism is Paul Lakeland's *Postmodernity: Christian Identity in a Fragmented Age* (Minneapolis: Fortress, 1997).

6. The sociological category of "total institution" was proposed by Erving Goffman, "The Characteristics of Total Institutions," *A Sociological Reader on Complex Organizatons,* ed. by Amitai Etzioni and Edward Lehman (New York: Holt, Rinehart, and Winston, 1980), pp. 319–339.

7. See *Gaudium et Spes* (The Pastoral Constitution on the Church in the Modern World), nos. 1 and 3.

8. The juridical, indeed legalistic, understanding of the vows that was adumbrated in the *Catechism of the Vows* (for example, Pierre Cotel, *A Catechism of the Vows* for the use of religious [Westminster, MD: Newman Press, 1962, c. 1926]) was somewhat counterbalanced by the treatment of the "virtue of the vows," which tried to express the ideal embraced by the one making profession but, in fact, most religious who went through formation prior to the Council equated the vows with the assumption of carefully specified legal obligations that exceeded those of other Christians.

9. The distinction between religious profession as a global life-orientation and the vows as specific expressions of this orientation is clear from the fact that one can undertake religious life in different congregations and Orders by profession of a variety of different vows. Some groups, e.g., male Dominicans, make one vow. Others, e.g., Jesuits, make numerous vows. In most congregations, the members make three vows and sometimes a fourth pertaining to a specific ministry. In other words, profession is the act by which one becomes a consecrated religious. The vows are ways of unfolding the potentialities of the act.

10. The vast amount of work on the parables in recent biblical scholarship was launched by the pioneering work of scholars such as Amos N. Wilder, *Early Christian Rhetoric: The Language of the Gospel* (Peabody, MA: Hendrickson, 1999). A particularly enlightening treatment is that of Sallie McFague, *Metaphorical Theology: Models of God in Religious Language* (Philadelphia: Fortress, 1982), esp. chapter one on metaphorical language, and chapter two on the parables. See also John R. Donahue, *The Gospel in Parable: Metaphor, Narrative, and Theology in the Synoptic Gospels* (Philadelphia: Fortress, 1988).

11. I have dealt with the vow of consecrated celibacy extensively in *Selling All: Commitment, Consecrated Celibacy, and Community in Catholic Religious Life* [Religious Life in a New Millennium, vol. 2] (Mahwah, NJ: Paulist, 2001), pp. 117–274.

12. Lewis Hyde, *The Gift: Imagination and the Erotic Life of Property* (New York: Random House, 1983). First published in 1979.

13. American free market capitalism is probably the most striking example in modern times of this aspect of the commodity economy. For a very sobering description of how rampant materialism and naked greed on the part of less than one percent of the population sentences most of the population to increasing poverty, see Charles R. Morris, "Economic Injustice for Most: From the New Deal to the Raw Deal," *Commonweal* 131, no. 14 (August 13, 2004), pp. 12, 14, 16–17.

14. Canon 668 (see *New Commentary on the Code of Canon Law,* ed. by J. P. Beal, J. A. Coriden, T. J. Green [New York/Mahwah, NJ: Paulist, 2000] for the English translation of the canon and commentary on it). The ways in which different Orders and congregations handle the question of patrimony,

earnings, gifts, etc., vary enormously, and most renewing congregations probably need to devote serious corporate attention to how previously clear policies and shared understandings have evolved over the last forty years. Especially in what were previously called "congregations of simple vows" (the 1983 *Code of Canon Law* no longer distinguishes simple from solemn vows, but particular laws of some Orders may specify the practice of poverty in the way that solemn vows did in the past) there is currently a considerable lack of clarity and even abuse due, probably in most cases, more to ignorance than malice.

15. The Greek actually says the owner agreed to a *dhnarivon,* which is a day's wage rather than a specific sum. This opens a literary path to reflection on the diversity of value in different cultural contexts. It is not the absolute sum but the needs of people in a given context that should determine what a person should receive. For a first-world professional to try to live on the resources that well sustains a farmer in a third world country is the kind of fruitless "imitation" poverty that creates such unease in contemporary religious congregations without helping to clarify policy or improve practice.

16. Augustine, in his rule, written in 400, handles the question of need versus want in chap. 3, par. 5: *"Melius est enim minus egere, quam plus habere"* ("It is better to need less than to have more"). The *Rule of St. Augustine* in modern translation is available on line at http://www.geocities.com/athens/1534/ruleaug.html.

17. This is by no means a new idea. Augustine, whose Rule has supplied the basis of numerous ancient, medieval, and modern rules and constitutions, including those of both monastic and ministerial congregations, wrote (chap. 1, par. 3): "Call nothing your own, but let everything be yours in common. Food and clothing shall be distributed to each of you...not equally to all...but rather according to each one's need. For so you read in the Acts of the Apostles that *they had all things in common and distribution was made to each one according to each one's need* (4:32, 35)."

18. Historically, there have been children in religious congregations, usually consigned to a convent or monastery by parents or guardians. Such arrangements are no longer possible. A candidate cannot be admitted to the novitiate until the age of 18 (canon 643), nor to perpetual profession until the age of 21 (canon 658). Furthermore, profession requires freedom on the part of the one making it (canon 656).

19. Historically, there have been double monasteries of women and men, and some very new communities are experimenting with "branches" of married members and celibates, priests and religious, in the same community. There have also been some experiments in recent times with male and female religious of different communities or congregations living together because of shared ministry. Discussing these arrangements is beyond the scope of this paper. However, it should be noted that double monasteries were precisely that, not two-sex, single monasteries, and often the head of the double monasteries was a woman.

20. Although I cannot develop it here, this means that consecrated celibacy—the expression of a particular and distinguishing relationship to Christ—is the foundational motivation of religious life itself and therefore of community and ministry.

21. *Gaudium et Spes,* no. 4.

22. Cf. *Perfectae Caritatis,* 2a; *Dei Verbum* VI, 21, VI, 24.

23. In the past there was a tendency to regard rules and constitutions as quasi-revealed. The oft-quoted dictum, "Keep the rule and the rule will keep you," captured this exaggerated notion of the divine authority of the rule. The participation by most religious today in the process of revising their foundational documents, often very extensively and profoundly, has demythologized the rule and constitutions. This poses a problem we cannot address here, namely, how to understand the real authority of the congregation's particular laws and valid traditions when their origin in "mythical antiquity" no longer cloaks them in an indisputable aura of holiness. However, the point here is that these documents enshrine a valuable wisdom-tradition that unites and guides the community, but for which the community must assume responsibility.

24. A remarkable reflection on how Jesus' revelation of God as "fraternal" rather than "paternal" empowers us to move beyond hatred and retaliation against oppression into nonresentful love is James Alison, "Jesus' fraternal relocation of God," *Faith Beyond Resentment: Fragments Catholic and Gay* (New York: Crossroads, 2001), pp. 56–85.

CONSECRATED LIFE AT THE SCHOOL OF THE EUCHARIST

Most Reverend Franc Rodé, CM
Prefect of the Congregation for Institutes of
Consecrated Life and Societies of Apostolic Life

Greetings!

With joy I invite you, General Superiors—men and women—consecrated people, invited guests, to reflect upon the challenges and hopes that inspire your *passion for Christ* and your *passion for humanity.* This twofold passion meets the expectations of the Church, a permanent sign of God's love among men and women, thanks to your commitment in favor of the poor and social outcasts.

I cordially greet the president and the secretary of the International Union of Major Superiors, who promoted and organized this Congress with competence and love. I greet you all, consecrated men and women, who represent your brothers and sisters who struggle and suffer for the Gospel all over the world.

You came here to reflect together on the origins of your life and on the evangelical meaning of your actions, as Christians and as consecrated people. You are united by the same desire of the Apostle

Paul: "God's love impels us" (2 Cor 5:14). Your passion for Christ urges you to become the visible sign of God's tenderness toward those who "lie in darkness and in the shadow of death."

Introduction

At the beginning of this third millennium of the Christian era, it is urgent to reflect together in order to recognize the new things that the Lord of history wants to bestow on consecrated life today.

Moral and social problems, so numerous and often dramatic, question us as Church, as institutes of consecrated life, and as societies of apostolic life. They spur us on to keep alive in the world "the way of life which Jesus, the supreme consecrated One and missionary of the Father for the sake of his Kingdom, embraced and proposed to his disciples."[1]

United with Christ in his consecration to the Father, we do not stop seeking his countenance. We wish to remain with him, and through him, as the Samaritan woman of the Gospel, to come to the well of living water to quench our thirst with his word and to enjoy his presence.

Sharing in his mission, we feel compassion as we listen to the "cry of the poor," who demand justice and solidarity, like the Good Samaritan in the parable, and we commit ourselves to giving concrete and generous answers.

Yet, instead of converging, these two forces—the desire to dwell with Christ and the compassion which prompts us toward humanity—often tend to oppose one another.

Unity of Heart and Spirit

The pressure exerted on us by the dominant culture presents a lifestyle based on the law of the strongest, on the tempting and easy way of making a profit, and on the total collapse of personal, family, and community values. All of this can influence our way of thinking, and can place our projects and prospects for service at risk of being emptied of the motivations of faith and Christian hope that brought them about. The numerous and urgent requests for help, support, and service that come from the poor and from the outcasts of society push us to look for solutions according to the logic of efficiency, with visible effects and publicity.

And so, consecrated life runs the risk of being unable to express the strong reasons for the faith and hope which animate it. It succeeds with difficulty in revealing evangelical values, because often the true reasons for its life and hope remain concealed.

Evidently the problem is to be found, first of all, in the hearts of consecrated people. Often, in fact, they do not manage to find the right words to witness to Christ in a clear and convincing manner because, "in addition to the life-giving thrust, capable of witness and self-sacrifice to the point of martyrdom, consecrated life also experiences the insidiousness of mediocrity in the spiritual life, of the progressive taking on of middle-class values and of a consumer mentality. The complex management of works, while required by new social demands and State norms, together with the temptations presented by efficiency and activism, run the risk of obscuring Gospel originality and of weakening spiritual motivations. The prevalence of personal projects over community endeavors can deeply corrode the communion of brotherly and sisterly love."[2]

It is necessary to recognize that we often do not succeed in carrying out a satisfying synthesis between the spiritual life and apostolic action. Yet this is absolutely necessary if we want to face the challenges of the "newness" to which Christ and the Church invite us and humanity eagerly expects of us. In a shattered and fragmented world, profound unity of heart, spirit, and action is required of everyone.

In the Light of the Eucharist

While the episode of the Samaritan woman at Jacob's well emphasizes the spiritual dimension of contemplation, and the Good Samaritan the altruistic dimension of assistance, both evangelical icons proposed for our reflection certainly have profound links.

If we highlight the connections and fix our attention upon Christ, who is seated at the well of Jacob and "who, though he was in the form of God, did not regard equality with God something to be grasped" (Phil 2:6), but rather came down to heal us with the oil of mercy and his blood, we find a unique spring from which to draw living water, a privileged setting where unity of consecration and mission is achieved; a place where light and power generate the "newness" of consecrated life. This unique source, this evangelical place is the sacrament of the Eucharist.

The Holy Father pointed this out in an urgent way on the occasion of the Day of Consecrated Life, on February 2, 2001, when he said, "Meet him, dear friends, and contemplate him in a most special way in the *Eucharist,* celebrated and adored each day as the source and summit of life and apostolic action."[3]

In the post-synodal Apostolic Exhortation, *Vita Consecrata,* the Holy Father states that "by its very nature the Eucharist is at the center of the consecrated life, both for individuals and for communities. It is the daily viaticum and source of the spiritual life for the individual and for the institute. By means of the Eucharist all consecrated persons are called to live Christ's Paschal Mystery, uniting themselves to him by offering their own lives to the Father through the Holy Spirit."[4]

In the Eucharist the basic demands of consecrated life find its role model and its perfect completion.

The Need for "Renewal"

Despite the atmosphere of discouragement and resignation noted in certain communities, the deep demand of "newness," the hope for a turning point, a future to be lived and lived together is long awaited by consecrated persons. Even for those who think "there's nothing else to hope for," their hearts may actually nourish the hope of a possible newness. And this is true for both individuals and communities.

In these past years, several General Chapters have been held to search for new fields of action and new ways to approach the charismatic identity of their institutes. They have looked for new ways of living fraternal community life, they have committed themselves to listen in a new way and to maintain a more dynamic approach to the plentiful requests for help stemming from the moral and spiritual poverty afflicting humanity today.

Yet, this commitment toward something new has not always been in line with discerning evangelical criteria. Sometimes "renewal" has been misunderstood and confused with an adjustment to the dominant mentalities or cultures, at the risk of losing authentically evangelical values. It goes without saying that "sensual lust, enticement for the eyes, and a pretentious life" (1 Jn 2:16), characteristics of the world and of its culture, have exercised their disorienting influence, thereby causing grave conflicts within communities and apostolic choices that have not always been faithful to the spirit and the original inspirations of the institutes.

As always in the course of history, the Church finds itself between the prompting of the Spirit, which opens new paths, and the seductions of the world, which distort the way and mislead.

This is why we need to go to the "well" of the Eucharist. Only a Eucharistic reading of the signs of the times can help us interpret the quality of new approaches.

Jesus in the Eucharist is waiting for us and he calls us: "Come to me, all you who labor and are burdened, and I will give you rest" (Mt 11:28). Melito of Sardis comments: "Come to me, all you who are oppressed by sins, and receive forgiveness. I am your pardon, I am your Easter of redemption, I am the Lamb who has given out my life for you, I am the cleansing water, I am your life, I am your resurrection, I am your light, I am your salvation, I am your king. I take you up in heaven. I will bring you back to life and will show you the Father who is in heaven. I will raise you up with my right hand."[5]

The "passion for Christ" must lead consecrated persons to place Jesus, present and at work in the Eucharist, at the center of their lives and activities. Around the table of the Lord, our apostolic orientation has a greater guarantee of fidelity to his spirit and a more certain ability to fulfill the right choices.

Jesus came to announce the "good news" and today he repeats what he once said to the Apostle Peter, returning from a fruitless night of fishing: *"Duc in altum"* ("put out into the deep").[6]

It is the challenge of the Eucharist. The consecrated life truly constitutes *"a living memorial of Jesus' way of living and acting* as the Incarnate Word in relation to the Father and in relation to the brethren. It is a living tradition of the Savior's life and message."[7]

This Eucharistic perspective strengthens spiritual motivation, gives new vitality to apostolic action, and brings to completion the baptismal consecration, which is the foundation of the identity and mission of consecrated persons.

In a particular way, I think that Christ, the Church, and humanity make three pressing requests of consecrated life: to reaffirm the primacy of holiness; to reaffirm the ecclesial sense; and to be a witness to the power of Christ's charity. The Apostolic Exhortation *Ecclesia in Europa* echoes this when it says that "there is always need of holiness, of prophecy, of evangelization activity and of the service of consecrated people."[8]

To Establish the Primacy of Holiness

The central message of the Holy Father for the third millennium emphasizes above all the primacy of holiness in Christian life.

Holiness, with its variety of forms and ways, has always been the supreme goal of those who, "leaving behind life in the world, sought God and dedicated themselves to him, 'preferring nothing to the love of Christ.'"[9] Especially today, in the secularized atmosphere in which we live, the witness of a life totally consecrated to God is an eloquent sign that God is enough to fill the human heart.

In *Novo Millennio Ineunte,* the Holy Father affirms, "First of all, I have no hesitation in saying that all pastoral initiatives must be set in relation to *holiness.*"[10] He continues that holiness "implies the conviction that, since Baptism is a true entry into the holiness of God through incorporation into Christ and the indwelling of his Spirit, it would be a contradiction to settle for a life of mediocrity, marked by a minimalist ethic and a shallow religiosity."[11]

The many different forms of consecrated life in every time and place has been raised up by the Holy Spirit precisely to offer to Christian communities the image of evangelical perfection.

It is a matter of making more vigorous and powerful the path of the following of Christ, he who in his incarnation made himself like us in all things but sin. Similarly, thanks to a wise inculturation, consecrated life assimilates the values of the society it is called to serve, putting aside what is damaged by sin and inserting into it the vital force of the Gospel. On this path, in the measure that an institute of consecrated life integrates the positive values of a particular culture, it becomes instrumental in the openness to Christian holiness for an entire group of people.[12]

Through the constant tension to fulfill "God's project for humanity," consecrated persons walk on the line of the common Christian ideal, and not outside or above it. The whole Church, in fact, greatly depends on the witness of communities rich "with joy and with the Holy Spirit" (Acts 13:52).[13] "If in fact it is true that all Christians are called 'to the holiness and perfection of their particular state,' consecrated persons, thanks to a 'new and special consecration,' have as their mission that of making Christ's way of life shine through the witness of the evangelical counsels, thereby supporting the faithfulness of the whole body of Christ."[14]

The common vocation to holiness of all Christians cannot be an obstacle but an incentive to the original and specific contribution of religious men and women to the splendor of holiness in the whole Church.

In the Light of the Eucharist

The Eucharist enlightens and gives vitality to the Church's journey toward sanctity.

Through the Eucharist, the sacrifice of Jesus is made present in every time and in every place; it is Jesus' offering to the Father, his handing himself over to humanity, which shows us the way to sanctity. The Eucharist proposes again, for humanity and for each one of us, the model, that is, the way in which Jesus "gave himself up" to men and the manner with which he "entrusted himself" to the Father in his death. In the Eucharist Jesus is always the one who "gives himself up" to humanity as gift. In it, consecrated persons learn, as did St. Paul, how to say, "I have been crucified with Christ; yet I live no longer I, but Christ lives in me; insofar as I now live in the flesh, I live by faith in the Son of God who has loved me and given himself up for me" (Gal 2:20).

The identity and mission of consecrated life is seen here in all its brightness as a continuation of Christ's mission and one that is totally dependent on him. Thus, the passion for Christ transforms itself into active energy, into passion for humanity.

According to the particular characteristics of people and institutes, in the celebration of the Eucharist Jesus shows us how to offer, in the present time, his suffering and death for the salvation of humanity. His passion and death becomes the keystone inspiring the lifestyle of consecrated persons, making every moment a moment of grace. Thus the exhortation of St. Paul concludes, "We always carry about in our body the dying of Jesus, so that the life of Jesus may also be manifested in our body" (2 Cor 4:10).

In the Eucharist an intimate bond is created between *our body and the body of Jesus:* that body given up into the hands of sinners and delivered to death, so that the Father's eternal glory may shine forth on the Son's countenance. Similarly, our body, an image of Jesus' body, contributes to the Father's project of love and salvation, sacrificing it out of love and showing the way to salvation.

This is the true face of sanctity that today's consecrated life is called upon to make real and present.

To Strengthen the Ecclesial Sense

The second pressing appeal made of consecrated life is to enlarge the ecclesial sense of its life and works, and giving to their communities the characteristic of being "houses and schools of communion."[15]

In these last years, we have come a long way in the study of the identity of consecrated life. However, the themes contained in the documents of the magisterium, especially the Apostolic Exhortation, *Vita Consecrata,* and in the two instructions of our dicastery, *Fraternal Life in Communion* and *Starting Afresh from Christ,* seem not to have yet penetrated the awareness of consecrated persons or of Christian communities.

Today in the Church, the notion of "communion" has become "the principal hermeneutic."[16] The identity of members is not defined by the individuals themselves, but by the ecclesial relationships and specific ways of participation in the mission of Christ and of the Church.[17] The strengthening of personal identity is always the fruit of the quality of relationships established with our brothers and sisters in the faith.

Therefore, it is indispensable to attend to the quality of ecclesial relationships with all those who, guided by the Spirit of God, "obey the voice of the Father and worship God the Father in spirit and in truth. These people follow the poor Christ, the humble and cross-bearing Christ in order to be worthy of being sharers in his glory."[18]

This leads consecrated persons to a strong experience of "exodus." Liberated from the norrowness of the "I," they will be invited to come out of themselves and together to look once more for the meaning of their life in community and the meaning of their apostolic work. Only in an ecclesial and social dynamic is the identity of charismatic gifts proper to an institute revealed and strengthened.

The image of a tree is often used to represent religious families, with the Founder represented by the trunk and the Superior Generals or saints represented by the branches. In a book published in Venice, in 1586,[19] the image of a tree was taken up again, but the image of a boat was added. In the boat, representing the Church, stood an immense tree branching out like a plant. The boat, sailing on violent seas, reached harbor with the help of holy religious. The image illustrates very well the way consecrated life develops when it is united in a vital way to its trunk and when it sinks its roots into the fertile soil of the Church.

Both illustrations—the tree and the boat—show two ways of understanding consecrated life. The image of the tree suggests stability, but leaves us to wonder if the religious family might not seek its own gratification. The image of the boat, on the contrary, introduces the idea of a consecrated life embracing a dynamism and service given to the Church to help it reach port.

A Renewed Vitality

A more dynamic relationship with Christ and his body, which is the Church, keeps on track the process of the renewal of institutes of consecrated life and societies of apostolic life. It is not a question of "refoundation" according to the logic of "human demands," but of allowing ourselves to be accompanied by Jesus, as the disciples of Emmaus on Easter, allowing his words to rekindle our hearts, the "broken bread" to open our eyes to contemplate his countenance. Only in this way will the fire of his charity burn sufficiently within each consecrated person prompting them to become bearers of light and givers of life in the Church and to the whole of humanity.

Moreover, from this perspective, the journey toward renewal will never be a pure and simple return to origins, but a reclaiming of the fervor of the origins, of the joy of the beginnings, of an experience of a creative repossession of the charism. A more open and free relationship with the origins will result in true growth and progress in the understanding and realization of the gift of the Spirit which gave birth to a family of consecrated life.

Every "renewal" will be a gift to the Church to help her reach the "port." With their brothers and sisters, consecrated persons are called to face the perils of navigation, to work in the boat, and not to remain on the shore of their certainties. They are not supposed to be "lighthouses," but sailors in the boat of the Church. A lighthouse does not know perils; sailors, instead, experience them every day, and these perils are their daily bread and pride.

Consecrated life, deeply anchored in the fertile soil of the Church, vitally grafted in the theology and spirituality of the *evangelical counsels* according to the teachings of *Vita Consecrata*,[20] will find the necessary light and strength to face the daring choices needed to respond effectively to the appeals of humanity. In line with the origins of their own charisms and constitutions, consecrated life will set out again with energy and enthusiasm toward a new though no less demanding interpretation. A renewed dynamism of a more ecclesial and communitarian spiritual life, more generous and enlightened in its apostolic choices,[21] will offer consecrated persons the occasion to revitalize their own roots within the fabric of the Christian communities in which they work.

In this quest for a renewed vitality, the Eucharist is the source and school of formation according to the characteristics of faith and service. The Eucharistic mystery wonderfully cultivates the ability to find the place and way to unite respect for sound traditions and the willingness to listen to the new voices coming from the wounded and oppressed humanity of our times.

In the Eucharistic celebration, Jesus repeats still, "Do this in memory of me" (Lk 22:19). In fact, all of Sacred Scripture is based on *recalling*. "Remember..." is one of the fundamental expressions of the Covenant. God asks his people to have as a principal and integral attitude of heart complete confidence in him and a listening and obedient attitude toward his Word. Without a memory of the "exodus" and Passover, Israel, God's people, would not have existed and would not have had the least amount of faithfulness. Remembering the past, facts and words, explains events and becomes a source of discernment for the present and orients us "prophetically" toward the future.

To recall is not a nostalgic souvenir of what no longer exists and what, in any case, is no longer viable. In the biblical sense, *to recall is a memorial,* that is, an effective memory that renews, realizes, and puts into action what it remembers, thus making it contemporary.

To learn how *to recall* means, above all, to rediscover the meaning of *gift* and of *listening.* For us the Eucharist, Jesus' Passover, his presence, his sacrificial death, his resurrection, is nourishment, source of life, communion with this gift, the summit and center of our lives as baptized and consecrated persons.

The Eucharist brings us back to the events and dynamism of the origins of the Church and of our institutes, makes them real and present in our hearts and in the life of the community. It is the fulfillment of Jesus' desire, "I have eagerly desired to eat this Passover with you before I suffer" (Lk 22:15).

Each and every institute of consecrated life is a realization in history of this desire of Jesus. Only by learning *to recall* will institutes find the way to face challenges and to discover anew the real dimensions of their own identity in the Church and to enliven the missionary ardor of humble and passionate service to the *new evangelization* that the world waits for from the Church.

To Bear Witness to Christ's Power and Charity

The third appeal or challenge that consecrated life faces today is that of being a "sign of the Lord's Passover among men" through charity.

The commitment to transform social reality with the power of the Gospel has always been and remains a challenge at the beginning of this third millennium of the Christian era.

Jesus Christ's "good news" of salvation, love, justice, and peace is not always welcome in today's world. However, now more than ever, the men and women of today are in need of the Gospel, of a saving faith, of an enlightened hope, of a self-sacrificing charity.[22]

History today places before us many new situations that sometimes nourish the hopes of a fuller life and sometimes the fear of suffering and death; situations that speak of a progress and freedom that try to hide the profound signs of new forms of slavery and struggle among individuals, peoples, and nations. In this *habitat,* consecrated persons run the risk of undermining the attitude of being on the side of the poor and the oppressed in struggles where there is no room for a truce, and instead of attracting people to Christ, humanity's only Savior, it drives them away.

The majority of people today live a hopeless life, one always more closed to an eschatological future. To them, the present life appears as their only chance to take everything they can: always more, always faster. There is something desperate in this attitude, especially when the satisfaction of desires becomes impossible, something that happens almost all the time.

This situation should be a special challenge for consecrated persons, who profess faith in the future and hope in the hereafter as the driving force of their lives.

Here the prophetic mission of consecrated life assumes new emphasis. In this field it possesses a specific ministry that, in a certain sense, we could define as "priestly." In fact, we read in *Starting Afresh from Christ:* "In imitation of Jesus, those whom God calls to follow him are consecrated and incited to continue his mission in the world. Indeed, consecrated life itself, guided by the action of the Holy Spirit, becomes a mission. The more consecrated persons allow themselves to be conformed to Christ, the more Christ is made present and active in history for the salvation of all. Open to the needs of the world as seen through the eyes of God, they point to a future with the hope of resurrection, ready to follow the example of Christ, who came among us so that we 'might have life and have it to the full' (Jn 10:10)."[23]

Even with regard to charity, the Eucharist is the place where consecrated persons can draw a new prophetic vigor for their community life and their service to humanity. It makes the cross, where Christ is immolated, real and present, supporting those who in the past, present, and future are prisoners of sin and death, so that in him all those who are distant can become brothers and sisters and have access to the Father. In this school, consecrated persons learn an authentic passion for humanity and listen to the invitation to live their mission as a sharing in the death that marks the body and soul of men and women, in order to bring them hope beyond death.

Enlightened by the Eucharistic celebration, consecrated life will learn to become the "Good Samaritan" in the manner of Christ and, with his Spirit, will know how to offer ways of hope to everyone encountered on the journey. In the Eucharistic celebration, the action *to recall* Jesus' violent death is transformed into "nonviolence," into a voluntary self-gift. Jesus is not sacrificed, he sacrifices himself. The principal of opposition makes room for the principle of solidarity.

The Eucharist is at the same time *sacrifice, memorial, and meal. The Word,* who becomes flesh, offers himself in *sacrifice.* One who adheres with faith to this mystery enters into communion with the gift of Christ and becomes "gift" in his or her turn, since in the Eucharistic celebration, *communion* is united to the sacrifice of Christ (Jn 6:49–58). When this gift, this immolation of Christ in the Eucharist, is rejected, then the drama and torment of the betrayal of Judas is relived, or the following of Jesus is refused as in the Synagogue of Capernaum when the people listened to his proclamation of the gift of the *body* and the *blood* for the life of the world (Jn 6:64–70).

On the other hand, any pastoral activity, any service of the humble, the poor, the sick, the downtrodden of society, if it stems from a profound participation in the Eucharistic mystery, becomes the realization of Jesus' commandment, "Do this in memory of me." The fire of Christ's charity embraces everything and becomes a commitment and self-gift. Consecrated life finds precisely here the strength to come out of "blocked situations," to overcome barriers, to win over self-indulgent attitudes, to enlighten a unilateral reading of reality.

The "sacrifice of praise" of consecrated persons will express itself in a new passion for humanity, prompting them to complete in their own flesh "what is lacking in the suffering of Christ." To *serve,* to be *small,* to be *joyful,* will always be rooted in the Lord's Pasch, welcomed, loved, and suffered for the salvation of all.

Toward a Universal Easter

Not only our brothers and sisters, but the whole universe is involved in this Eucharistic energy that renews everything. Through the Eucharist, the life Christ transmits, the gift of himself, goes further than we imagine. Its influence reaches out to all material dimensions and to the entire cosmos. All creation is present in the Eucharistic bread and wine, elements of nature cultivated by man. In the Eucharist, creation and human labor are profoundly united in one salvation history. "For creation awaits with eager expectation the revelation of the children of God" (Rom 8:19), and humanity, transformed by the Eucharist, will labor to renew the whole universe, bringing it along toward the fullness of life. Thus, consecrated life will find in the Eucharist the light to guide in truth the way of those seeking a deeper and more fruitful relation with nature, without idealizing or exploiting it, giving proper value to everythings in the logic of "gift" and "service."

To Start Anew from "Formation"

One last point of fundamental importance: formation is a decisive element in all areas of ecclesial life. This is particularly true for consecrated persons.

From the initial formative journey, it is indispensable to educate people to commit their energies, abilities, and affective strength to the radical following of Christ, to discover the "unique" One, the "one thing necessary," he who is the source of life and the only one who can fill and satisfy every human heart.

The encounter with the One "who, though he was in the form of God, did not regard equality with God something to be grasped"(Phil 2:6), but who humbled himself to the point of death, even death on a cross, in order to communicate his divinity and make humanity more like himself, gives birth to a "proposal," that is, a project of a life completly permeated by the presence of Christ, a life focused on him, learning how to cultivate "the same attitude that is also yours in Christ Jesus" (Phil 2:5).

The experience of God's strong love will guide young consecrated persons to give back this love in an exclusive and spousal manner, so that little by little all other loves and values will disappear from the horizon of their life. In words that would come to be read as a synthesis of the project of consecrated life, St. Paul explains: "Whatever gains I had, these I come to consider a loss because of Christ. More than that, I even consider everything as a loss because of the supreme good of knowing Christ Jesus my Lord. For his sake I have accepted the loss of all things and I consider them so much rubbish, that I may gain Christ and be found in him..." (Phil 3:7–9).

The depth and totality of this *passion for Christ* will almost spontaneously become a total and unconditional participation to the *passion for humanity.* Young consecrated persons will feel the irresistible need to proclaim the Gospel of the Beatitudes to all the poor, the hopeless, and the oppressed. They will feel urged to become their companions on the painful journey of life after the discreet and strong style of Jesus. They will open their hearts to hope, walking along the demanding road of a love that is self-giving.

It is necessary to reconsider the formation of consecrated persons as limited to a moment or period of life. In a world that changes at a frenetic pace, it will be indispensable to develop the willingness to learn all one's life, at any age, in any environment, from any person and from any culture, from any fragment of truth and beauty. Above all, it is necessary to learn and allow ourselves to be formed by daily reality, community life, brothers and sisters, by daily things—ordinary and extraordinary—by prayer and apostolic work, in joy and in suffering, to the moment of death.[24]

Conclusion

May the experience of our Lady, Mary, Mother of Jesus and Mother of the Church, who allowed herself to be shaped by all the circumstances of the life of her divine Son—"She kept all these things, reflecting on them in her heart" (Lk 2:19)—guide consecrated life to persevere in the devotion to the Lord and walk the paths of the new evangelization with free and generous charity.

Notes

1. *Vita Consecrata,* no. 22; cf. Mt 4:18–22; Mk 1:16–20; Lk 5:10–11; Jn 15:16.

2. *Starting Afresh from Christ,* no. 12.

3. John Paul II, Homily (February 2, 2001), *L'Osservatore Romano,* (February 4, 2001); cf. *Starting Afresh from Christ,* no. 26.

4. *Starting Afresh from Christ,* no. 26; cf. *Vita Consecrata,* no. 95.

5. Melito of Sardis, *Homily for Easter,* 2–7.

6. *Novo Millennio Ineunte,* no. 1; cf. Lk 5:4.

7. *Vita Consecrata,* no. 22.

8. *Ecclesia in Europa,* no. 37.

9. *Vita Consecrata,* no. 6.

10. *Novo Millennio Ineunte,* no. 30.

11. *Ibid,* no. 31.

12. Cf. *Ecclesia in Africa,* no. 87.

13. *Vita Consecrata,* no. 45.

14. *Starting Afresh from Christ,* no. 13.

15. Cf. *Novo Millennio Ineunte*, no. 43; cf. *Starting Afresh from Christ,* nos. 25, 28, and all of the third part.

16. Cf. Congregation for the Doctrine of the Faith, *Communionis notio* (Vatican: May 28, 1992), no. 3; cf. John Paul II, Discourse to the Bishops of the Church in the United States, September 16, 1987, no. 1.

17. Cf. John Paul II, Apostolic Exhortation *Christifideles Laici,* no. 8; *Pastores Dabo Vobis,* no. 12; *Vita Consecrata,* no. 16ff.; *Pastores Gregis,* no. 22; Tenth Ordinary Synod of Bishops: "Bishops serve the Gospel of Jesus for the hope of the world," *Lineamenta,* intro.

18. Second Vatican Council, *Lumen Gentium,* no. 41.

19. Pietro Rodolfi da Tossignano, *Historiarum seraphicae religionis...;* cf. DIP 4, 518.

20. Cf. *Vita Consecrata,* nos. 20–21.

21. Cf. *Starting Afresh from Christ,* no. 20.

22. Cf. Pontifical Council for Justice and Peace, *Compendium of the Social Doctrine of the Church* (Vatican: 2004), presentation.

23. *Starting Afresh from Christ,* no. 9.

24. Cf. *Ibid.,* no. 15.

THE PARTICIPANTS' VOICE:
A SYNTHESIS

The themes of the study groups dealt with fifteen areas that might be considered a "monitoring system" of the positive or negative life signs, which aid or impede consecrated life today. The syntheses presented to the Assembly and given to the participants before the end of the Congress list the signs of vitality, obstacles, convictions, and lines of action that emerged. Although it is impossible to convey in a few lines the wealth of the discussions, the summaries below give some idea of the main points addressed.

1. A structural transformation of our life and our works is needed. There is a need for simpler structures and more open and accepting communities, in order to globalize a "compassionate" solidarity and a network of justice at the service of a culture of peace, so that the poor may be listened to.

2. Dialogue with cultures is an important part of the mission of consecrated life. There are many signs of the vitality of the consecrated life in the world, through which it continues to have meaning: the growth of multicultural, international congregations; during initial formation the accent is put on the culture of origin; the Congress itself is a sign of openness and sharing. Obstacles to inculturation exist, among which are the difficulties of expressing the affective element in worship and in the various expressions of faith.

3. The poor, cultures, and religions are the object of a triple dialogue that consecrated life has to conduct. In many contexts Christianity is perceived as extraneous, as an imported religion. The very fragility of our faith, our wounds, the spirit of domination are obstacles to dialogue, as is the fundamentalism diffused in so many cultural and religious areas. Dialogue has to become a choice, a lifestyle. Our communities have to be places of reconciliation and pardon.

4. Art and beauty are icons for all cultures; artists help communities of consecrated life fight against a consumerist mentality, create beautiful spaces for prayer, and find new symbols to tell new stories to the hearts of the men and women who listen. This communication of beauty will give birth to joy and life in the midst of violence and death.

5. We need to change our mentality toward communication and to know how to take risks, both within the Church—where we are often divided or criticized or too clerical—and outside the Church, in our relations with the world and the media. We have to prepare men and women religious to be experts in this field; to encourage those who work in it to collaborate with each other to provide resources and to work in close contact with competent lay persons. It is necessary to interact with the mass media in a creative way, ready to respond and not to run away from it. We have to have the courage to show ourselves as we really are, with our values and our weaknesses, and to speak a language that people of today can understand.

6. We must dare to launch some projects in our lives to give primacy to the Word of God; to review, from the viewpoint of the poor, our lifestyle and our works, and to learn how to live provisionally; to promote the presence of the consecrated life in world forums and in decision-making organizations such as the United Nations, where the future of humanity is decided; to be present where life is most threatened.

7. Consecrated celibacy brings one into a deeper relationship with Christ and enables one to share the love of others. Celibacy

for us is a free choice; it is our call; it is for us a healthy and balanced way of living our sexuality. Today we feel more at home with our bodies, with our feelings, and with our emotions. We believe, as Nicodemus of old, that we were born again. The choice of our chastity is mostly resplendent when we make visible the fact that ours is a journey toward the Reign of God.

8. We have to make of the Bible our companion of life and to embody it in our ministry. To reach authentic community discernment it is necessary to base our journey in the Word, giving it more space in our daily prayer; *lectio divina* has to become the element of transformation of our style of life.

9. Speaking about the thirst for God, we noticed that we touched a fascinating topic. Our experience of God is that of an incarnate God. To make this experience dynamic it is necessary to modify our interior structures and begin again from an intimate and radical love for Christ. It is necessary to have a human, personalized formation, a critical style of thought, a formation to dialogue, all of which leads to personal change in looking at the world and life in a spirit of faith. We also need to learn how to share the experience of faith.

10. Ongoing formation means above all an active and intelligent disposition of a spiritual person to learn from life throughout all of life. Ongoing formation involves different levels: the individual, the institution, etc.; ordinary and extraordinary experiences. Ongoing formation must be organized around the model of integration and have as its point of reference the paschal experience of the Easter Triduum—life, death, and resurrection. Formation directors and community are needed that are able to accompany persons in moments of crisis.

11. We are witnesses of increasing pluralism, which is an irreversible process. It is necessary that our structures be built on solid values preparing us to live the mission. Updating and adaptation of structures must be seen as a continuous process of change. We have to promote a spirituality of communion to intensify the efforts of

intercongregational collaboration. We need to ask for changes in canon law, in order to arrive at real equality in institutes with clerical and non-clerical members.

12. Young people, in particular, thirst for community life as an expression of mission and as a place for sharing faith and relationships. Some religious today live in community as if they were in a hotel. Our present structures of government reflect times when there were many more members living in community. They are not suitable for today's situation. Every institute has to keep developing means of ongoing formation, so that community life is more human and meaningful. The community has to be open and hospitable.

13. Lay persons help us discover that our charisms are gifts for all Christians, for the Church, and for the world. In spite of our difficulties and the aging of our members, the Spirit makes us productive. It is necessary to develop the ecclesiology of communion and the theological foundation of relationships between religious and lay persons, in order to intensify common formation, religious and lay; to favor a shared mission and bond with the local church; and to have flexible structures to share experiences among congregations.

14. The unity of our congregations comes without doubt from a common vision, but it is sustained by a network of relationships that create unity and break down barriers. There is still a great deal of road to travel so that women may really assume their role in society and in the Church. To lead a group to a shared decision is a difficult art: superiors need to be witnesses of enthusiasm if they want to sustain the passion of the members. If love and creativity cooperate, our journey will be stimulating.

15. Consecrated life gives catholicity and openness to universality to the local church; we contribute to opening the horizons of the Church. Twenty-five years after the proclamation of *Mutuae Relationes,* we must continue dialogue at all levels in the Church, and work harder to harmonize the activities and plans of the con-

gregation and those of the diocese. It is important to be trained for dialogue with lay persons, men and women religious, and diocesan clergy; consecrated life has to be an experience of communion. This implies a strong call to community life.

FINAL DOCUMENT: WHAT THE SPIRIT SAYS TODAY TO CONSECRATED LIFE— CONVICTIONS AND PERSPECTIVES

"There was a great multitude...from every nation, from all tribes and peoples and languages.... The Lamb...will guide them to springs of the water of life" (Rev 7:9, 17).

The Congress on Consecrated Life, celebrated in Rome from November 23–27, 2004—the last week of the liturgical year—and organized by the two Unions of Superior Generals of women and men, was an unprecedented event. Participants included 847 religious from all parts of the world:

- 95 from Africa,
- 250 from America,
- 92 from Asia,
- 16 from Oceania,
- and 394 from Europe.

The majority were Superior Generals, but also represented were presidents of most of the national conferences of religious from every part of the world, theologians, directors of reviews and publications on religious life, and young religious. Bishops and several members of the Congregation for Institutes of Consecrated Life and for Societies of Apostolic Life, and of the Congregation for the Evangelization of Peoples also participated.

"Passion for Christ, Passion for Humanity" was the theme of the Congress, born of contemplation of two icons: that of the Samaritan woman at Jacob's well at Shechem, and that of the Samaritan man—the Good Samaritan—on the road from Jerusalem to Jericho. With this final synthesis, we offer consecrated life the essence of the reflection and discernment that has absorbed us during these days. The perspective we have chosen for this final declaration is to do "what the Spirit inspires us to do today in consecrated life." We have been moved to do this by the Word of God, proclaimed and celebrated during these days: the Book of Revelation and the eschatological discourse of Jesus has placed us face to face with the gravity of the present moment and the dawning of a passionate hope for the future.

The Congress gave priority to the experiential aspect of consecrated life in its diverse sociocultural and ecclesial contexts. It used a process that involved everyone in discernment. A preparatory paper distributed in advance set forth observations concerning trends in consecrated life worldwide. This generated a fruitful sharing and dialogue. During the Congress points made in the paper served to stimulate reactions and discussion in groups, whose conclusions were shared in plenary sessions. This sharing made apparent what the Spirit is bringing into being in consecrated life in the pluralistic world in which we live. The challenges of the signs of our times and places became tangible as we interacted. The need to insert ourselves into the reality of our time, into the life and mission of the people of God, with "a new 'creativity' in charity" (*NMI,* no. 50) became evident to us.

I. Thirst and Water, Wounds and Healing: Our Context

"I know where you are living.... I know your affliction and your poverty" (Rev 2:13, 9).

1. In the Light of Two Icons

The two icons, that of the Good Samaritan and the Samaritan woman, are like a mirror in which we see reflected our situation of woundedness and thirst, our situation of need for healing and for living water.

a) In humanity

We are part of humanity in our:

- thirst for wellbeing in a world of consumption of goods and of poverty; for love in the midst of chaos and disordered loves; for transcendence in the midst of political and existential discord;

- need for great wells at which to quench our thirst (like the Samaritan woman) and need to build new wells (like Jacob);

- desire to know and to develop knowledge and technology;

- establishment of institutions (the Temple, the inn) to fulfill our transcendental needs, and generating of prejudices about race, religion, and gender;

- experience of ourselves as wounded, in the midst of death, excluded and impoverished, homeless, in the midst of violence and insecurity, sick and hungry (like the man left dying by the roadside)—all as a result of violence, wars, and terrorism; of the concentration of power and arbitrary injustice; of perverse economic systems and uncontrolled egoism.

In the mirror of the two icons we see our own face:

- of ecclesiastical institutions (the priest, the Levite, the Temple) far from the poor and from the sorrows of humanity;

- of a spouse prostituted by alliances of convenience (our idolatries).

We are in a transition time, marked by:

- great advances in science and technology, still incapable of resolving the great problems of humanity;
- powerful means of communication that sometimes "colonize the spirit";
- globalization that makes us interdependent while it simultaneously undermines particular identities;
- *kairos* moments in which we are surprised and realize that the God who speaks is the Lord of history;
- a thirst for and crisis of meaning that holds out to us a thousand proposals and promises.

We examine and understand this time with the Gospel criterion these two icons offer, challenging us to interpret through:

- the thirst for meaning;
- the sorrow of humanity;
- a passion for Jesus Christ, mediator of our covenant with God;
- a compassion called forth by the sorrows and needs of humanity.

This Gospel criterion leads us to discover the ambiguities, the limitations, the fragility, and the influences of evil in our world and in ourselves. At the same time, the Gospel criterion helps us see that passion and compassion are movements of the Spirit that give meaning to our mission, that animate our spirituality, and that impart quality to our community life.

b) In the Church

We seek our place in the Church, the People of God, home and school of communion (cf. NMI, no. 43).

- It is not easy to re-situate ourselves within the Church as men and women, as brothers, sisters, and ordained.

- We thirst for a new level of "mutual relations" with our pastors and with other groups and movements in the Church, animated by equality, sisterhood and brotherhood, and a greater mutual trust and openness to one another.

We affirm that we are a gift for the whole Church (cf. VC, no. 1).

- We give thanks to God for this, and we desire to move forward in a spirit of renewal and generosity.
- We recognize that our different charisms and ecclesial ministries are a great gift for us.
- We see that in the mutual sharing of gifts the Body of Christ will recover its vigor (cf. 1 Cor 12:12–31).

We understand that "consecrated life" must reach out beyond the boundaries of our institutes, of our Catholic faith, of our Christian faith. For this reason:

- We support ecumenism and dialogue between consecrated life and other religions.
- We support solidarity with other groups who struggle for human dignity, peace, justice, and ecology.
- We join with those lay sisters and brothers who share our charisms, in such a way that we identify ourselves not as an Order or congregation, but as family, sharing life and mission.

2. "To Be Born Anew"

For some time now something new has been coming into being among us beyond other realities of death (obsolete traditions and styles, dying institutions). The agony of what is dying and trust in what is being born affects us.

Although we do not yet see clearly what the Spirit is bringing to birth in consecrated life, still we identify as sprouts of newness:

- the desire to be born anew—fulfilling the implications of the Incarnation (cf. NMI, no. 52) and entreating the Spirit for the grace of re-founding;

- the fascination exerted over consecrated life today by the person of Jesus, who showed forth the fullness of the beauty and love of God from the cross (cf. VC, no. 24), and by his Gospel;

- the centrality of *lectio divina,* in which we proclaim, meditate on, share, and pray in obedience to the Word of God;

- the fundamental importance of our mission realized in accord with our particular and shared charisms, a mission that excites our imagination and impels us to undertake bold and prophetic new initiatives; to go beyond our frontiers to proclaim Jesus Christ through inculturation, interreligious and interconfessional dialogue; to express our option for the lowly and excluded ones in society; to explore new means of communication: a mission and an option for the poor (poverty);

- the search for communion and community, based on deep and inclusive relationships; the progressive extension of community living to the parish, diocese, and city; to society and to humanity (celibacy and communion);

- the need for a new spirituality that integrates the spiritual and the corporal, the feminine and the masculine, the personal and the communal, the natural and the cultural, the temporal and the eschatological, and is with us in all our living and doing;

- the transition from a consecrated life that separates us from the world to a consecrated life that is incarnate and a witness to transcendence.

II. In the Footsteps of the Samaritan Woman and the Good Samaritan: Following and Learning

"If you knew the gift of God" (Jn 4:10).

"I am standing at the door knocking" (Rev 3:20).

The desire to respond to the signs of the times and the places where we serve led us to describe consecrated life as a "passion"—for Christ and for humanity. This spiritual state is more a point of departure than a mere passing sentiment. It is, above all, a pathway to growing passion.

Jesus tells us, "I am the Way" (Jn 14:6):

- He loved us and gave himself for us. His passion precedes our passion. His passionate love for his Abba translated into passion for humanity.

- Moved by divine compassion, he took on our thirst, our wounds; he loved us without distinction, even to being our Good Samaritan and our Spouse who holds out to us the cup of the new covenant: his blood poured forth, his body immolated.

- From the cross, Jesus "draws all people to himself" (Jn 12:32), and we have experienced this attraction.

Along this way of following the Master

- we are always drawn more strongly;
- we are formed more and more in Jesus' image and likeness;
- we are introduced little by little, like the Samaritan woman, to the mystery of Jesus' mission;
- we learn, like the Good Samaritan, to transform our passion into deeds of compassion;
- our ambiguities and infidelities with respect to power, possession, and sexuality are redeemed; and
- the Spirit counsels us interiorly and strengthens us for the struggle (cf. Rev 2, 3).

In the school of following

- the Samaritan woman and the Good Samaritan become for us a mystagogy of contemplation and of commitment to contemplative mercy;

- in the two we harmonize contemplation and action: the Samaritan woman encounters Jesus and goes to proclaim him; the Good Samaritan discovers the face of God in that of his neighbor who suffers, and reaches out to help him.

III. "Do Likewise and You Shall Live": Toward a New Praxis

1. Seven Contemporary Virtues

The following of Jesus we intend to realize through consecrated life in our time calls forth in us certain attitudes to which we have given the symbolic title "seven contemporary virtues." We have drawn them from the rich group reports, conscious that we may have omitted some. They enable us—as the Pope has suggested—to quench thirst, to heal wounds, to be the healing balm on open wounds, to respond to the longings of our brothers and sisters for joy, for love, for liberty, and for peace (cf. John Paul II, Message to the Congress, no. 3). With these, we assume the new face of consecrated life as the "sacrament and parable of the Reign of God."

- Depth: Gospel discernment and authenticity,
- Hospitality and gratitude,
- Non-violence and meekness,
- Liberty of spirit,
- Boldness and creativity,
- Tolerance and dialogue,
- Simplicity: valuing the resources of the poor and despised.

2. Convictions for Deciding to Go Forward

The themes of the study groups dealt with fifteen areas that might be considered a "monitoring system" of the signs of vitality and obstacles that consecrated life experiences today. From the syntheses presented to the Assembly and given to the participants, convictions and lines of action emerge. Let us begin with the convictions:

1. A structural transformation of our life and our works is needed. There is a need for simpler structures and more open and accepting communities in order to globalize a "compassionate" solidarity and a network of justice at the service of a culture of peace, so that the poor may be listened to.

2. Dialogue with cultures is an important part of the mission of consecrated life. There are many signs of the vitality of the consecrated life in the world, through which it continues to have meaning: the growth of multicultural, international congregations; during initial formation the accent is put on the culture of origin; the Congress itself is a sign of openness and sharing. Obstacles to inculturation exist, among which are the difficulties of expressing the affective element in worship and in the various expressions of faith.

3. The poor, cultures, and religions are the object of a triple dialogue that consecrated life has to conduct. In many contexts Christianity is perceived as extraneous, as an imported religion. The very fragility of our faith, our wounds, the spirit of domination are obstacles to dialogue, as is the fundamentalism diffused in so many cultural and religious areas. Dialogue has to become a choice, a lifestyle. Our communities have to be places of reconciliation and pardon.

4. Art and beauty are icons for all cultures; artists help communities of consecrated life fight against a consumerist mentality, create beautiful spaces for prayer, find new symbols to tell new stories to the hearts of the men and women who listen. This communication of beauty will give birth to joy and life in the midst of violence and death.

5. We need to change our mentality toward communication and to know how to take risks, both within the Church—where we are often divided or criticized or too clerical—and outside the Church, in our relations with the world and the media. We have to prepare men and women religious to be experts in this field; to encourage those who work in it to collaborate with each other to provide resources and to work in close contact with competent lay persons. It is necessary to interact with the mass media in a creative way, ready

to respond and not to run away from it. We have to have the courage to show ourselves as we really are, with our values and our weaknesses, and to speak a language that people of today can understand.

6. We must dare to launch some projects in our lives to give primacy to the Word of God; to review, from the viewpoint of the poor, our lifestyle and our works, and to learn how to live provisionally; to promote the presence of the consecrated life in world forums and in decision-making organizations such as the United Nations, where the future of humanity is decided; to be present where life is most threatened.

7. Consecrated celibacy brings one into a deeper relationship with Christ and enables one to share the love of others. Celibacy for us is a free choice; it is our call; it is for us a healthy and balanced way of living our sexuality. Today we feel more at home with our bodies, with our feelings, and with our emotions. We believe, as Nicodemus of old, that we were born again. The choice of our chastity is mostly resplendent when we make visible the fact that ours is a journey toward the Reign of God.

8. We have to make of the Bible our companion of life and to embody it in our ministry. To reach authentic community discernment it is necessary to base our journey in the Word, giving it more space in our daily prayer; *lectio divina* has to become the element of transformation of our style of life.

9. Speaking about the thirst for God, we noticed that we touched a fascinating topic. Our experience of God is that of an incarnate God. To make this experience dynamic it is necessary to modify our interior structures and begin again from an intimate and radical love for Christ. It is necessary to have a human, personalized formation, a critical style of thought, a formation to dialogue, all of which leads to personal change in looking at the world and life in a spirit of faith. We also need to learn how to share the experience of faith.

10. Ongoing formation means above all an active and intelligent disposition of a spiritual person to learn from life throughout all of one's life. Ongoing formation involves different levels: the individ-

ual, the institution, etc.; ordinary and extraordinary experiences. Ongoing formation must be organized around the model of integration and have as its point of reference the paschal experience of the Easter Triduum—life, death, and resurrection. Formation directors and community are needed that are able to accompany persons in moments of crisis.

11. We are witnesses of increasing pluralism, which is an irreversible process. It is necessary that our structures be built on solid values preparing us to live the mission. Updating and adaptation of structures must be seen as a continuous process of change. We have to promote a spirituality of communion to intensify the efforts of intercongregational collaboration. We need to ask for changes in Canon Law, in order to arrive at real equality in institutes with clerical and non-clerical members.

12. Young people, in particular, thirst for community life as an expression of mission and as a place for sharing faith and relationships. Some religious today live in community as if they were in a hotel. Our present structures of government reflect times when there were many more members living in community. They are not suitable for today's situation. Every institute has to keep developing means of ongoing formation, so that community life is more human and meaningful. The community has to be open and hospitable.

13. Laypersons help us discover that our charisms are gifts for all Christians, for the Church and for the world. In spite of our difficulties and the aging of our members, the Spirit makes us productive. It is necessary to develop the ecclesiology of communion and the theological foundation of relationships between religious and laypersons, in order to intensify common formation, religious and lay; to favor a shared mission and bond with the local church; and to have flexible structures to share experiences among congregations.

14. The unity of our congregations comes without doubt from a common vision, but it is sustained by a network of relationships that create unity and break down barriers. There is still a great deal

of road to travel so that women may really assume their role in society and in the Church. To lead a group to a shared decision is a difficult art: superiors need to be witnesses of enthusiasm if they want to sustain the passion of the members. If love and creativity cooperate, our journey will be stimulating.

15. Consecrated life gives catholicity and openness to universality to the local church; we contribute to opening the horizons of the Church. Twenty-five years after the proclamation of *Mutuae relationes,* we must continue dialogue at all levels in the Church, and work harder to harmonize the activities and plans of the congregation and those of the diocese. It is important to be trained for dialogue with laypersons, men and women religious, and diocesan clergy; consecrated life has to be an experience of communion. This implies a strong call to community life.

3. Lines of Action

During the Congress we reflected at length on the situation of consecrated life in different parts of the world. The working groups identified action steps to confront contemporary challenges. We refer you to the reports which were presented. The richness and detail of the various proposals may be found in these reports.

This gathering of men and women religious from all parts of the world, from different cultures with different languages, to dialogue, debate, and plan together concerning the present and future of our life and mission, is an unprecedented event. For this reason, the perspectives offered here and actions proposed have an extraordinary value.

We hope that this Congress—not only its discernment but also its methodology—may give us a fresh point of common departure in the beautiful adventure of following Jesus in our times.

IV. Where the Spirit Leads

"...Let everyone who is thirsty come. Let anyone who wishes take the water of life as a gift" (Rev 22:17).

At the conclusion of the Congress we can proclaim that the Spirit has comforted us and opened up new horizons to us. Though the Spirit is as invisible as the wind, and we know not where the wind comes from or where it goes (cf. Jn 3:8), we have listened to the murmur of the Spirit's voice in the signs of our times and places, and have sought to discern its meaning with a shared and prayerful faith.

Like Mary and Joseph, her spouse, we have understood that to follow Jesus we must live open to God and near to the needs of our neighbor, always ready to respond to the God of surprises whose ways and thoughts are not ours (cf. Is 55:8–9).

The celebration of the Congress has ended, but its implications and demands continue. They begin now. The responsibility is ours—UISG, USG, national conferences of religious, communities and consecrated persons—to translate the Congress implications into attitudes, initiatives, decisions, and projects. The way of understanding and living religious life that bore fruit so abundantly in the past is yielding to another way more in accord with what the Spirit asks of us. "We have a glorious history to remember and to recount, but also a great history still to be accomplished! Let us look to the future, where the Spirit is sending us in order to do even greater things!" (VC, no. 110)

Perhaps more than ever before in history we are experiencing our poverty and limitations. In the midst of these the voice of the Lord resounds: Fear not, I am with you! This certitude renews our hope and trust in the goodness and fidelity of the God of hope, who fills us with all joy and peace in believing, so that we may abound in hope by the power of the Holy Spirit (cf. Rom 15:13). God is our hope, and "hope does not disappoint" (Rom 5:5).

GREETINGS TO THE HOLY FATHER, POPE JOHN PAUL II

Therezinha Joana Rasera and
Álvaro Rodríguez Echeverría

Holy Father,

With great joy the participants—men and women religious—at this International Congress for the Consecrated Life send you their best greetings. We greet you with the affection, admiration, and gratitude we have toward your person, and we express to you our deep thanks for the concern you have always shown for the consecrated life.

The 850 participants at this International Congress came from all over the world: 95 from the African continent; 250 from North, Central, and South America; 92 from the Asian continent; 16 from Oceania; and 394 from Europe.

With gratitude and deep communion with the Church, Mother and Teacher, we have rejoiced in the presence of some of the bishops who have shared with us in moments of reflection and commitment. In a special way we would like to underline the presence and the contribution given to the Congress by his Excellency, Most Reverend Franc Rodè, Prefect of the Congregation for Institutes of Consecrated Life and Societies of Apostolic Life, as well as the presence of other members of the above-mentioned Congregation.

We are here from all over the world to reflect upon our being and our acting in today's world. As His Holiness states in the Apostolic Exhortation, *Vita Consecrata,* "the consecrated life is at the very heart of the Church as a decisive element for her mission" (no. 3). Thus, the main topic of our Congress is "to perceive together where the Spirit of God takes us and, therefore, how we respond to today's challenges to build up the Kingdom of God in response to the signs of the times emerging in today's world" (no. 5).

For that reason we are grateful first of all to God for having raised up and always keeping alive the consecrated life as a priceless gift; and to the Church and to His Holiness, for acknowledging the great fruits of martyrdom, holiness, missionary work, and witness that the consecrated life has constantly borne. His Holiness has repeatedly outlined his confidence in us and has offered valid guidelines to maintain it and increase it in the commitment to follow Christ.

The theme of this international Congress is "Passion for Christ, Passion for Humanity." The passion of Christ for humanity is seen in his whole life and above all in the cross, as an unchanging factor which accompanies the entire history of humanity; many are the signs that today confirm this extraordinary richness. Today, at the beginning of the twenty-first century, Christ shares in the cross of millions of women and men who, wherever on our planet, bear the brunt of the most inhumane injustices which most often hit the poorest of the world.

Our hopes and anxieties in this Congress receive inspiration from two emblematic and paradigmatic icons for us, men and women religious of the twenty-first century: the Samaritan woman and the Good Samaritan. In the Samaritan woman we find "the spiritual and passionate search for the living water, the contemplative passion" (no. 59) which is to inspire our consecrated life. In the Good Samaritan we find "the image of a wounded and abandoned society and the compassion of God who, through his Son, bends down over the countless wounds to heal them" (no. 67). The words of Jesus, "Go and do likewise" (Lk 10:37), are a challenge for us, to which we want to respond with the same insight and courage.

We are convinced that it is the love of God, who loves us passionately, which links us with the "wellspring of living water" and invites us to commit ourselves for the sake of justice, peace, and mercy. We are called to live in solidarity with everyone, particularly the poorest, to build up his Kingdom. For this reason we pray to the Virgin Mary, ever present in the life of Jesus and the newborn Church, that she may transform us through her intercession and grant to His Holiness every good.

United in Christ we implore your blessing.

MESSAGE OF POPE JOHN PAUL II TO THE PARTICIPANTS AT THE INTERNATIONAL CONGRESS ON CONSECRATED LIFE

Dearest Brothers and Sisters!

1. To you all, called by God with a special vocation to a closer intimacy with Christ, my heartfelt greetings. At the end of the International Congress on the Consecrated Life, which took place in these days in Rome, I am very pleased to send a special message to all the participants: to the Presidents of the Conferences of Major Superiors, men and women; to the General Superiors, men and women; and to all of you, consecrated men and women gathered together to delve into the problems and prospects distinguishing your choice of life.

2. Today's humanity is spiritually impoverished to the extent of not being able to realize its own poverty. In our times we have to face forms of injustice and exploitation, the selfish use of justice and indulgence in corrupt practices by single people and entire groups, that has never been heard of before. For many it results in that "darkening of hope" that I mentioned in my Apostolic Exhortation *The Church in Europe* (cf. no. 7). In this situation, consecrated men and women are called upon to offer to this confused, spoiled, forgetful

society credible witness of Christian hope, "showing forth God's love which never abandons anyone" and offering "to today's misguided humanity true reasons for hope" (ibid., no. 84). "For to this end we toil and struggle, because we have our hope set on the living God..." (1 Tm 4:10).

3. In the face of a society in which love has no room to express itself in a gratuitous manner, consecrated men and women are called to witness to the logic of the gratuitous gift: their choice finds expression "in a radical gift of self for love of the Lord Jesus and, in him, of every member of the human family" (VC, no. 3). Consecrated life is called upon to protect the patrimony of life and beauty able to refresh the thirsty, to bandage the wounded, to soothe the injured, and to satisfy the desires of all for joy, love, freedom, and peace.

4. "Passion for Christ, Passion for Humanity" has been the guiding theme for your reflection during this Congress. In it is expressed your commitment to base everything in Christ as the cornerstone so that you may learn how to love your neighbor as he did, he who "came not to be served but to serve, and to give his life a ransom for many" (Mk 10:45). St. Mary Magdalene de Pazzi, the Carmelite mystic, called upon the souls of consecrated men and women to love him who is Love, the Love not loved: "O souls created from love and out of love, why do you not love him who is Love?" And she beseeched the Loved one: "O Love, which is neither loved nor known. O Love, may all creatures love you, you who are Love" (PR 2, 188–189). This passion, this fervor for Christ and for souls, this unquenchable thirst for divine love and the desire to bring all humankind to share in it, must constantly nourish your commitment to personal conversion, to holiness and evangelization.

5. All of you, consecrated men and women, are called upon to follow Christ in an intimate way, to share in his feelings (cf. Phil 2:5), to learn from him who is meek and humble of heart (cf. Mt 11:29), to accomplish together with him the will of the Father (cf. Jn 6:28), and to follow him in the way of the cross. This is the only way for

the disciple. There is no other way. Every day, with joyfulness and gratefulness, we have to embark upon following the Master's narrow path to draw from the fountain of living water the necessary strength. Let us open our hearts to the Spirit's vital whisperings, vying with each other in mutual love and service, opening the doors to the weak, the lonely, and the downtrodden. By witnessing a chaste, obedient, and poor life, you will become, at the dawn of the third Christian millennium, transparent windows of the loving countenance of Christ.

6. You, virgins for the Kingdom of heaven, more than anyone else are called upon to put on Christ's feelings of humility, meekness, and patience. May your vow of chastity point out the fruitfulness of a nuptial relationship between creature and Creator, and be a sign that only God can fill the human heart.

Called upon to share joyfully in the poverty of Christ, who for our sake became poor although he was rich, so that by his poverty we might become rich (cf. 2 Cor 8:9; Mt 8:20), you bear witness with your detachment that your being is fully projected toward heaven, "where neither moth nor rust consumes and where thieves do not break in and steal" (Mt 6:20).

Always be obedient in Christ. Let your communities be responsible places in which the assignments given to some do not represent lack of commitment to others; communities in which everyone exercises discernment, exemplary charity, and fraternal correction. Show to the world that the renunciation of your own will, your own projects—in freedom, love, and faithfulness to the Gospel—is the source of joy and opens the way to self-fulfillment.

7. When you are immensely loved, you cannot take part in the mystery of self-giving love by looking at it from far away. You must let yourself be consumed by the fire, which burns the holocaust to become love.

Openness—first of heart and intelligence, then of hands—has always placed you, consecrated men and women, in the forefront in facing all kinds of poverty found in the concrete situations of daily life. Even today, you have to be ready to face the challenges that men and women of good will, individual believers, the Church, and society have to overcome.

Throughout the centuries, love for one's brothers and sisters—especially for those who are helpless, the young and children, and for those who have lost hope in life and been rejected by all—has pushed consecrated men and women to adopt an attitude of total self-giving. Continue to spend yourselves for the world, always conscious that the only measure of love is to love without measure. Be contagious with this preferential love for the smallest of those whom you meet, especially the laity who would like to share in your charism and mission. Be always ready to listen to the new calls of the Spirit, trying to pinpoint, together with the ministers of the local churches where you are called to live, the spiritual and missionary urgencies of the present moment.

By urging you to keep your eyes fixed on Jesus, the leader and perfecter of our faith (cf. Heb 12:2), I impart to you, and to all consecrated men and women the world over, a special and affectionate apostolic blessing.

From the Vatican, November 26, 2004

Joannes Paulus PP. II

THE "FASCINATION" OF CONSECRATED LIFE

Álvaro Rodríguez Echeverría, FSC
President of USG

Introduction

As this international Congress on consecrated life draws to a close, I am sincerely grateful for the participation of each one of you. In a special way and in the name of everyone I want to express our profound thanks for the thorough and excellent work of the Central Commission and of all the Commissions; thanks also for the work done by the Secretariats of the two Unions of Superior Generals and that of the Congress, the team of facilitators and the team that prepared the *Instrumentum Laboris;* thanks as well for the reflections with which the theologians have enlightened us and the contribution of those who helped make the Congress a reality, those near and far, those who helped directly or indirectly. A heartfelt thanks to Archbishop Rodé, to the members of the Congregation of Institutes of Consecrated Life and Societies of Apostolic Life, and other guests who have been present with us.

I want to make special mention of those men and women religious who, in their silence and anonymity, perhaps in their suffering, and through their lives of dedication and sacrifice in the cause of the Kingdom, are making real what we have said here and much more besides. Their contribution has been no less effective and useful at the time for final assessment and drawing conclusions. These men and women are a sign of the new model or paradigm for consecrated life that we should all search for and live.

My remarks, more than a farewell, are intended to reinforce and to launch the work that we have sown during the preparation and realization of this Congress with such determination, sacrifice, and hope, in order to make real the proposed objective: "To discern what God's Spirit is causing to emerge among us to respond to the challenges of our time and to build up the Kingdom of God."[1] Even though this task is challenging, I would like to try to comment on this, without attempting to offer any definitive solutions, so that the work of this Congress is not reduced to a few days of study and reflection. Besides the spirit and letter of this Congress, I was encouraged by the Instruction *Starting Afresh from Christ* when it stated that consecrated life, in order to be an expression of the Risen Lord, has to "develop and experience new forms."[2] What should they be like and how can this be done?

1. "Fascination" and "Disenchantment"

It seems to me that the greatest challenge that confronts us is to give back to consecrated life all of its enchantment. The word "fascination" refers to everything that produces contagious joy, strong attraction, gentle freshness, and stimulating optimism. It awakens grace and friendliness, imagination and fantasy. By its very nature, it gives rise to strength, enthusiasm, and hope.

In opposition to "enchantment," we speak of "disenchantment." This includes everything that brings about frustration, monotony, and disillusion. Those who are affected by it take on an attitude of "letting things happen," to the point of placing in another's hands decisions that should be made personally. Disenchantment produces annoyance and tiredness; it is like a graveyard for hope and may even include remorse for having chosen the consecrated life.

In many parts of the world we are experiencing a highly complex and pluralistic post-industrial period. In a digitalized and globalized world, pessimism and disenchantment, nourished by the social and political problems that at this time have taken control of humanity, also affect the Church. Consecrated life "is at the very heart of the Church as a decisive element for her mission."[3] Therefore, it is not exempt from the global crisis that we are undergoing. As Dolores Aleixandre said, "We are experiencing the frustration of not having totally succeeded in the search for the fullness of life to which we have committed our lives." The challenge that arises for all men and women religious is how to make possible the "maturing" of consecrated life, so that it becomes something attractive and awakens not just a kind of admiration for it, but an affinity, a willingness to commit oneself, calling one's attention, captivating and, above all, being an instrument of salvation for the world.

2. Structural Elements That "Enchant"

By way of some broad strokes, I am going to indicate a few things that might contribute to consecrated life recovering its "fascination," so that it might be "the proclamation of an alternative way of living to that of the world and the dominant culture."[4]

The "Freshness" of the Centrality of Jesus

The foundational element of consecrated life has been and continues to be the person of Jesus Christ and his message. This has never been in doubt. The principle for renewal that the Council proposed, said: "The adaptation and renewal of the consecrated life includes both the constant return to the sources of all Christian life and to the original spirit of the institutes and their adaptation to the changed conditions of our time."[5] It goes on to say: "Since the ultimate norm of the consecrated life is the following of Christ set forth in the Gospels, let this be held by all institutes as the highest rule."[6] I believe that we have all made an extraordinary effort in recovering our charisms and congregational spirit, but I am not so sure that our highest rule is the Gospel.

The two icons that the Congress chose as the center of reflection, "the Samaritan woman and the Samaritan man," are an encouraging sign concerning what must hold the first place in all Congregations and institutes. The Working Paper, when speaking about the new model of consecrated life that is emerging, took up the Council's invitation to "take up again the Gospel as the first rule."[7] There could be an objection made that the charism is designed to reveal the different facets or the richness of Jesus Christ, which nothing nor anyone can embrace in its totality. This is true. But there is a world of difference between holding something up as the means when it is really the end and holding something up as the end when it is really the means.

Everyone is familiar with the freshness and newness that the person of Jesus always has for letting go of the old and taking on the new. He invites a response at all times and in all circumstances, both personal and social, in accord with the spirit of the Gospel, not to pre-established specific parameters. Here, too, we can apply the words: "New wine is poured into fresh wineskins" (Mk 2:22). The figure of Jesus by itself awakens enthusiasm and it attracts, more than particular charisms, although these naturally can fix our gaze on Jesus and direct our lives toward him.

The "Appeal" of Spirituality

Connected with the above is the topic of spirituality. The person of Jesus has awakened a certain spirituality in those who have known him and have meditated on him. Christian spirituality is nothing more than taking on the very spirit of Jesus in order to make the journey which every human being has to do in order to go toward God. What characteristic is most appealing to men and women today? One of the most outstanding current wonders is the thirst for God which the world manifests in thousands of ways and forms, both within and outside the Church. Every human being has a "passionate thirst for living water"[8] and "thirst for an encounter with Jesus."[9] But we have to recognize that not all roads lead to an encounter with God in the same way.

St. John of the Cross spoke of "disregarding" any mediation that comes between us and God: "If you do not disregard them, they obstruct the Spirit; since the soul is distracted by them and the Spirit may not fly toward the invisible; this is one of the reasons that led Jesus to say to his disciples that it would be better for him to go, so that the Advocate could come (Jn 16:7). In the same way, after his resurrection, he did not allow Mary Magdalene to hold on to him (Jn 20:17)"[10] Don't we have to make a fundamental change in our style of prayer? In many cases, the formulas and devotions—which become repetitive and routine—have served to substitute the "freshness" which an encounter with God produces.

The true mystic—like Jesus—does not lose sight of history but encounters it; he connects his spiritual and consecrated life with daily life and with commitment to his neighbor; he experiences the world and everything in it—persons and nature—as an extension of himself and forms in which God is made manifest. Whoever experiences God in all things will necessarily act as Jesus did, especially toward the poor in his life and as part of his plans; he will look at his existence, environment and society according to Gospel criteria and he will live a simple life.

The "Force" of the Mission

The attraction of consecrated life, rather than in and of itself, is in the lifestyle and objective specific to each institute. The mission has authored some of the most beautiful and valiant pages in history. Consecrated life, by its very nature, ought not to be centered in itself but in its commitment and giving spirit, like that of Jesus, in service of the most vulnerable. Furthermore, "...consecrated life itself is a mission, as was the whole of Jesus' life."[11] Continuing and collaborating in the plan of Jesus, the Kingdom, is the most effective incentive to take on voluntarily and joyfully the trials and difficulties which the option for consecrated life carries with it. All this goes to prove a very common saying: "Any *how* is possible as long as there is a *why.*" Whoever is convinced of the fundamental objective of consecrated life will overcome all obstacles to achieve it and a cheerful, optimistic, and encouraging presence will be the best call to communicate to others that this vocation is worth the trouble and does give meaning to life.

The signs of the times, read in the light of faith, are the best incentive for awakening the enthusiasm and attraction for mission and, therefore, a renewed life and following the Lord faithfully. Few times in the history of humankind has there been such a profound crisis of values. And few times, also, have we had the opportunity, keeping in mind the Gospel and our collaboration in making it real, to be able to look for a new model of consecrated life that responds to the challenges presented.

The "Heartbreaking Cry" of Humanity

One of the things that is most worrying and upsetting to men and women today is the lack of humanity. The extremes of violence and terrorism, hunger and exclusion have reached alarming levels. The heartbreaking cry for a world that is more just and more humane has become stronger day by day, and at the same time this cry has become attractive to the younger generations, calling them to respond to it and to make the world more humane.

It is obvious that we religious cannot live on the margin of this human trend that engenders optimism and hope amid so much sadness and suffering. This human trend must be a part of our structures, not in theory but in practice. We must be the human face of the Church, the bearers of life, like the Samaritan, and we must be the manifestation of humanitarianism, which the world today appreciates so much: "Consecrated persons make visible, in their consecration and total dedication, the loving and saving presence of Christ...they become, in a certain way, a prolongation of his humanity."[12] Sometimes, structural interests take precedence over the humanitarianism that we should be bearers of, and we sometimes find certain approaches and a rigidity that have nothing to do with the Gospel nor with a radical following of Jesus Christ.

To be human does not mean making consecrated life "light," but it does mean making it possible to always place persons first, before established norms or particular interests. This has never been easy. True communities emerge in this way, where people come first and where common ideas and ideals lead to unity and to sharing. The Working Paper has some words in it that perhaps have been overlooked, but they reflect what we have been saying: "If attention is not paid to the human layer that must support consecrated life, it is probable that it may be built on sand."[13] Experiences of Founders and Foundresses, along with their co-workers, are an example of what we just said. They were not united by any rule or regulation, but by a common ideal and the desire to make a charism real that was considered to be worthwhile for evangelization and presence within the Church.

The "Enchanting" Balance Between Persons and Structures

Persons are the reason for and center of the mission of the Church, as Paul VI forcefully stated at the close of Vatican II. Both moral and human science agree that the person is the strongest element or the nucleus of all reality. Everything converges toward persons and everything must be assessed in the light of how persons are affected, how they are fulfilled, and how they mature. Both in Jesus' approach as well as in his teachings, we see these principles made real. In his own words, Jesus says without exception that "The sabbath was made for man, not man for the sabbath" (Mk 2:27). John Paul II, in his first encyclical, considered as the defining document of his pontificate, also clearly stated: "The human person is the primary route that the Church must travel in fulfilling her mission: the person is the primary and fundamental way for the Church, the way traced out by Christ himself."[14]

However, this route, in practice, is loaded with obstacles. In our ministry we condemn, rightfully, the evils of globalization, wanting all nations and peoples, with no regard for their own culture, needs, or interests, to have to accept a certain political line, to take on certain financial criteria that they do not understand and which will not benefit the population, etc. The reason for this condemnation is because human rights, cultures, and the individuality of each person are not respected. These same reasons have to mark the life and structures of consecrated life. It is easy to lose balance, to forget that each person is one-of-a-kind and inimitable and to apply the "culture of control," common in modern society, as Radcliffe says, to consecrated life.[15]

At the same time as keeping a balance between persons and structures, the decentralization of consecrated life must also be kept in mind. The Eurocentric style is still the dominant one, which is the same thing as saying that inculturation within consecrated life still needs to be done. It is important to respect and to appreciate multiple spiritualities and various ways of living consecrated life, even within institutes themselves. Community is formed not by the fact of living under the same roof, but by participating in the same objectives, each with his or her own qualities and culture. In this sense it is necessary to let Eastern spirituality and that of emerging continents help us to enter into the Gospel more deeply, at the same time being open to allow ecumenical and interreligious dialogue to enrich us, aware with Peter that "God shows no partiality. Rather, in every nation whoever fears him and acts uprightly is acceptable to him" (Acts 10:34–35).

Conclusion

Today, more than in the past, we need to divest ourselves and to invent, to innovate and to go forward (Gabriel Ringlet).

To invent new responses that connect to the social, economic, and political changes of nations where we are not established, attentive especially to those who are still excluded from the benefits of globalization, both in rich countries and in poor countries.

To innovate our structures of meeting with God, community life, service to our neighbors, our professional lives shared with our co-workers.

To go forward divested, in imitation of Jesus Christ and with the fire of his passion. We need to be aware that none of this can be lived authentically if we do not open ourselves, in conversion, to the powerful action of God, Father, Son, and Holy Spirit, who reignites our heart with a passion for humanity.

To structure consecrated life around these items that were mentioned is not an easy task. Perhaps this may move us away from places where we find our security and lead us to a different ordinary routine. But let us recall that it was here, in the ordinary events of life, that the Samaritan man and woman found what was attractive and new in Jesus. And from the daily routine also—lived in the style and spirit of the Gospel—we can give back to consecrated life its "enchantment."

Notes

1. Working document for the Congress, no. 4. This document will hereafter be cited as IL.

2. *Instruction of the Congregation for Institutes of Consecrated Life and Societies of Apostolic Life* (March 12, 2002), no. 2.

3. *Vita Consecrata* (March 25, 1996), no. 3.

4. *Starting Afresh from Christ,* no. 6.

5. *Perfectae Caritatis,* no. 2.

6. *Ibid,* 2a.

7. IL, no. 73.

8. *Ibid,* no. 59.

9. *Ibid,* no. 63.

10. *Ascent to Mount Carmel* II, L, II, chap. 11, 7.

11. *Vita Consecrata,* no. 72.

12. *Vita Consecrata,* no. 76.
13. WP, no. 40.
14. *Redemptor Hominis,* no. 14a.
15. *Consecrated Life after September 11,* no. 9.

BOOKS & MEDIA

The Daughters of St. Paul operate book and media centers at the following addresses. Visit, call or write the one nearest you today, or find us on the World Wide Web, www.pauline.org

CALIFORNIA
3908 Sepulveda Blvd, Culver City, CA 90230   310-397-8676
5945 Balboa Avenue, San Diego, CA 92111   858-565-9181
46 Geary Street, San Francisco, CA 94108   415-781-5180

FLORIDA
145 S.W. 107th Avenue, Miami, FL 33174   305-559-6715

HAWAII
1143 Bishop Street, Honolulu, HI 96813   808-521-2731
Neighbor Islands call: 800-259-8463

ILLINOIS
172 North Michigan Avenue, Chicago, IL 60601   312-346-4228

LOUISIANA
4403 Veterans Memorial Blvd, Metairie, LA 70006   504-887-7631

MASSACHUSETTS
885 Providence Hwy, Dedham, MA 02026   781-326-5385

MISSOURI
9804 Watson Road, St. Louis, MO 63126   314-965-3512

NEW JERSEY
561 U.S. Route 1, Wick Plaza, Edison, NJ 08817   732-572-1200

NEW YORK
150 East 52nd Street, New York, NY 10022   212-754-1110
78 Fort Place, Staten Island, NY 10301   718-447-5071

PENNSYLVANIA
9171-A Roosevelt Blvd, Philadelphia, PA 19114   215-676-9494

SOUTH CAROLINA
243 King Street, Charleston, SC 29401   843-577-0175

TENNESSEE
4811 Poplar Avenue, Memphis, TN 38117   901-761-2987

TEXAS
114 Main Plaza, San Antonio, TX 78205   210-224-8101

VIRGINIA
1025 King Street, Alexandria, VA 22314   703-549-3806

CANADA
3022 Dufferin Street, Toronto, ON M6B 3T5   416-781-9131

¡También somos su fuente para libros, videos y música en español!